A PATHWAY THROUGH PARKS

Stan-
I hope that you've
enjoy these stories and
rekindle the memories of
travels with your friend
Sharon

Carl S. Chavez

Printed in Victoria, Canada

Cover Photo: Carl, Margaret and Abigail Chavez;
Bodie, California, 1967

Co-published by Trafford publishing and c2 Publishing.

A cataloguing record for this book that includes the U.S. Library of Congress Classification number, the Library of Congress Call number and the Dewey Decimal cataloguing code is available from the National Library of Canada. The complete cataloguing record can be obtained from the National Library's online database at: www.nlc-bnc.ca/amicus/index-e.html
ISBN 1- 4120-2273-8

TRAFFORD

This book was published *on-demand* in cooperation with Trafford Publishing. On-demand publishing is a unique process and service of making a book available for retail sale to the public taking advantage of on-demand manufacturing and Internet marketing. **On-demand publishing** includes promotions, retail sales, manufacturing, order fulfilment, accounting and collecting royalties on behalf of the author.

Suite 6E, 2333 Government St., Victoria, B.C. V8T 4P4, CANADA
Phone   250-383-6864   Toll-free   1-888-232-4444 (Canada & US)
Fax   250-383-6804   E-mail   sales@trafford.com
Web site   www.trafford.com   TRAFFORD PUBLISHING IS A DIVISION OF TRAFFORD HOLDINGS LTD.
Trafford Catalogue #04-0101   www.trafford.com/robots/04-0101.html

10   9   8   7   6   5   4   3

A PATHWAY THROUGH PARKS

A PARK RANGER'S REMINISCING

CARL S. CHAVEZ

DEDICATED

IN MEMORY OF THE FINEST RANGER I EVER KNEW

MY DAUGHTER

ABIGAIL ROSE
JUNE 23, 1967-NOVEMBER 19, 1996

CONTENTS

The drawings throughout the text are by the author

ACKNOWLEDGEMENTS

I am a journal keeper. When I first began to think about writing these tales of my adventures as a Park Ranger with the California Department of Parks and Recreation (DPR), I used my journal entries to jog my fading memory. Still, I did nothing about writing, I just thought about it.

It took the motivation of my Life Partner, my Dearest Friend and Loving Wife, Margaret, to offer me the encouragement to "Quit talking about it. Shut up. Just do it!" Little did she know how involved in this project she would become. Through it all, sometimes with a shake of the head and eyes rolling, she would humor me as my editor and critic. Living the somewhat nomadic life of a park ranger's wife, she offered our children, Abigail and Christopher, the stability and grounding of our shared park experiences that was to serve them so well in their own careers. This is her book as much as mine.

Then there is my "other family". That is the **Park Family**. It is made up of the friends, coworkers, employees and "Cast of Characters" of the California Department of Parks and Recreation of whom I write. In researching this book I talked to many of them, some retired, some still working. Without their dedication and support this would have remained an unwritten story and "A Pathway To Nowhere".

Finally I would like to thank my friends Becky Stockdale and Bill Morris for helping me get to the end of the pathway.

I appreciate all of them.

Carl S. Chavez
"c2"

PREFACE

Carl Chavez, California State Park Ranger I. Oh the sound of that title! At last a change of life style for a 21-year old, recently graduated, unemployed, starving college student with a wife to support and a baby on the way. I was starting a career with California Department of Parks and Recreation that was to be a part of my life for the next 33 years and beyond. A career that was to make me the person I am today. But I get ahead of myself. It is October 24, 1966 and I have just been appointed as one of two full time employees who will reside in the ghost town known as Bodie State Historic Park. Before my tale begins here is a little about how I got to this starting point.

Born on April 13, 1944, I was the only son of Salomon and Josefita Chavez and the first of my family, which included five sisters, to be born in California, my parents having moved to the San Diego area from New Mexico during World War II. Growing up in Linda Vista and Fletcher Hills, I spent much of my time with cousins and friends exploring the canyons, hills, mountains, desert, and lakes/reservoirs of the area. Early on I knew I liked and enjoyed the freedom of exploring the hidden "Secret Spots" that even the relatively developed areas of San Diego County offered. Places like Tecolote Canyon, Black Mountain (Cowel Mt.), Cuyamaca Rancho State Park, the Laguna Mountains, Anza- Borrego Desert State Park, or Pauma Canyon near Mt. Palomar. My parents expected that I would follow in my father's footsteps as an engineer. Do you know you have to take a lot of mathematics to be an Engineer? This drawback was enough to convince me that engineering would be "a path not taken". Besides, I liked the outdoors and enjoyed working with people. What would fill that bill?

The answer to that question came to me through my best high school friend, Sam Miles. Sam and I had known each other since elementary school in Fletcher Hills where his father was the school principal. Over the years, all the way through high school, Sam and I had developed a hunting and fishing partnership. At every opportunity we were out exploiting the resources of San Diego County. That is not something I'm particularly proud of, but perhaps something I made up for later in life.

One of our more memorable episodes involved a rabbit hunting foray in the vicinity of Anza-Borrego Desert State Park. On this occasion we decided to try our luck outside the park in the wilds southwest of the Vallecito County Park. In the middle of what appeared to be a desert wasteland we came across an authentic street sign at the junction of two dirt tracks that read: "Hollywood & Vine" and decided this was as good as anyplace to start hunting with our trusty .22 cal. rifles in hand. In truth we were blissfully ignorant of the State Park boundary or any applicable rules and regulations as we stalked our quarry, the elusive jackrabbits, that inhabited creosote bushes and arroyos of the area. At least we were ignorant until we crested a small scrub covered sand dune and found ourselves staring at the back of a State Park Ranger who was standing next to his patrol vehicle scanning the area with his binoculars.

With our hearts thumping we quickly beat a hasty retreat and fled in full flight over, under, around and through bushes, cacti, and arroyos feeling guilty as sin. In our effort to elude the law we made it to the relative safety of a canyon surrounded by sandstone cliffs. It took a minute to catch our breath before we peeked out from our hiding place to see if the long arm of the law was still after us. He was and it was obvious that our pursuer was trying to follow our tracks.

To make a long story short, just let me say that we managed to evade that park ranger by taking a circuitous route over hard ground back to the shack where we were staying. That was my first (near) encounter with a California State Park Ranger. Many years later I met longtime Anza-Borrego Park Ranger, George Leetch, who had a vague recollection of just such an incident. In all probability it was he with whom I almost had "A Close Encounter" of the embarrassing kind!

In any event, sometime in my high school senior year of 1962, while on another hunting or fishing expedition with Sam he mentioned in passing that it would be neat if we could get a job doing something like this and get paid for it. I asked him what he meant and he said he had thought about going to Humboldt State College in Northern California and checking out a major in Forestry or Wildlife Management. Sam never did pursue that idea and instead he became a successful house-remodeling contractor in Jackson Hole, Wyoming. It is to Sam that I owe a great deal of gratitude for helping to plant a seed in my mind that led me to begin thinking about an alternative career to engineering. He had provided me with a way to escape the potential drudgery and daily grind of a desk job I was sure I would have detested, assuming I could have passed the mathematics of Advanced Algebra and beyond.

After graduating from high school I appeased my parents by enrolling in San Diego State University as an "Undeclared Major". The more mathematics and chemistry I took the more and more I became convinced I wasn't cut out for this line of work. It was time to make a run for it, meet new people and enjoy the outdoors.

Unbeknownst to my parents, in the spring of 1963, I had begun to seriously research the possibility of transferring to Humboldt State College in Arcata, California. Now, understand that Arcata was the furthest North I could go from the San Diego area and still attend a State College in California, which was an important budget consideration for me. My research into the Forestry Program indicated that there would be quite a bit of engineering involved, for example, when tearing up the landscape for logging road construction - Yikes again! That would mean I would actually have to put into practice some of the theoretical math I had fumbled through. But wait! The College Catalog also listed something Sam had mentioned called "Wildlife Management". Hey, I could do that. How hard could that be? I like to hunt and fish and I loved the outdoors. Further research in writing to various Departments of Fish & Game and State and National Parks confirmed that indeed I could get paid for having fun. True, the pay wasn't going to be spectacular, but how much does a single, carefree kid need to live on anyway? This was beginning to sound more and more like something I could do.

Now all I had to do was graduate from college, find a job in a park somewhere, collect my paycheck and go fishing and hunting. The pathway to my future was clear to me now. All I had to do was follow it!

A PATHWAY THROUGH PARKS

MAJOR PARK ASSIGNMENTS

STARTING DOWN THE PATHWAY

In September of 1963 I boarded a Greyhound bus for the 24-hour bus ride up the California coast and US 101 to an uncertain future, a college I had never seen, and people I did not know. My parents, to be sure, were not happy with my decision and dire predictions of a bleak and uncertain economic future that would send me to the poor house seemed a sure thing in their minds. But I was determined, even to the extent of taking my beloved pet "Mike the Dog" down to the animal shelter for adoption since no one at home would offer to care for him in my absence.

Despite this sad farewell, everything fell into place shortly after my arrival in Arcata. Within days of my arrival the most significant event of my life occurred. That is, I had the good fortune to meet a girl named Margaret and with that, the most focused pursuit of any goal in my life began as I started courting her in an effort to acquire a wife. As things turned out it took me one more year to obtain a college degree than it did to get a wife!

Life at Humboldt State College (HSC) in Arcata was good. The first year I lived in the Redwood Hall dorm, Room 305. As part of my courtship efforts I organized many of my dorm mates to help me serenade Margaret with songs that drifted across the Dorm Quad to her listening ear over in the adjacent Sunset Hall Dormitory. Occasionally, I did find time to study and managed to do well enough to maintain good enough academic standing to remain in college.

The next school year I moved out of Redwood Hall and, along with my good friend John Bosworth, took up residence in Arcata with Mrs. Cora Hunt Taylor at 630 11th Street. It was such a deal with room and board for only $40/month. I should say a word about dear Mrs. Taylor. She was in her late 70's or early 80's when we lived with her. John and I were something like the 42nd and 43rd students,"her boys", that had boarded with her during their college years. She was a spry and delightful lady who could cook the best chicken and dumplings I've ever had. While John and I struggled to identify birds in the yard as part of our Ornithology class exercises, Mrs. Taylor would chuckle in the background as she identified birds by song alone, more often right then we were. Mrs. Taylor had a house rule that no "girls" were allowed in the house. That rule remained in effect until she met Margaret and made an exception for her.

Margaret and I were married on June 12, 1965 at the end of my Junior year. Margaret, being a year ahead of me and smarter too, had graduated in January of 1966. While I finished up my last year of college she supported us by working at a drug store across the street from Mrs. Taylor's home. Margaret, still a welcome guest, would often lunch and visit with Mrs. Taylor during our first year of marriage. Both Margaret and Mrs. Taylor brought stability to my life that was a new experience for me. But again I get ahead of myself.

I knew that once I had gotten to HSC (now HSU) that it was important to do well in school, but also equally important to obtain a summer job "in the field". I figured out very early on that my interest really was in the realm of a park ranger's duties. Except for trips to various parks and forests over the course of my early life, I knew very little about them and I understood no distinction between the various classifications of our land resources. Like most people today, they all fell into a category of "forests" and anyone who worked in them was a "forest ranger" whether he/she was a forester, fish & game warden, firefighter, wildlife manager or park ranger. It is what I call the "Lassie Syndrome" because so many folks associated the television program featuring a Forest Ranger and Lassie the dog with the romanticized view of the forest ranger and their work adventures and exploits. In any event, beginning in the summer of 1964 and for the following two summers I found a niche in summer work which seemed to fit my evolving career goals.

I was hired that first summer as a back country patrol ranger on the Mammoth District of Inyo National Forest after having submitted over 25 applications to various national and state agencies throughout the United States. I had received two job offers. One was as a Range Management Conservationist for the Bureau of Land Management in Worland, Wyoming. That job entailed advising ranchers who knew more about things I knew nothing about - nope that was not for me. The other job sounded more interesting. It was as a backcountry patrol ranger. Of course, I knew nothing about packhorses either but the job sounded much more exciting and glamorous then identifying grasses on the prairie. I had been a Boy Scout, went camping and backpacked. Maybe I could "fake it". After all, I had been hired sight unseen and they didn't know I wasn't a horse person who would probably need more help than those I was supposed to assist. It was worth a try for this privilege of being paid to have fun!

I knew that it was too good to be true. On July 1, 1964 my bubble had already burst! As luck would have it, I arrived at the District Office in Mammoth Lakes, California only to find that the person who I was to replace that summer as the Back Country Patrol Ranger had a change of heart and decided to returned for one more season. Secretly, I gave a sigh of relief because now I wouldn't have to figure out on which side of the horse to get up on or our how to tie a Diamond Hitch on the packhorse or packmule (what's the difference?). But now the Forest Service had the problem of what to do with me.

The solution was to send me down to a place called Red's Meadow near the Devil's Postpile National Monument. I was to be part of a three-man "recreation" crew responsible for management and operation of five campgrounds strung out along the upper reaches of the San Joaquin River. This was my first real job and the manner in which I obtained it set a pattern of unorthodox selections for employment that was to follow me throughout the rest of my career. To this day I am still left wondering what a "normal" hiring, promotion, or job selection process is. All I know is, as the reader shall see later on, it is something I rarely experienced.

My living quarters at Red's Meadow were unique. Along with my work partner, Al Woodard, we lived in a one room vertical log cabin situated above the Red's Meadow Campground. Al was returning for his second summer season at Red's Meadow. A year or two older than me, Al was the one who "showed me the ropes." He was a happy-go-lucky fellow from Apple Valley, California who would soon be graduating from college and getting married. I could, and did, learn a lot from him – both on and off the job.

The cabin, itself, was adequate though a bit spartan. You could see daylight though the vertical cedar logs that made up the walls and provided excellent cross ventilation in the heat of the summer. The only real problem we had was with the numerous pack rats that came each night to visit and rummaged through our food stores. We managed to solve that problem by amassing a pile of objects that were placed upon a chair strategically set between our beds. In the middle of the night whenever we heard their stirrings we would automatically reach over and grab something to throw at the offending critters. Each morning we gathered up the stuff we had thrown the night before and rearmed for the next night's assault.

In the meadow below our cabin was a natural hot springs shower that we maintained for the campers, and backpackers who frequented the area. We had our own private natural hot springs tub secreted in the meadow for our personal use. The 4'x8'x3' sunken concrete tub was a joy to soak in after a day's labor. At night the Milky Way showed brilliantly overhead in the clear mountain air. If anybody had bothered to look, we would have been a strange sight indeed with our heads protruding above the Sierra flora surrounding our natural hot tub.

Our cabin was the only place along the John Muir trail where supplies could be cached for pickup about half way along the trail's route from Mt. Whitney to Yosemite National Park. Talk about outdoors! I thought I had died and gone to heaven. Fishing at our doorstep, wilderness at our front and back doors and lots of friendly folks. Our boss Bill Martin, and his wife Patty, lived in a new US Forest Service house up the road a couple of miles near the Pumice Flat Campground. Supervision was far enough away so that we could create some mischief both on and off the job to make things really interesting. I couldn't believe my good fortune. I was actually getting paid ($3.74/hr) to work outdoors just like I had planned. Never mind that I was hauling garbage, cleaning 22 sets of pit toilets, collecting camp fees and occasionally settling camper disputes amongst "friendly" folks. On top of this my girl friend, Margaret, had a summer job working up the road about 40 miles away at the Tioga Lodge on the shores of Mono Lake. It couldn't get any better than this-but it did!

In 1964 the paved roadway to Red's Meadows ended

at Minaret Summit, just beyond the Mammoth Mountain Ski Resort. It is a spectacular vista looking across the valley West to the Minaret Wilderness Area (today called the Ansel Adams Wilderness Area) before you began the steep descent on a rough dirt road into the valley along the upper reaches of the San Joaquin River.

"WHAT'LL IT BE?"

Starting from the north end of the Red's Meadow Valley and going south the first campground you come to is Agnew Meadows Campground (CG) and pack station, then Pumice Flats CG, Minaret Springs CG, Soda Springs CG, and finally Red's Meadow CG with it's pack station, store, and rental cabins. The five campgrounds had perhaps a total of 250-300 campsites. Each of these informal campgrounds had its complement of trashcans that needed pickup and pit toilets that needed cleaning. That was our job. It really was too much for a two or three person crew. There simply wasn't enough time in the day to clean all 22 sets of toilets and collect the garbage.

Then on top of this came the day when we were also expected to register campers and collect camping fees. The day before, the main boss, Charles Bucklew, had come down from the Mammoth District Office to give us the news that we were to begin collecting camp fees on the following day. A new Federal program, something called the "Golden Eagle Pass", was to start that day. Charles had brought down almost everything we would need. In the metal collection box were passes, rolls of tickets, camper registration cards, a moneybag, and of course no change. Al, Bill, and I were given hurried instructions on procedures. When we asked when we were supposed to collect fees in the midst of our other duties, we were told that that was our problem to figure out, and with a call of "good luck" and wave of goodbye we were left literally holding the (empty money) bag. Camping families had been coming to this area on vacations for years. They liked the rugged outdoor life that this valley had to offer and they liked it for its beauty and semi - primitive campsites. They also liked it because it was free.

The next day was not much fun as we began making our rounds and collecting fees. Though there had been some advanced notice through posted signs, the message really had not registered on the minds of the campers. Al and I did most of the fee collection and fast talking. We struggled through the first couple of weeks but soon we established a routine and we had figured out a system that seemed to work. Since there was never enough time to do all that was expected of us, we would start each morning by asking ourselves "What'll it be?" That meant should we collect fees today, pick up garbage, or clean toilets. We might be able to do two of three of these tasks but we could never get to all three in a single day, especially if other assignments like burning the dump once a week were expected of us

Neither Al nor I especially liked to cook and there were no nearby restaurants. We quickly discovered, however, that we had an untapped resource right under our noses – the campers! If we made our fee collections during the time dinner was being prepared we were sure to get a dinner invitation from at least one out of several hundred campers we had come in contact with during our daily maintenance rounds. Besides we had developed a friendship with many of the families (daughters). Undoubtedly the Forest Service would have (and probably still does) frowned heavily upon this practice had they known what we were doing. If it was not illegal it was most likely against Forest Service policy. Al and I were able to rationalize that we were only performing public relations duties, and besides that it was on our own time and it gave us more time to do other work the next day. We were actually saving the Taxpayers money! How's that for rationalizing?

Trash and garbage pickup was another problem. As I said before it was not something we could do every day.

There were no large trash bins set out in those days, only individual trash cans, almost a hundred of them. Bears and other animals were a constant problem. They were almost as messy as the campers were. We had no garbage truck, only a standard US Forest Service ½ ton pickup truck. We quickly learned that there was no way in hell we could pick up the cans from the five campgrounds strung along our five-mile valley. Any attempt to haul them to a dump that was situated midway in the valley and return the cans for a repeat trip over and over again would never work. We resorted to just dumping the trash and garbage in to the bed of the truck. We could get a bigger load that way and reduce the number of trips to the dump. Of course by the time it came for fee collections later in the afternoon or evening the truck usually didn't smell too good.

This method of trash pickup almost turned to disaster one day when I was on duty all by myself. As I drove down the road I thought I smelled smoke. I glanced in my rearview mirror and I saw not only smoke, but fire! Someone had put still hot barbecue briquettes in the trashcan and the hot coals had ignited the trash in the bed of the truck. I slammed on the brakes and skidded to a stop. Quickly I got my McCloud fire tool, dropped the tailgate and pushed the flaming debris out onto the gravel roadway. I was able to stomp the flames out and prevent any damage to the truck, or worse, to the forest around me. I was a bit shaken when I cleaned up the mess and drove off to give it another try.

The "highlight" of each workweek was a trash fire, not in the back of a pickup, but rather, at our dump near Pumice Flats. Today such a dump would be strictly illegal. In 1964 it is the way we did things. It was our practice to save all of the "empty" Coleman fuel containers and backpacker's propane cylinders we collected during the week and set them aside at the dump for our very own weekly 4th of July celebration (I still can't believe we did this). On the prescribed morning we would telephone up to the District Ranger Station in Mammoth to advise them that we would be burning the dump that morning so they could notify the fire lookout and they wouldn't be alarmed by the smoke coming from our direction. Let me tell you, we had some pretty good explosions!

The job in the trilogy of tasks we were suppose to do after fee collection and trash pickup was cleaning restrooms (not necessarily in that order). Now you would think that that would not be fun. You would be right, but we still tried our best to make it so. It was our most thankless job, but probably our most appreciated task. We got a lot of lunches out of it (don't take that literally!). What I mean to say is those campers who were feeling sorry for us often invited us to have lunch with them. We of course, though in uniform, rationalized this too by thinking we were saving time by not having to rush back to our log cabin for lunch. It never occurred to us to bring a lunch with us to work.

One gets used to cleaning 22 sets of pit toilets. We had a standard procedure that worked pretty well. We were on a schedule that while not providing daily service of each facility usually got us around to each one every second or third day. Not great, but good enough to keep most campers satisfied. In addition to this cleaning schedule we would also, about every two weeks, give them a more thorough cleaning and spray them with a disinfected called "Berkaline" (with that many toilets, even after 40 years, you don't forget the name or the smell!). We used our portable fire pumper unit to do the spraying. Once in a while, before beginning to clean and spray the interior of the structure, we would forget to announce ourselves. This could prove embarrassing to both the occupant and to us.

Keep in mind that these restrooms were "two holers." That is they had two separate stalls, but a common pit. One day we were spray cleaning the walls and the pits with our trusty sprayer full of Berkaline. Al opened the door to one stall and began spraying the walls and down into the pit. Suddenly, he saw movement down below. He recognized it as a rat and began spraying even more. It became a game to try and drown the rat! Al began to laugh and shout louder and louder, "It's alive! It's alive!" Berkaline was splashing everywhere, including up into the next stall. Suddenly there was a roar and a string of expletives from the other stall. We were not alone! There was someone next door using the facilities and he definitely did not want, nor expect a disinfectant treatment on his bottom. We beat a hasty retreat without saying a word and worried about that incident for a day or two before laughing about it for the rest of the summer. I wondered "what'll it be tomorrow?"

"BASQUE(ING) IN THE MOONLIGHT"

It wasn't all work and no play at Red's Meadows in the summer of 1964. In fact, it was probably more play and some work! My work partner Al and I were for the most part on our own and left to our own devices with our supervisor Bill out of sight and out of mind. We did our work and had fun at what we did. The evenings were our own time and we made the best of it by visiting with the campers and their teenage daughters, collecting fees, and gratefully accepting any dinner invitations that might be offered. On my days off I was usually out fishing or hiking or, more often than not, driving up the road to visit with my girlfriend, Margaret, at Tioga Lodge a few miles north of the town of Lee Vining.

I had always accused Margaret of being a "Cradle Robber" when she chose me as a mate. After all she was an older woman (at least older than I was). In fact she was soon to become a legal adult while I still languished in the minority.

July 18th was Margaret's 21st birthday and I had been thinking about it all day at work but I had failed to get her a gift or card, a fault I have to this day. Al could tell that I was moping about and my spirits were down thinking that there had been no mention of a party or anything. Who was there at Mono Lake who would even know it was her birthday, much less prepare a special rite of passage birthday? Al, who had fond memories of his 21st birthday party, suggest we drive up to Mono Lake after work and have our own celebration (I wasn't 21 years old yet) birthday party with her.

We left the cabin after getting a quick bite to eat and drove up the steep winding dirt road from Red's Meadow to Minaret Summit, where the pavement began. That seven-mile journey took over half an hour. It was about another hour drive from there, through the town of Mammoth Lakes, and then north on Highway 395 to the town of Lee Vining and Mono Lake. I was very excited at the prospect of surprising Margaret with this unexpected birthday visit. As we approached Tioga Lodge I could see that the restaurant/bar across the street from the post office and cabins where she lived and worked seemed very quiet. I got out of the car and walked up to her cabin and knocked. There was no answer and no other employees appeared to be about. I walked back across the highway and into the restaurant. There were only a couple of tables occupied and there didn't seem to be any action in the bar. Normally the bar and restaurant was a beehive of activity.

This was the local hangout for the Basque sheepherders who grazed their flocks in summer pastures around the lake. After imbibing a little too much, the Basque became "friendly intoxicated singers." I'll say this for them; they had beautiful voices as they sang their mournful tunes of home in the Pyrenees of Spain. They were a sharp contrast to the local Native American Paiutes, who frequented the bar and drank sullenly and quietly until they too might have had a bit too much to drink - then you better watch out! Tonight it wasn't like that. It was quiet, too quiet.

I was very disappointed. Al suggested we ask the bartender if he knew where Margaret might be. We did, and he told us he wasn't sure but he had heard something about a party down at the Sheep Ranch. Where was the Sheep Ranch? He said it was somewhere down near the lakeshore to the north. Darkness was approaching as we turned off Highway 395 and drove a mile down a gravel road toward the lights we had seen in the distance near the shore of Mono Lake.

We had found it! As I got out of the car I could see a roaring fire with many people standing around it and a whole lamb on a spit being barbecued. The next thing I was aware of was Vic, the local Deputy Sheriff, in uniform, walking toward the fire. Someone at the fire turned around and started walking in his direction. It was Margaret and she had one of the sheepherder's bota bags in her hand! I thought, "No, she wouldn't dare! Yes, she would!" - and did! A stream of "full bodied" red wine shot from the sheepskin bota bag as she "offered" Vic a taste of her party. Later he might have some explaining to do about the wine stains on his shirt, but for now he stayed for food and fun. When Margaret saw me she squealed with delight and ran towards me with bota bag in hand and proceeded to "contribute to the delinquency of a minor." A good time was had by all as we partied into the night.

It was a wonderful, warm, crystal clear night here on the east slope of the Sierra Nevada Mountains. Above, a full moon shown brilliantly in the sky, and for those not too blurry eyed to see it, the Milky Way, a sparkling river of stars, streamed overhead. Around 11:00 pm someone suggested that we should move the party to the Hot Springs near Bridgeport. Okay, what and where are they? About 15 miles north of Mono Lake on Highway 395, over Conway Summit, and just south of the town of Bridgeport are some natural hot spring pools that at the time were only know to a few locals. They sat in open ground among a few scattered and scrawny juniper trees. As I recall the one we went into was about 10' x 20' and about 6'-8' deep. About 10 or 12 of us piled into several cars and proceeded to caravan to the hot springs in order to continue celebrating Margaret's birthday.

Al, thank goodness, was our designated driver and for some reason he had the presence of mind to count everybody when we all stripped away our inhibitions and jumped into the water. The water was warm and soothing. Later when I went back in daylight I found my mind had played tricks on me. Actually the water was pretty awful with gobs of green algae floating about and the detritus of human activities strewn about. Some might even say it was disgusting, but on this 21st birthday night it was perfect.

"Who's missing?" Al asked. The count didn't add up and someone was missing! About this time someone stepped on Jose at the bottom of the pool! He was quickly pulled up sputtering and coughing and placed in the back seat of our car. He **seemed** all right, but his condition was enough to have a sobering effect that put a damper on the party. So it was that we broke up the party and taking Jose with us we returned to Tioga Lodge after dropping him off at his abode near Mono Lake. It had been quite a night and quite a memorable party for Margaret after all. Al and I drove back to Red's Meadow, arriving at our log cabin around 3:00 am in the morning.

Who was that banging on the cabin door? Oh God, we'd over slept! When we opened the door, there stood our boss, Bill, and he was not happy! It was 9:00 am and there was work to be done. Because of our tardiness, Bill decided to teach us a lesson. He took us to the Group Campground near Pumice Flats and told us to start digging. Was he going to shoot and bury us for our transgressions and sins? Was this our grave? No, we were to dig a new pit for a "two-holer" toilet. As Bill sat on the ground next to the hole we were trying to dig he sternly lectured us. Digging this hole was not easy. Pumice Flats didn't get its name for being firm ground. It was loose pebbly pumice that was many feet thick, the result of the volcanic activity the area is known for. You dig one shovel full and two fall in. By noon we were finished. Bill invited us over to his house for lunch and cool drinks. We had paid the price for our "Basquing" in the moonlight at Margaret's 21st birthday! Oh yes, and what about Jose? We discovered too late that he did not know how to swim! Jose ended up in the hospital with pneumonia but recovered to sing and dance the Jota again.

"WHERE THERE'S SMOKE, THERE'S FIRE"

As summer came to an end in 1964, I was the last of our Red's Meadow crew still working. Bill had left to return to Los Angles to pursue a job as a police officer and Al had returned to college in Southern California. HSC classes didn't start until mid-September so I could get in a little extra work and earn some much-needed money. I winterized all of the facilities and when I had completed that job I was called up to the District Ranger Headquarters in Mammoth Lakes to fill in as a seasonal fire crew member. I had had minimal training as a firefighter, just the basics shortly after I had reported to duty. During the summer I had only been on one major wildfire. That had occurred on my days off so I was glad to earn the extra overtime, but I was appalled at the amount of waste of manpower and materials that went into putting out a forest fire. The most damaging fire I did see occurred when the refuse disposal site (dump) for the town of Mammoth Lakes ignited and flames overran and destroyed one of the Forest Service fire trucks that had been sent to extinguish the flames.

Living in the barracks at Mammoth only reinforced how lucky I had been to be assigned to Red's Meadow. The few seasonal employees that remained in the barracks had no idea how good we had it compared to them. At least when there weren't fires we didn't have to do "make do" work. Here it was rake the grounds, clean the barracks. It was all very **boring**. The most exciting thing that happened during my first week on "fire standby" was that I was sent over to the Lee Vining Ranger Station to "standby" there. They too were lacking crews and needed another "grunt" in case they needed to send the truck out. One day we did take the Lee Vining truck out, but only to "patrol" around the Mono Cone Craters. That was interesting and fun. For the most part though, there wasn't much to do.

The U.S. Forest Service in the 1960's was still in the "Smokey the Bear" mode of fire protection. If it smoked or burned you put it out - regardless. There were little, if any, control or prescription fires and certainly no opportunity for a natural wildfire to run its course. On one occasion when I was back at Mammoth Lakes I joined two experienced firefighters as part of a crew trying to track down a report of "smoke" east of Highway 395 between Hot Creek and the Owens River. We did not succeed in finding any fire that day as we spent most of our time digging our stuck fire truck out of the soft, sagebrush covered ground. Not to be deterred, we returned the next day in a 4-wheel drive fire truck but only succeeded in getting that truck stuck too.

The second week of my stay in the barracks I finally got some action. The District Fire Control Officer came over to the barracks and found me there. I was the only one left of the summer seasonal crews. He took me outside to a clearing near the highway and pointed to the mountains in the direction of Convict Peak, miles away. He asked if I could see the smoke that was barely visible about halfway up a mountainside. If I squinted hard I could see it. Yes, it was definitely there. **Fire!**

There had been a thunderstorm a few days earlier and with it the accompanying lightening strikes. One of these strikes had hit an old snag and that was what was burning. The Fire Control Officer told me that he had sent a three-man crew with chain saws and other fire equipment, carried by a pack mule, out earlier that morning. They had left in such a hurry they did not take any food with them. I guess this was a real emergency. He wanted me to take lunches up to them. He handed me a backpack with the precious food inside and told me to hurry. The crew had a three-hour start on me and they would surely be hungry by the time I got there.

Dutifully I took the backpack from him. He also gave me a map with the location of the fire marked on it since there were no trails in that area. I drove as close to the area as I thought I could. This wasn't going to be easy. From Mammoth, several miles away the smoke was visible. Here in a forest at the base of 9,000'-10,000' mountain peaks you couldn't see much. I had parked in the area that the Fire Control Officer said was the best starting point. He thought that once I was there I would see the vehicle and trailer of the fire crew. No such luck and no sign of them.

I slung the pack up on my back and started hiking through the pine forest in search of them. After about an hour of hiking I broke out of the forest above the tree line. I had come out onto what appeared to be a rocky avalanche chute. I was in a river of huge boulders and rocky scree. Best of all, straight ahead of me high up the mountainside, maybe a mile away I could see the burning tree. I took a moment to scan the vista around me. The town of Mammoth Lakes was spread out before me like a map. I could pick out familiar landmarks in all directions except the direction I was traveling. Neither in the vicinity of the tree nor in any other direction did I see any sign of the fire crew. Onward and upward I went, making my way hopping and scrambling over the rocks. In another hour I was at the burning tree. Let me get this straight. I left three hours after an experienced fire crew and got here first. Humm... I had a clear view back down the way I had come and still could see no sign of the other fellows. Shouting, I go not response.

I sat down to ponder what to do next and take notice of my surroundings. The burning tree was a large Ponderosa Pine. Several large limbs had burned and fallen to the ground. Pieces from the top of the tree were scattered all about, apparently by the explosive force of the lightening strike. Flame was still visible at what remained at the top of the tree. Most apparent, however, was where the tree stood. It stood **isolated** in the middle of the rocky scree. How its seed initially ever found a foothold and nourishment to grow into such a tall and beautiful specimen is beyond me. **There was nothing else growing here that could burn.**

I continued to wait by the burning tree for another hour with still no sign of the crew. Now I was getting hungry! Nobody, including myself, had thought to pack a lunch for me. Finally, I opened the pack and took out one of the box lunches and ate it. I had no sooner finished when down slope, just above the tree line I saw movement and heard voices carried on the wind. At last, the protectors of our forest! I could see three people but I could not see any pack animal. When they were about half way to me I shouted to them and could tell they were surprised to see someone else up here. It took them a good hour to reach me after I spotted them coming out of the trees.

Once they had reached me they were just as curious as to how I got here ahead of them, as I was curious as to what took them so long. I told my story and they told me theirs. Apparently they had trouble with the mule and took it back to the trailer. That coupled with the fact that they went to the wrong area first had contributed to the delay. I explained that I had gotten hungry and tired of waiting and had eaten one of the lunches. No problem, they had brought food with them after all. I gave them the remaining box lunches anyway. I stayed to watch them do the dangerous work of falling that old burning snag. To what purpose they cut that tree down I haven't a clue.

It had been an unexpectedly long day by the time I got back to the barracks and I was ready to return to college.

RED'S MEADOW, 1965

I was to come back for my second season in the summer of 1965 as part of the Red's Meadow crew. As it turned out neither Bill nor Al returned that second summer so the Mammoth District was hard pressed to find someone to put in charge that was familiar with the Red's Meadow operation. The Red's Meadow unit operated independently from most other forestry and recreational operations of the Mammoth District, situated as it was in blissful isolation below the Minaret crags. I was notified in the spring that I would be "promoted" to Crew Chief for the summer operation and would have the Pumice Flats house for my use. Of course this was an extremely powerful ego boost, but in hindsight I now know that I got the job by default because no one else was available. As I said before, that was to be a pattern that was often to be repeated early in my State Park career.

In any event, the first thing I did was recruit two other HSC acquaintances to apply for the other positions. That is how Bill Supernaugh (now Superintendent of Badlands National Monument) and Norm Cook (now with LA Division of Forestry) came to be on my crew. But wait! You say I get the house in the deal? By now my romance with my sweetheart Margaret was in full bloom. We decided not to wait for graduation and take advantage of these latest developments and get married earlier than we originally had planned. So we did and we drove off in our little Austin-Healy Sprite for another summer at Red's Meadow. As we began our descent into Red's Meadow over Minaret Summit on the rough, dusty, unpaved road Forest Service road we knew not what lay ahead except a little stacked cedar log house at Pumice Flats that was to be our honeymoon abode. It was a summer to remember in married bliss that took the edge off the toiling drudgery of cleaning pit toilets, hauling garbage, and collecting fees while Margaret worked at the Red's Meadows Pack Station store. As blissful as it was that summer, Margaret is quick to remind me that it was also a summer of **no electricity, rats, poison grain** in the floor furnace and **herds of horses** peering in our bedroom window. She also had the chore of trying to press uniform shirts with an antique flat iron (with no handle) heated over the stove. She claimed that it was like ironing with hot rocks! I wouldn't know about that.

When summer came to an end the honeymoon was over. We packed up all of our belongings in our little Sprite and headed up the steep road over Minaret Summit back to college. Stopping briefly at the Summit we looked west to the Minarets, unsure of where our path would take us in the coming year. Would we back?

RED'S MEADOW, 1966

I learned what faith was in 1966. It was in June that I successfully completed the requirements for a Bachelor of Science Degree in Wildlife Management. I still didn't have a full time job of any kind, much less in my chosen field of work. During my senior year at HSC I had taken numerous Civil Service tests for jobs with the US Forest Service, National Park Service, Fish & Wildlife Service, Bureau of Land Management, Nevada State Parks, California Department of Fish & Game and the California Department of Parks and Recreation. Of course there was always the Vietnam War and I was sure a "job" could be found for me there.

After graduation I had decided that in the event that I could not get a good job, my fallback position was to work one more summer at Reds Meadow for the US Forest Service and return to HSC for graduate school in the hope of better things to come. So that is what we opted to do. Margaret and I did not even wait around to go through graduation ceremonies despite the threat that we would not receive our diplomas. Instead, we decided to take our first real vacation to the Grand Canyon before reporting to work at Mammoth Lakes. We had the faith that something would turn up. When we finally did report to the Mammoth Lakes Ranger Station to start the summer season, my return, though welcomed ("out of sight/out of mind"), was not exactly enthusiastic. No one seemed to know if the Pumice Flats house was habitable because no one had been there since we had left the previous fall. Question such as, "where are the keys? Is there propane? Does the generator work? is the water hooked up" all fell on deaf ears and blank faces. There was only one way to find out.

This time we took our new VW Bug over Minaret Summit and down into the valley over the muddy, recently plowed road. Snowdrifts and remains of avalanches were abundant and the Minaret Wilderness Area at our front door was still blanketed in snow. Spring was springing but nights were still cool and before we could enjoy it we had to take care of business and make our home livable again. That meant we had to get into the house since we had no key. Initially, much to our dismay we discovered the house had been broken into via the kitchen window. That made entry easy for me too. Our inspection proved that nothing was missing. In fact, the culprits had forgotten and left a nice single reflex camera that I added to my photographic equipment. It took a couple of days to get the house in order and we even had electricity from the generator for a couple of days before it again went out for the rest of the summer. The biggest problem was again clearing the floor furnace of poison grain that the wood rats and mice had carried off and stored by the bushel in the crooks and crannies of the heater.

As it turned out the summer of 1966 at Red's Meadow was very prophetic for us because it was that summer that we first heard from friends of a place called "Bodie". Our friends told us that it was a very interesting old gold mining town that we should visit if we got the chance. So on a day off from work in August we decided to venture forth to see this ghost town. Bodie is located north of Mono Lake at an elevation of over 8300 feet. It is in some of the most barren, godforsaken, high desert sagebrush country one can imagine. Once a thriving gold mining boomtown of ten thousand inhabitants, it was now a shell of some 180 dilapidated buildings, mine shafts, and few residents other than a small State Park staff.

There were two main washboard roads into Bodie. The **bad one**, a rough 13 mile dirt road off of Highway 395 (now paved) or the **worse one**, up Cottonwood Canyon off of the Hawthorne, Nevada "Poleline" road. We took the ten-mile Cottonwood Canyon road, which steadily climbed, to a ridge that overlooked the "Bodie Bowl" where the townsite lay. To this day I can still remember saying to Margaret "What a neat place, but who in the world would ever want to live here, especially in winter?" Beyond that I have little memory of our visit other than it was indeed an interesting place. After that visit we returned to our summer home at Pumice Flats and didn't give Bodie another thought.

As the summer ended we returned to HSC and our little trailer at Mac's Mobil Manor in the Arcata Bottoms. Margaret went back to work at the drug store and I enrolled in Graduate School. We weren't back in Arcata long before job offers began to come trickle in. Amongst them was an opportunity to join the Navy as a navigator (Math?), a job with the US Forest Service in Oregon, a job with BLM in Battle Mountain, Nevada and even a job as a clerk at Mare Island, California.

Remember the tests I said I had taken in my senior year? One of them had been with the California Department of Park and Recreation. I had taken the test at the Post Office in Eureka, dutifully passed the written exam and for the experience decided to venture down to San Francisco for the oral interview. I knew little of California State Parks, most of the time not even knowing when I was in one. I had never met or talked to a park ranger, having spent most of my time eluding them at Anza-Borrego or evading them to avoid paying camping fees at other parks. During the interview I distinctly remember saying I would like the job because..."I like the outdoors and I like working with people", a phrase I would hear often repeated throughout my career when I sat on the other side of the table conducting interviews. Mr. James Tryner, who for many years was Chief of the Resource Management Division, saw fit to pass me on the interview. I ended up 47th on the hiring list that was issued in March 1966.

Much to my surprise, I did get three different offers as a park ranger for three different parks with the California Department of Parks and Recreation. The first was for Huntington State Beach and the second for Bolsa-Chica State Beach in Southern California from whence I had come and escaped. In those days if you turned down three offers you were placed on an inactive list. Then came the third and final offer. You guessed it. BODIE STATE HISTORIC PARK. Who in the world would want to live there? – **US!**

RED'S MEADOW SKETCHES

Carl S. Chavez

WHAT A WAY TO START

I had accepted a State Park Ranger I position at Bodie State Historic Park at the amazing and stratospheric salary of $530/month! Bursting with pride I couldn't believe I had been selected for the job. Then it dawned on me that being 47th on the list probably meant that 46 others had turned it down. but why?

I grew a little suspicious when I considered my so-called job interview. The only relevant question asked was "When can you get there? because it will be snowing soon." I was told that housing would be provided, but was given no further information as to furnishings or general living conditions other than to be prepared for cold and snow. Incidentally, in passing, I was told there had been some previous personnel problems in Bodie and a new Supervising Ranger would also be reporting about the time I was to arrive in late October. That meant that the only two full-time employees would be **new** to this assignment. Oh yes, because conditions were considered too harsh in Bodie during the winter for children, employees with children were not allowed to be year-round residents. That led to the only other significant question I was asked which was: "Do you have any plans for children in the near future?" That is a question that could not be asked today. At this point I sort of crossed my fingers and answered "No". This at the same time I had told the Navy that "Yes" we had a child on the way. In truth we didn't really know if Margaret was pregnant at the time but we knew there was always that possibility and we were having fun trying to make it happen! I figured, heck, once we were in Bodie what could "They" do about it?

With all our belongings in our little red VW bug and small rental U-Haul trailer we headed for our first adventure. with the Department of Parks and Recreation (DPR). Near Bridgeport, California we had a flat tire just before turning off the paved highway to take the 13-mile washboard dirt road into the ghost town. On October 24th we arrived in Bodie. It had been only three months since our first and only other visit to the ghost town where we had once wondered "Who would ever want to live here?" It was a surprising beehive of activity as State Employees scrambled to complete work shoring up buildings to "a state of arrested deterioration" and struggling to put a new waterline in town. The employees were a summer restoration crew that was anxious to complete their work and be gone before the winter storms arrived.

I identified myself as the new ranger to one of the employees and was directed to Link Covington, who was the Acting Supervisor in Bodie on temporary assignment from Grover Hot Springs State Park. He advised me that there had been some recent staffing problems at the park and the previous Supervisor, who apparently had a drinking problem, was nowhere to be found and hadn't been seen in several weeks. The other permanent employee, John Myers, whom I was replacing, was in the process of moving out of the D.V. Cain residence that we were supposed to occupy. Link explained to me that the new Supervisor, Bob Frenzel and his wife Dorothy had arrived a few hours ahead of us with a moving van and were going to occupy that house instead of us. The problem was that the other house, the J.S. Cain residence, was still occupied by relations of the former Park Supervisor. Link was very apologetic and embarrassed at this inauspicious beginning to my park career. He too was surprised that I really hadn't been thoroughly interviewed about the prospects and living conditions of the job and felt that a ten-minute telephone interview just wasn't sufficient for the challenge that lay ahead. In any case, just as with my first job with the US Forest Service, the immediate problem was to decide what was to be done with us and where we would live until the other house was vacated. The answer was to introduce us to Bob and Dorothy (better known as Dot).

Bob and Dot were promoting and transferring to Bodie from Anza-Borrego Desert State Park. Talk about going from hot to cold! Bob came from a previous career as a Merchant Marine captain, mean and gruff in outward appearance but a "pussy cat" on the inside. Dot was a friendly, out-going, grandmother type. Since they were considerably older then we were, they immediately took us under wing and made us feel comfortable and welcomed. For the most part we were able to forge a good working and living relationship with them. In those first two weeks it was a necessity because we moved in with them! As if that wasn't enough, our best friends from college, John and Judy Calhoun arrived for a stay of several days and moved in with us too!

The time finally did arrive when we were able to move in to our own place at the J.S. Cain House. It was an upscale place for the 1880's, once being the town banker's residence. It had two stories, a huge kitchen with a trap door root cellar, two bedrooms upstairs and one downstairs, a parlor, living room, dining room, bathroom. The park office was also attached off of the dining room. With plenty of propane heat and an abundant wood supply to burn, it was comfortable most of the time though snow often did accumulate on the **inside** of the windowsills during blizzards.

I should say something about my first day of actual work on the job as a Park Ranger. Remember that Bodie is at 8375' elevation. We had recently moved from Arcata which is basically at sea level. That first day found me with pick and shovel in hand, digging a ditch for the water line. Actually, we had to blast the ditch out with dynamite and then muck out the rubble. You could say I got a bang out of my first day on the job. In any event it was hard work for someone not acclimated to that altitude. This time I didn't think I had "died and gone to heaven", I just thought I had died!

Bodie State Historic Park is considered by many as the best-preserved ghost town in the United States. It is registered as a National Historic Site. The uniqueness of Bodie is that it has been preserved in a "state of arrested decay." Buildings are not restored to their original condition. If a structure is leaning, it is stabilized in that position. Over 180 structures remain of this boomtown that once had a population of over 10,000. Bodie Bluff dominates the scene, where an estimated $90-100 million in gold and silver was mined from the deep shafts of the bluff. Still standing on the flanks of the bluff is the Standard Mill where the gold ore was processed. Vehicles are no longer allowed in town and that only adds to the desolate ambiance of the stark terrain

In its heyday between 1879-1881 Bodie was a rough town with over 60 saloons, dance halls and brothels that fueled the reputation of a town that was said to have "man for breakfast" every day in reference to the numerous shootings that took place in Bodie. Perhaps most telling are the words often quoted and attributed to a little girl. When told she was moving to Bodie she is said to have said either, "Goodbye, God, I'm going to Bodie" or "Good, by God, I'm going to Bodie." I think one of those two sentiments applied to us at our first assignment. Only time would tell which meaning applied.

Bodie grows on you. It has a magic, a history, and a stark beauty that we grew to love. Living and working there gave me a strong sense of self-reliance and foundation for a career in State Parks. There are many stories and events I could relate about the year we lived and worked in Bodie. Everyone who has had the privilege of being assigned to Bodie State Historic Park has stories to tell. Bodie had only become a unit of the California State Park System in 1962. Now four years later, it turned out that I was probably one of the first park rangers that really **wanted** to be there and looked forward to the assignment.

WINTER

Neither Margaret nor I had any prior experience living in real winter conditions. After all, there is winter and there is **Winter**, but there is nothing like a Bodie **WINTER**. It is hard to imagine the life of miners and their families in the heyday of Bodie. The hardships they endured are evidenced by a stroll through the cemetery. Winters were tough in those days and took their toll. In our winter of 1966-1967 we did not have telephones, reliable radio communications, TV's, or snowmobiles. What we did have was a Tucker SnoCat for transportation, electricity, propane, firewood and our wives (one of whom was now definitely pregnant) to keep us warm. We also had -20°F to -35°F temperatures to deal with and snow drifts that prevented any vehicle traffic in town from December 5, 1966 until May 11, 1967. Our personal vehicles were kept in a tin shed at the "Goat Ranch" located about a mile from the paved "Poleline" road and about 9 miles from Bodie. We stationed one of the park's old Four Wheeled Drive (4WHD) vehicles at the snow line, wherever that might be at a given time, to shuttle out to in the SnoCat and then drove that vehicle to our cars at the shed. Most of all when you really got right down to it, the only two full time Rangers assigned to this

Unit had a tremendous lack of knowledge and experience of the harsh winter conditions and operational problems that lay ahead. If it had not been for one of the restoration crew members I don't know how we could have survived that winter. Bobby Bell had been born and raised in Bodie as had his father before him. The house he grew up in is still there. Bobby was a wealth of knowledge and he remained in town offering his wisdom and suggestions on enduring the winter until that day in December when snow and the icy grip of winter closed the town. The last thing he did before heading out of town was hand me a hand-crank battery operated telephone and showed me where to climb a telephone pole and tap into a nearby telephone line in the case of a real emergency. Wait a minute. If there is a nearby telephone line, why don't we have a telephone? "Cost" I am told. My God, I thought, what have I got Margaret in to?

The worst experience I encountered that winter occurred on December 13th. As a new Ranger, with little formal job orientation, I didn't know what was expected of me. On that day Supervising Ranger Frenzel and I had left in the morning for Bishop, California as storm clouds were building. Taking care of business in Bishop I returned ahead of Bob to the Goat Ranch vehicle storage area and awaited his arrival in another vehicle he had picked up at a repair shop. I waited and waited and waited. The wind began blowing and it was now snowing to beat the band but still no sign of Bob as darkness approached. I thought he should have been right behind me but I had now waited over an hour for him and I was becoming increasingly concerned, not only for him, but also for our wives who were all alone in Bodie with a blizzard in progress. At last at about 5:00pm I saw some wavering headlights coming up the Cottonwood Canyon road. I opened the garage door so Bob could park his vehicle. What should happen next but he backed in very fast and slammed into my little red VW!

As Bob got out of the vehicle he started at my

presence and mumbled some incoherent words about wanting to go have a drink with Curly, the Goat Ranch foreman. My God! Bob was more than a little inebriated and he had driven, in uniform, all the way from Bishop to the Goat Ranch! Actually, he was falling down drunk. What was I to do? I'd been on the job a little more than one month and was still on a year probation period that had to be evaluated by this man. Bob kept insisting that we had to go visit and have a drink with Curly. I insisted we had to get back to Bodie and to our wives who surely would be worried about us. Youth won out over Bacchus as I manhandled Bob into the SnoCat for the trip back to Bodie. He immediately passed out on my shoulder as I started up the SnoCat for the hour ride back to town. It was now snowing so heavily I had difficulty following the road as visibility was down to near zero and the vertigo effect of the headlights on the blowing and falling snow disoriented my senses. As I reached the summit ridge leading into the Bodie Bowl I caught a glimpse of glowing lights from our two houses. Old, abandoned telephone pole snow markers helped me find my way along the road as the snow obliterated the lights from town. At last, around 6:30pm, after driving over several feet of drifting snow, we arrived in front of Bob's house. Dot came out to greet us, worried, as I knew she would be. I was upset and fit to be tied. All I managed to say to her was "Take the #@*+/!" as I shoved him out of the cab into her arms.

Now what do I do? I worried all night about what I should do about today's events. Do I ignore this obviously unprofessional, and to say the least, dangerous lapse in my Supervisor's judgment? Do I report him to higher ups in the organization? Do I do nothing? Help, I'm still on probation. They didn't cover this situation in a college course in Wildlife Management!

This is what I did. I had been in the habit since my arrival in Bodie of keeping a daily typewritten journal. I went to the journal and typed in a brief account of what had occurred. The next morning I waited again for Bob to

31

come in the office which, as I mentioned before, was part of our residence. I spent the next morning waiting for Bob to come in. 8:00am...9:00am...10:00am came and went. Finally, at 11:00am there was a knock at the door. Bob stuck his head in and asked "What are you going to do about yesterday?" I didn't say a word and merely pointed to the typewriter with my journal account there for his reading. I finally said, "If this ever happens again and you endanger our lives or that of our wives this goes in to the Stockton Headquarters Office". That ended the problem.

THE GREAT SNOCAT ROBBERY

You have heard previous mention of the SnoCat. For those of you not familiar with a Tucker SnoCat let me try to describe one. Envision a large cab-enclosed vehicle that sits upon four large pontoons with rollers and tracks much like an army tank. When it works, it is an ideal and generally reliable vehicle for travel over snow. Our SnoCat at Bodie had two seats up front and bench seats along the sides, all passengers and cargo being enclosed. The enclosed cab was not, however, lockable. We also had a sled trailer that could be pulled behind for transporting additional cargo. It was International Orange in color over its aluminum skin.

Our major problem with the SnoCat was that it did require constant maintenance, especially the greasing of all of the roller bearings on the four pontoon tracks. Under "normal" circumstances this might not have been a problem. Our situation was not normal. We had no heated garage to work in or store the SnoCat. Consequently, in the cold temperatures it was difficult to service. In order to start it one had first to squirt ether into the carburetor to get the engine going. Next, a flexible metal hose had to be connected from the exhaust to ports built into the sides of the pontoons in order to heat and thaw the rollers and loosen the tracks from the previous night's icy grip. If the SnoCat needed gasoline we had to go through another elaborate process of transferring gas from a storage tank near the "County Barn" into a 55-gallon steel drum and then hand pump the gasoline into SnoCat.

Despite its shortcomings, the SnoCat was our link to the outside world. This was just before snowmobiles were a common mode of winter transportation. If the SnoCat didn't work we either stayed put in town until it was fixed or we walked. Indeed, Margaret and I did walk out on several occasions. In one instance in March, when Margaret was 6 months pregnant, we hiked out for an hour and fifteen minutes over snow in the early morning to reach the park's 4WHD at the snow line. We kept the SnoCat stocked with emergency gear such as sleeping bags, snowshoes, spare parts and tools and first aid equipment in case we were stranded or needed to assist others.

On the morning of April 19, 1967 I went through the routine of preparing the SnoCat for a trip out of Bodie. Because we had had 5" of snow the previous day I had to scrape the ice and snow from the windshield. In doing this I utilized a unique "Tony the Tiger" (thank you General Mills) ice scrapper that was kept in the SnoCat for that purpose. Today we were going in to Bridgeport to pick up the mail, do some shopping and keep an appointment with Dr. Elliott who was looking after Margaret's pregnancy.

Except for the usual rough bouncy ride that was particularly difficult on Margaret in her "with child" state of affairs, our trip out was uneventful. We made the transfer to the park's 4WHD at the snow line and drove the remaining 5 miles on slushy snow and mud to the paved highway. On previous trips out I had noticed that several people had attempted to drive their vehicles up the road to Bodie only to be stopped by snow at the higher elevations. In order to stop this I had put up a series of signs in "Burma Shave" fashion warning people of the conditions ahead so they wouldn't continue on and get stuck. I would put a scratch mark on the sign each time I discovered that a vehicle had gotten stuck. There were over 20 marks by the time the road opened in May.

We concluded our business in Bridgeport early because, as it turned out, Dr. Elliott was unavailable. Because of this we made the return trip back to the SnoCat sooner than originally planned. As we drove up the muddy road back to the SnoCat I noticed a new set of vehicle tracks that hadn't been there before indicating that someone in a vehicle had obviously ignored my warning signs. Rounding the last bend in the road to where the SnoCat was parked we came upon a vehicle pulling a U-Haul trailer stuck sideways across the road. Two male characters, of dubious appearance, were standing next to the stuck vehicle. I was immediately suspicious of the situation, noting that these two individuals were not dressed appropriately for the severe winter conditions. One of them actually had on a light short-sleeve, Hawaiian type cotton shirt while the other had on only a light jacket. At this point I noticed that the one wearing the jacket had a familiar "Tony the Tiger" ice scrapper sticking out of his pocket. In fact I was sure it was the one I had used that morning as I prepared the SnoCat for the trip. Next I noticed the driver's side door on the SnoCat was open a bit. I was positive I had closed it tightly when we left a few hours earlier. Trying not to show my concern, I offered to help the two "tourists" free their vehicle from its predicament. We were successful in this but I noticed their car's taillights were not operating properly. I offered to take a look and fix the lights and asked if they would open the trunk. They declined my offer and appeared anxious to be on their way. I did nothing to stop them, as I did not have the means to do so. State Park Rangers at this time were not fully sworn Peace Officers, had little training, and we carried no firearms or other defensive weapons. Our mouth and brains and/or ignorance were the total extent of our protection.

As soon as these folks departed I jumped into the SnoCat and tried to start the engine. Nothing happened. I then noted the latches to the engine hood were unlocked and the battery was gone! In a flash I was in the truck and chasing after the culprits. At this point reason took over in the form of my wife who said something like "Slow down, what are you going to do if you catch them?" With that sound advice I did slow down and trailed the thieves at a safe distance from which I thought we wouldn't be seen. Once we reached the Poleline road it was easy to see the crooks had not headed east on the straight and narrow road toward Hawthorne, Nevada. Instead we saw them and their trailer heading west toward Highway 395 before we lost sight of them in a series of dips in the road ahead. Our plan was now to head for Mono City, along the north shore of Mono Lake off of the Poleline Road, where we knew Mono County Deputy Sheriff Vic lived. Vic was the sheriff that Margaret had doused with wine at her 21st birthday party two year earlier.

Imagine our surprise when we pulled up to Vic's house only to see, two doors down the street, the dumb criminals we had been chasing parked in a vacant lot. Fortunately they did not spot us as I pulled out of sight screened by Vic's house. Now I only had to roust the deputy. Alas, he wasn't home and the door was locked! The nearest telephone for help was located at the Mono Inn about 5 miles further down the road on Highway 395. We decided to make a break for it and hoped that we wouldn't be seen as we left. At the Mono Inn we called the Sheriff's Office and were told that the nearest assistance was from a Highway Patrol officer who would be enroute from June Lake, another 20 miles away.

The CHP Officer finally did arrive and we told him our story as we drove with him in his vehicle back to Mono City. If we were surprised before, we were really in for a shock now as we drove up to the vacant lot with the suspect vehicle still parked there. Both the suspects were partially out of sight inside the vehicle as we drove up. On hearing our approach they raised their heads and lo and behold, one of them was wearing my snow hat which I had left in the SnoCat that morning!

The CHP Officer placed them under arrest and searched their vehicle. Inside was not only our SnoCat battery, but our tools, sleeping bags, tow chain, etc. The Officer also relieved the suspects of the numerous knives they were carrying. While we waited in the relative comfort of the CHP officer's warm sedan he had the "bad guys" waiting in the freezing wind for over and hour with their hands on the roof of their car until the backup sheriff unit arrived from Bridgeport to transport them to jail.

It was obvious that these two "treasure hunters" had been on their way to Bodie to steal all the artifacts they could get their hands on. As it was, the culprits were convicted of petty theft misdemeanor charges. They had been "kind" enough to leave our snowshoes in the SnoCat. If they had taken them they would have been charged with a felony as the amount of the theft would have exceeded a $200 limit.

Several months later, in the vicinity of Bishop, California we spotted "our friends" who were hitchhiking along the roadway. One had to be amazed that they weren't in the hospital recovering from pneumonia or worse after their ordeal standing in the cold along the shores of Mono Lake awaiting transport to jail. Needless to say we didn't stop to pick them up! Thus ended the Great SnoCat Robbery.

ALL ALONE, ALMOST

Because it was often such a struggle to journey out of Bodie in the winter, when we did leave we usually went out for more than a day. It was our practice to always have one of the rangers on duty each day. This usually meant that Margaret and I or Bob and Dot would be gone for two to four days at a time with the remaining party transporting them out to the vehicles in the SnoCat and by pre-arrangement picking them up on their return. That is how it was supposed to work.

Occasionally there were glitches in our system. For

our part, Margaret and I always had a contingency plan that we used on several occasions. Margaret's former employer at Tioga Lodge, Norm Cunningham, had given us a key to one of the A-frame cabins he owned for our use in an emergency. Because the cabin was winterized, we did not have water but we had electricity and heat so we could hole up for the night during a storm and be picked up by Ranger Frenzel the next day. That was better than our option of last resort which was to stay at the Goat Ranch with the ranch caretaker, Mr. Clair "Red" Clark. We did that only once during a blizzard of January 21st and never again. "Red" did provide us a meal of sorts and offered us a filthy bed for the night. It was the "only room in the inn". We slept nary a wink that night as "Red's" nightmare induced groans, shouts, and expletives and talking in his sleep kept us wide awake that long night.

Previously I mentioned that the winter population of Bodie was four: two rangers and two wives. Actually there was a fifth member of our crew. That was a dog named "Smokey". She had been left with us by one of the summer restoration crew members. Though rather rotund and elderly, Smokey was a lovable Australian sheep dog and a good companion. Usually her only exercise was the walk between our house and the Frenzel's home as she went in search of the best warming fire to lay beside and the most scrumptious, tasty food to chow down on.

A recent review of my "Bodie Journal" reminded me how lonely Bodie could be. One day in March, Margaret and her brother Larry, along with a cousin and her three young daughters, who had been visiting us, had to walk out due to the breakdown of the SnoCat. I had also made the trek cross-country the previous day hauling out their luggage on a toboggan to the park vehicle. The five-mile hike out over the snow the next day was an adventure in itself in the freezing temperatures because some of our guests did not have proper winter footwear, but we all made it okay as you will later read.

Margaret and I continued on to visit her parents

and I returned back to Bodie a couple of days later, leaving Margaret with her folks. I had to walk back into town as the SnoCat was still broken down with cracked wheel bearings. The next day I was able to replace the bearings and get the SnoCat operational. It was then that Bob and Dot decided to drive to Folsom, leaving Smokey and me alone in Bodie. That wouldn't have been too bad but they took the SnoCat with them. Here are a few entries from my journal:

"March 27- Bob left the SnoCat up on the ridge. I can see it from here".

"March 28-It has begun to snow with the wind really humming (through) the wires. Smokey and I are bored without Margee around to play with. Oh, how I hope the snow won't stick."

"March 29- ...0° last night...I can't believe how quiet it is around here. I wish some ghosts would drop in so I could talk to somebody else besides dear Smokey. She always falls asleep when I get her into a conversation."

"March 30- Bob and Dot didn't show up today as I hoped. I am definitely beginning to crack up I think. Haven't seen anybody since the pilot of the jet circled low enough to wave at me!"

At this point I couldn't stand the complete isolation any longer so the next morning Smokey and I hiked out to the SnoCat in search of Bob and Dot. I found them in Bridgeport and proceeded on to pick up Margaret.

My previous mention of the pilot in the jet plane is interesting. One lonely day as I was going "stir crazy" I decided that Smokey and I should take a hike up into the hills behind town. The stark desolation and isolation of the moment still haunts me occasionally. We had reached the summit of a small hill about a mile from town when the silence was shattered by a formation of four A4D Skyhawk fighter planes streaking down through the Bodie

Bowl. I knew they were probably from the Fallon Naval Air Station in Nevada.

The jets were actually flying **below** my level on the hill and very, very close to me. At the time I was wearing a bright red snow parka which I proceeded to take off and wave at the jets, never thinking for a moment that they would actually see me. They did! One of the fighter planes peeled off and began circling around me. He was close enough that I could see his face. It was then that I realized that he might have thought that I was in trouble. I frantically waved my arms trying to make the pilot understand all was okay but soon I realized that my arm waving probably only made things worse. I finally gave up and just turned around and headed for home. I worried all the rest of that day and the next that a false alarm search and rescue operation might be in progress. Then I worried that one had **not** been put into action and what would have happened if I had actually needed help. So it was I found out that even when you are alone in Bodie you are only **almost** alone.

A WALK IN THE PARK

As I said before, in winter and spring there were several occasions when we had to walk out of Bodie because the SnoCat broke down. One of the most memorable of these "walks" I briefly mentioned previously. That was when Margaret's brother and cousin's had come for a visit.

The adventure started innocently enough one day in March when Bob and I drove out in the morning in the SnoCat to shuttle our park vehicles further up the road to the retreating snow line. This was necessary to prevent having to drive the SnoCat over mud and gravel between patches of snow. The mud and gravel caused havoc to the roller bearings on the SnoCat. It was not a simple procedure to get all the vehicles moved and it took four hours by the time we had moved two vehicles to the snow line. That included the time it took to dig them out from the mud several times after we had managed to get them stuck.

At about 4:00 pm Margaret's brother Larry, radioed us from the Mammoth Lakes Sheriff station informing us that he and Margaret's cousin Celia and three daughters ranging in age from 8 to 12 years old would meet me at the Goat Ranch. I drove the SnoCat back to where Bob and I had earlier left the 4-WHD truck and picked up our guests for the SnoCat ride back to Bodie. It was great fun for them. It was hard work for me. We finally got back to town about 7:00 pm.

The next two days we entertained guests with snowshoe hikes, snowman building and toboggan runs whizzing past the schoolhouse on Green Street. In preparation for our guests leaving the next day, I began to get the SnoCat ready for the trip out. As I was pumping gasoline from a 55-gallon drum to top off the SnoCat's gas tanks, I noticed that one of the pontoons was off-center from the axle. Closer inspection showed that a bearing had disintegrated, probably as a result of the mud and gravel we had traveled through earlier. I knew immediately that this meant we would have to walk out the next day.

Walking out of Bodie did not pose any special problem for either Margaret or me, even though Margaret was 6 months pregnant. We had done it several times before and we would do it again after this episode. It was a different story for our guests. They were "flatlanders" from Los Angeles not used to, or prepared for the extreme cold and snow conditions. For example almost all of them had brought only tennis shoes as footwear. There was still 3'-4' of snow on the ground. The problem was that late in the morning, as the temperature rose, the surface of the snow would become slushy and difficult to walk on. The other problem was that they had brought so much "stuff" with them. There were suitcases, sleeping bags, and even a typewriter. Bringing their belongings into Bodie on the SnoCat had been easy, walking out and carrying everything with us would be difficult, if not impossible.

I decided I would have to make a trip by myself in order to shuttle some of the gear out to the parked vehicle. That would lighten our load for the hike in the morning. The roadway out to the truck at the snow line circled around and between several peaks. I was not looking forward to a four or five mile hike lugging suitcases, sleeping bags and a typewriter. Then I thought, "the shortest distance between two points is a straight line." Brilliant, I would go cross-country, on a direct line to the truck, and save several miles of walking.

I loaded up the toboggan with three suitcases, sleeping bags, and typewriter and departed at 3:30 pm, hiking to the top of Green Street near the old railroad station. From there I cut across to the Red Cloud mine building. I rode on top of the toboggan down a steep slope into a snowfield below. That was fun, except that I got going so fast that I lost the flashlight I was carrying (I found it later in the spring after the snow melted). Well, maybe this was not going to be such fun after all. I was now down at the bottom of a snow bowl and would have to slog my way up, breaking snow trail all the way and pulling a toboggan, up to a gap in the ridge I could see above me. I figured that gap was just above where the truck was parked. Of course I didn't have a clue what was on the other side of that ridge.

I struggled through the snow, sometimes sinking in as deep as my thighs. I knew I could not bring the others out this way tomorrow. My shortcut wasn't a shortcut after all. Once I reached the top of the ridge I could see the truck below me off in the distance, parked near what we called the "Silver Mine." It was a long way off, but at least it was all down hill from here, and I had a toboggan!

I had to make a choice. The safe, but longer and slower way, winding down across the hillside, or the more hazardous, but direct route straight down a long snow filled gully. I choose the latter and climbed atop the suitcases, typewriter and sleeping bags for the trip of my life. Olympic bobsledders had nothing over me. I skimmed over snow, rocks, and sagebrush, ending up at the bottom in a tumble of gear and snow. I had a few bruises and minor cuts and scratches but no broken bones

I gathered everything together and pulled the toboggan the remaining short distance to the truck and locked everything inside. Prudently, I decided not to take my "shortcut" back to town. I walked up the road back to Bodie arriving at about 6:30 pm.

That evening I told the others the plan for tomorrow. We would all have to get up early and leave before the sun began melting the snow surface. I told them it would be very cold in the morning, probably around 20°, so they should dress as warmly as they could with their remaining clothes. Footwear was going to be the main problem. We told the kids to wrap their tennis shoes in plastic bags for the hike out but they would have none of that.

The next morning the alarm went off at 4:30 am. We prepared for the trip out and had a hearty breakfast, leaving the house at 6:20 am via the Cottonwood Canyon road. Despite, cold feet, and a little whining from the kids, they all did surprisingly well and we made it out to the truck in about two hours. Our guests departed south for Los Angeles with tales of adventure. Margaret and I departed north and west to Sacramento for repair parts for the SnoCat. For us it was just "another walk in the park."

SAGE(HEN) ADVICE

As lonely as Bodie appeared, there was actually plenty of life around us. Frequently we saw a herd of pronghorn antelope in the hills behind town. Sometimes they would race alongside our car on the old Masonic Road leading north out the back way to Bridgeport. We saw coyote, even in winter, and then there was the badger that made his home down the road at the dump. Occasionally we also saw deer or bobcat, but most often we would see the bobcat's most common prey, the brush rabbit. Birds were plentiful in the spring. Golden Eagles and other raptors, Flickers, Blue Birds, Dickcissels, seagulls, quail, and Sage Hens were common. If the wildlife didn't spark your interest you could always get thrill from being chased by a "domestic" Santa Gertrudies bull that might wander into town to rub his behind against one of the leaning buildings. One of our jobs was to move the cattle out of the town so they wouldn't knock buildings over with all of that rubbing!

It was the Flicker and not the cattle that initially had me "buffaloed". Early one morning in the spring, a knocking (I thought) on the door awoke us. There were still several feet of snow on the ground and I knew that no one could have driven into town. Perhaps someone had hiked or skied in, but why so early in the morning? Was there some kind of emergency? I got up, threw on a robe, and went to the door expecting to find someone in need of help. I opened the door but there was no one there. Had I been dreaming? I went back to bed. Again the knocking at the front door. Once again I got up and went to the door and quickly yanked it open. Still no one was there. Was this some kind of joke? If so, I wasn't finding it funny. I was now too alert to go back to sleep and Margaret was also wide-awake. The third time the knocking occurred I slowly got out of bed and snuck over to our bedroom window and peaked outside to see who was doing this. I couldn't see anyone, but this time the knocking continued. I gave up, got dressed and went out into the cold air and snowy front yard. The knocking stopped. I stopped. There it was again. I slowly crept towards the bedroom corner of the house, hugging the wall as I went. When at last I reached the corner of the house I peeked around it only to find that our early morning guest was a Red-Shafted Flicker that had decided to bore a hole into the exterior wall of our bedroom. The mystery was solved and I was no longer mad at the world for interrupting my sound sleep.

We also had a resident pair of Great Horned Owls

that lived and nested high up in the rafters of the Standard Mill. They were interesting year round companions and I often hiked up to the mill to check on them. Usually when I went into the mill the big birds took little notice of me as I made winter inspections of the impressive stamp mill where so much gold had been processed. The owls would maintain their stately, dignified posture, seemingly twisting their heads off their necks and peer down at me. I always found it interesting to inspect the area under their roosting site for the "owl pellets" (regurgitated remains of their meals) that accumulated there. The bits of bones, skulls and hair gave an indication of how truly efficient these night hunters were in reducing the rodent population.

One day in the spring, May 14, 1967 to be exact, we had some friends from Mammoth Lakes visiting us. I decided to give them a tour of the Mill. Since the spring thaw was in full progress we had to hike through mud and slush to reach the mill. The lighting inside the Mill when we entered was of very low intensity and very diffused. What light there was streamed through the window openings and the dust in the atmosphere scattered the light giving it a golden hue that mixed with the dark shadows. The only sounds to be heard was the drip of snow melting from eaves onto lower levels of the corrugated tin roof. The feeling was surreal and a bit eerie.

Suddenly from high in the rafters, completely unexpected and surprising to us, one of the owls took flight above our heads. It headed straight for one of the window openings. I guess we must have surprised the owl more than it surprised us because at that moment it had chosen to fly through a window that still had its glass panes. The owl crashed right through the window shattering it and sending glass raining down upon us.

Apparently the Great horned Owl was uninjured and none the worse for wear in "crashing our party". If nothing else he was surely a wiser bird for this miscalculation of his normal flight pattern.

The other interesting ornithological event we witnessed was the spring arrival of the flocks of seagulls from their Mono Lake nesting area. Hundreds of these birds would fly in each afternoon to feast upon the gigantic bullfrog pollywogs that inhabited the intermittent streams and ponds that were the result of the spring thaw. The seagulls would gorge themselves to the point of sometimes appearing too heavy to take flight again. The incongruity of seagulls in a ghost town like Bodie always has amazed me.

Later, in the spring and summer the Sage Hens arrived. Flocks of these chicken-size birds would cover the hillsides. In the fall there was a two or three day hunting season on them. That didn't seem fair. Even chickens were smarter than these birds. Heck, you didn't even need a gun to get one of them. That summer I had caught several Sage Hens by hand. I had read somewhere that these birds could not fly very far. They flew in a similar fashion to pheasants, suddenly bursting from cover and then flapping wildly only to glide to another location. The Sage Hens were not capable of this flight behavior too many times in quick succession before they became exhausted. If they were quickly flushed from their cover without much time to rest, the distance they could fly would be less and less until they simply "hunkered" down and froze. At that point you could walk up to them and pick them up.

I tried it and it worked! It was best to have several people in the hunting "pack" in order to run relays so you could quickly tire out the birds. If the Sage Hens were on a hillside and had a long slope to glide down the task was impossible. At the 8300′ elevation one did not have the stamina to run very far, at least I didn't. But if you surprised a flock on flat ground you had a chance.

I documented such an event in my Bodie Journal on August 23, 1967. In the afternoon we noticed a school bus stopped beyond the park boundary on the Cottonwood Canyon road. Earlier in the day the bus had brought a group of Job's Daughters from the Los Angeles area into Bodie for a visit and history lesson. After their visit the group left in the bus but stopped along the road about a mile outside of town.

At first we took no further notice of the bus as Jack Bogle and Gene Reed, our two Park Aides, and I assumed the bus had stopped to look at something they found of interest. However, after three hours the bus was still there. We figure that something was wrong so the Park Aides and I got in our truck and drove the mile out to where the bus was parked. We could see that the engine compartment was open and the bus driver was busy fiddling with the engine. He told us that he thought he had the problem just about fixed but he had a busload of teenage girls who definitely were not happy with the situation. The three of us boarded the bus and began to entertain them and regale them with stories of Bodie. At some point one of the girls noticed a flock of Sage Hens run across the road. I saw them too and began an explanation about the birds and how you could catch them by hand. They did not believe me and thought I was just telling them another tall tale from Bodie. Gene and Jack had no luck convincing them that we were not kidding. Finally, I told them that if some of them would help us I would prove my thesis.

Several of the girls volunteered to help, probably anxious to get out of the cramped bus where they had been sitting for the past three hours. We spotted the flock of Sage Hens again and I placed Jack, Gene and the girls in what I deemed strategic positions in order to force the birds to fly in a direction that was most advantageous to us. We forced the Sage Hens to fly up slope. This must have been a lazy flock because it only took us two runs to tire one of the birds out. I was able to walk right up to it as I had described to the girls and grab it. We took the bird back to the bus and showed it to the rest of the group who squealed in delight.

Shortly after that the bus driver got the bus working again and off they went headed for Yosemite National Park. The three of us, with bird in hand got in the truck to return to town. We had never eaten Sage Hen before and wondered how it tasted. We had no legal right to the bird, but we hadn't captured the Sage Hen within the State Park boundary. That was enough justification for us to decide that in the interest of "scientific research" we should find out what this bird tasted like. As we drove back to town we began a discussion of how and who would kill and cook the bird. None of us wanted to play butcher. At this point, the bird, which I was holding suddenly made a funny gurgling sound, convulsed in a series of jerks, and died in my hands. We felt terrible! Had our talk of killing this Sage Hen resulted in its death? If so it was "sage advice" that should have been ignored by the bird!
We did end up cooking the specimen. We also now know why it is called **Sage** Hen.

SIGNS OF THE TIMES

Today as you enter Bodie via the Cottonwood Canyon road you will see a rustic entrance sign and flagpole off to your right. It reads "Bodie State Historic Park, EL. 8375'". There may still be an old ore cart spilling its cargo of ore next to the sign. When you see this sign you will be looking at a labor of love. It is the creation of Park Supervisor Bob Frenzel.

Bob was a Ranger from the "Old School." He could drink with the best of them, be it alcohol or coffee, and he had to have his cigarettes. As a former sea captain, he loved the ocean, yet he had spent most of his park career in the desert. He was most comfortable when he was doing maintenance work. His strength was that he was straightforward and honest and had a big heart. His weakness was that he was a procrastinator.

When the snow began to melt with the spring thaw

in May of 1967 Bob decided he needed a project that he could work on in the outdoors as the weather warmed. He decided that the park needed two new signs. One of the signs was to be a new entrance sign and the other was to be a sign directing visitors to the parking lot adjacent to a building know as the "County Barn". Bob described to me what he had in mind and asked me to make a drawing of the entrance sign for him. The parking lot sign was much simpler he said and he didn't need a drawing for that one. I designed about a 4' x 8' sign made of four thick weathered boards and gave him the drawing. He liked the design but thought the routed letters should be burned to give the sign a more rustic and weathered appearance. I too thought that was a good idea.

My Bodie Journal indicates that Bob started working on the entrance sign around May 5th. Margaret and I watched with growing interest as Bob set up his work area for the sign between his house and the Red Barn. We couldn't understand why the setup was taking so long. Not long as in hours, but long as in days. We thought all that he really needed was a couple of boards, two sawhorses, a skill-saw, a router, and an extension cord. But we were unaware that this took so much time. First you had to think about gathering up the materials and equipment. Then you had to tell us about it and then you had to tell Dot about it, and then you had to ask Carl, Margaret, and Dot if you had told us you are about to start work on the sign. You get the idea.

The day finally arrived that the first significant progress was apparent on the sign. Bob had actually cut the boards and doweled and glued them together. Now it was time to watch the glue dry. That must have taken at least a week or two. We figured that Bob must have already been through at least one can of Folger's Coffee in the weeks since he had started on this project.

In June, when the road was clear of snow and park visitors began to arrive in greater numbers, Bob had actually started work with his router to do the letters and numbers needed for the sign. There were 36 characters that needed to be routed. Progress was being made, as Bob completed five letters: **"BODIE",** by the end of May!

June was a little better month for letters as he got as far as "**STATE HIST**", a new monthly record!

July had not been a good month because there were distractions. Those darn tourists who were always wandering around town would come over to see what he was doing and interrupt his work. Then there were the Santa Gertrudis cattle that became curious and wanted to inspect the job too. Bob took to shooting them with his pellet gun to shoo them away. To us it looked like he was standing guard over his masterpiece. To the park visitor he looked like a Ranger in uniform shooting wildlife. Maybe I'm being too critical because, after all, he was now working on **two** signs. He had begun work on the **PARKING LOT** sign and that was no easy task because it had to have a directional **arrow** routed on it.

Bob rebounded in August and added **"ORIC PARK"** and **"ELEVATION"** for a grand total of 17 characters! Go Bob! Not only that, but he finished the parking lot sign that month. I went over to inspect his completed work. It looked okay but I then asked him exactly where he intended to place the sign. He told me he was going to put it on the right side of the roadway before the vehicles turned **left** into the parking lot. I then asked, "Then why does the arrow point **right**?" Bob went stomping off into his house. I guess it must have been time for a smoke and coffee again. The next day Bob told me to come over and look at the sign again. He had rip-sawed the arrow portion of the board and re-doweled and glued it **with the arrow on it turned upside down** so that it now pointed in the opposite direction! Very clever.

The first week of September showed us what Bob was made of. He not only finished routing **"8375'"** but he burnished all of the letters to give it the rustic appearance he wanted. The sign was officially completed and installed on September 15th, a little more than 5 months since work had begun. It was a **sure sign of our times**. I guess things just went at a slower pace in those days!

BODIE BABY

In truth when we arrived in Bodie we didn't know that Margaret was pregnant. The policy at the time was that employees with children were not assigned to Bodie because of the perceived harsh conditions. When we first realized that we were to be parents we kept quiet about the situation. However, as with most pregnancies, there comes a time when it becomes obvious. Dr. James Elliott was our trusted physician in Bridgeport. In the winter he would fly over our house in his airplane and buzz us to see how we were doing. I guess he expected us to come outside and give him a thumbs up. We did.

Eventually we told Bob and Dot about our situation (even though Dot had already figured it out much earlier) and the word went up the line that the population of Bodie would be increasing sometime in June. Once the word was out we were carefully watched over by friends, family, the Parks Department, and the citizen of Bridgeport. Suddenly we were news.

The pregnancy seemed to go well. Dr. Elliott thought the baby would be due around the first week of June. Throughout the winter Margaret was in good health as I mentioned before, and had even been able to walk out of town over the snow on several occasions. The one worry we did have was would we be able to get out of town to the hospital in Bridgeport when the time came for delivery of the baby. The problem, of course, was that there was still plenty of snow around and little hope of getting a vehicle, other than the SnoCat, in or out of town through the snow even as we entered the first week of May.

What is that yonder speck on the ridge? Could be, yes it is. The Mono County bulldozer was coming to clear the road at last! We now could bring our own vehicles into town. A few park visitors began arriving. Of course drivers had to be careful not to run a vehicle over the soft muddy ground where the waterline had been put in back in November. I had placed a sign at the entrance of the park advising visitors to utilize the parking lot next to the County Barn and warning drivers not to park in town. I kept score on the sign with marks indicating the number of vehicles that had been stuck. Over the next few weeks 30-40 vehicles, including a Mono County grader, and Supervisor Frenzel failed to heed the warnings to stay off of the waterline route and paid the consequences by sinking up to their axles in the morass of mud.

In Bob's case he got so mad about the stuck truck that he abandoned it in the ditch and stomped off home for a cup of coffee muttering, "Leave the damn truck there". Of course the park truck, stuck in the mud up to its axles, was a great source of amusement to the many tourist walking about town. Finally, Bob came back to the office and asked me if I thought we should get the truck out of the ditch. Of course I said, "Yes" and we did. In any event, if we avoided the ditch, we now had the freedom to come and go as we pleased in our private vehicles.

With the road open and travel easier we were ready for the baby's arrival. I tied Margaret's boots on her and dragged her out on long walks each day in an attempt to speed up this stubborn kid. The doctor even tried to induce labor to no avail. Nothing we could do would convince this kid to make an appearance. But all was not lost as the hikes provided a great opportunity to see colorful spring wildflowers all about us and spot the occasional antelope, coyote, badger, or Sage Hen in the surrounding hills. The snow melt produced numerous ponds and streamlets which provided habitat for hoards of huge tadpoles which hundreds of seagulls, flying in from Mono Lake, feasted upon. Before going to bed on the night of June 22nd I had Margaret lift the window shades and look out at the full moon. I was getting tired of waiting, as I'm sure Margaret was, and perhaps this would have a positive effect on the pending birth.

At 1:30 am Margaret awoke me and said "Carl, I think something is happening". What a memory I have of walking under a full moon, all alone on the Bodie boardwalk, on my way to get the car from the parking lot. It was not silent. Spring was still in the air and even at this early hour the Dickcissels were singing out their mating calls. These birds, similar to, but smaller, than Meadowlarks happily serenaded me with their songs of joy as the echoes of my footsteps fell in step with ghosts of the past. The 13-mile trip on the rough dirt road to Highway 395 and then seven more miles into town didn't seem to bother Margaret though inwardly I was in a mild panic. We got to the hospital at 3:00 am

Abigail Rose was born on June 23, 1967 at 4:27 am, the 35th anniversary of Great Bodie Fire of 1932, a fire that destroyed most of the buildings in Bodie and left it at it's present size. Abby was also the first child born in Bodie in those intervening 35 years and with her arrival she increased the permanent full-time population by 20%. It was a magic moment and as the meaning of her name suggests, she was truly "Her Father's Joy"! Little was I to know then that she would later grow up to be a park ranger following in her father's footsteps.

Abigail's arrival meant, with the "No Children" policy of DPR, that we would have to depart. We would stay through that summer and fall of 1967 and then make ready to move on. I was told to write a letter to our Personnel Department and list three parks to which I would like to be transferred. Still being a naive young ranger I thought that was a very liberal policy. I wrote my letter requesting a move either to Grover Hot Springs State Park, McArthur-Burney Falls State Park, or Plumas-Eureka State Park. The response I got was less than satisfying. My naiveté ended with the opening of the letter addressed to me from our Personnel Department. The parks that I had requested were unavailable and I would be transferring immediately to Folsom State Recreation Area (SRA). "So be it", I thought.

BODIE SKETCHES

Carl S. Chavez

PATHWAY SOUTH

Sometime in early October I went into Bridgeport to telephone the District Office and advise them that we would soon be heading to Sacramento to look for a place to live since there was no park housing available for us at Folsom SRA. Instead of saying to go ahead, I was told by Assistant Superintendent Carl "Andy" Anderson that the Folsom position had been filled and there was a change of plans. Now my choices were San Buenaventura State Beach (SB), Leo Carrillo SB, or Point Mugu State Recreation Area (SRA). All three of these units were on the Southern California coast between Ventura and Malibu.

I knew of the first two beach parks but had never heard of Pt. Mugu except as a Naval Air Station facility that was located south of Oxnard, California. When I was told that it was a brand new park that hadn't even opened yet I did not hesitate to pick that one. I immediately saw an opportunity to get in on the ground floor and bring a new unit on line. So here I was again, this time heading south to a park I had never seen, a position with no job description, a staff at the moment consisting of one park supervisor and me on the way with no place to live. Sound familiar? Bless Margaret's heart, she didn't even bat an eye and just asked, "When are we going?"

We left Bodie at 9:00am on October 27, 1967, almost a year to the day of our arrival. It dawned on me that I had also passed my probationary period during that year and was now a full-fledged State Park Ranger I. Ironic as it may seem, we had a flat tire as we left Bodie just as we had a flat tire on the day we arrived. Was there a hidden meaning to this? Probably not, just poor roads and cheap tires! The last entry in my Bodie Journal was: "We came as two and leave as three".

Ah, yes. Southern California. I'm not a beach person so Southern California wasn't exactly my idea of the place or lifestyle I wanted to live in and raise a family. This is what I had worked to get away from, but I figured that if we worked hard and made the best of it, I could eventually work my way back up north. To be sure this was going to be a different experience than Bodie.

To begin this job I first had to find this park called Pt. Mugu SRA and report for duty. Easier said than done. The problem was that it was so foggy I could hardly see the roadway, much less, locate the park. Up and down Pacific Coast Highway we drove in the vicinity of the park following the directions I had been given. Was this a phantom park? We finally gave up and drove north to Ventura to find someone who could give us more precise directions to our park. Certainly it did not look like we would find it until either the fog or our brains cleared. When I finally did find a sympathetic park employee at McGrath SB, he informed me that he had heard of the new park and said we had definitely been in the right area. He knew that someone was assigned there but didn't think that there was even a telephone installed yet. He did, however, have a phone number for what he thought was the park supervisor's residence in Oxnard.

From the park kiosk I dialed the telephone number that the park maintenance man had given me and was surprised when a women answered. She identified herself as Nancy and told me she was the wife of the park supervisor in charge of Pt. Mugu SRA. I explained to her who we were and what difficulty we were having locating the park. She seemed more excited than we were because she said she didn't think her husband, Jim, even knew he was getting an addition to his staff. Somehow that didn't sound too good to me.

In any event, Nancy told us to come to her house in Oxnard and she would take us out to the park. We found her place without any trouble but were exceedingly tired and little Abigail was crying and fussing something terrible. We had been driving halfway down the Central Valley that morning and it was already mid-afternoon. The last thing we wanted to do was any more traveling. Nancy, however, insisted we follow her to the park. How could we refuse my new boss's wife?

The fog was still thick along the Pacific Coast Highway as we followed Nancy and retraced our previous route. Yes, we had seen that CalTrans highway maintenance Station before. Hidden a little way beyond it, in the gloom of fog, was the park entrance at Sycamore Canyon. We had found it! As we drove up to the park kiosk/office the ranger inside looked up to greet us, a little surprised since the park wasn't officially open. I said to Jim Geary, "I'm your new Ranger". That's how we met. He obviously hadn't received the news that the park staff at Pt. Mugu was doubling, but I think he was pleased that it was. Now after our brief pleasantries I hoped we could leave and go find a place to stay for the night to rest our tired minds and bodies.

We weren't to be so lucky, however, as Jim insisted that all of us should go for a ride in their Jeep for a tour of the 12,000-acre park. The trip, under normal circumstances, would have been wonderful but we were beat. Bouncing on mile after mile of rough backcountry roads with a squalling baby wasn't my idea of fun. But how could I turn down the boss? We made the two-hour trip around the park but our headaches prevented us from enjoying it as we put up a brave front with smiling faces. That night, back at a motel in Oxnard, we turned on the TV only to find for our viewing pleasure a travel film on Bodie!

Eventually we did get settled into an apartment in Oxnard. Life there was really different with the daily half-hour commute to work and all sorts of stores and new fangeled convenience items available for our use. Apparently we had returned to civilization of sorts.

Pt. Mugu SRA was really a rather nice park. Once part of the Broom Family Cattle Ranch, it had nice beach frontage, beautiful Sycamore Canyon, and the splendid backcountry interior of La Jolla Valley. There was also a rich culture of Chumash Native American history as well as an abundance of coastal flora and fauna. When I reported to work on November 1, 1967 the Monarch butterflies that winter in the area were in great abundance hanging by the thousands from the Sycamore trees.

SYCAMORE SAGAS

Jim and I had our marching orders soon after I arrived. Because of very specific funding concerns, we **had** to get the park campground at Sycamore Canyon open by July 1, 1968. This proved to be a great opportunity for me to become involved in planning as well as the purchasing of supplies and materials necessary for operating a facility. This was not something that many State Park Ranger I's were involved in at this stage of their careers. Rangers and Park Attendant staff hired on their return from the

World War II had built many of our early State Parks. It seemed to me that I was sort of a 'transitional" ranger between " the old school" and the new breed of college educated and trained professional rangers that would soon make up the bulk of the ranger cadre.

As July 1st approached we worked at a fever pitch to meet the opening deadline. We were able to hire seasonal park aides to assist us in readying and operating the unit. Once again, as a State Park Ranger I, I was able to participate in the selection of the young college students we hired. I am proud to say that several of those individuals went on to careers as park rangers in our organization and are Park Managers today.

However, preparing the campground for opening day wasn't without delays. We had a major problem with Milk Thistle that had completely overrun the campground, a legacy of the cattle that once (over) grazed the area that had to be taken care of. Also we suffered another setback in the Spring prior to opening when a flash flood struck and left Jim and me in an embarrassing position.

At the time we had only two vehicles assigned to us. One was a ½ ton pickup truck, and the other a 1 ton stake-side truck. Because of all of the rain that had been falling, I became concerned about the hundreds of "Presto Logs" that we had stored in a shed that was not entirely waterproof. The shed was located about a mile up Big Sycamore Canyon above the campground. To reach it we had to drive up across Sycamore Creek at several low-water fords.

I went up in one of the vehicles and discovered that the building had almost literally "exploded" when water leaking in through the roof and sides of the shed saturating the Presto Logs. The logs are basically made of saw dust, that when wet expands dramatically. Hundreds of containers had burst open and were ruined. I told Jim what had happened and for some reason we took both vehicles back up to the shed. No sooner had we crossed the last ford than we heard a loud roar, followed by a rushing wall of water that swept down the creek. A flash flood had struck, leaving us stranded on the wrong side of the creek. We abandoned our vehicles and began hiking back downstream looking for a place to cross the creek. Eventually we found a fallen Sycamore tree that spanned the creek and we crossed to the other side on it.

Chagrined to say the least, we were forced to telephone the park supervisor at Leo Carrillo SB and ask (beg) for the use of a vehicle until ours could be retrieved after the water receded and the road was repaired.

Despite these occasional set backs We met our deadline and shortly after we had opened the park for business I found myself as the "Pseudo Supervisor" of Pt. Mugu SRA, and I faced the first of the much-dreaded reorganizations I would encounter over the next 30 years

The organization of the California State Park System when I was hired at Bodie in 1966 and later when I transferred to Pt. Mugu was one of unit operations. That is, a park supervisor managed each of the individual 150+ parks at the time and any number of subordinate staff as deemed appropriate. A short time after Pt. Mugu opened to the public the Department undertook a reorganization that combined several adjacent park units as one consolidated "Area" under the direction of an Area Manager. In the instance of the newly formed Pt. Mugu Area our unit was combined with Leo Carrillo SB. This did pose an interesting situation when Jim, my supervisor, was appointed Area Manager and the headquarters was moved to Leo Carrillo SB, much to the dismay of the supervisor at that unit. The initial effect was to leave me alone in charge of my own unit at Pt. Mugu.

Eventually, the operations of both Pt. Mugu and Leo Carrillo grew in size with additional staffing and further campground and beach facility developments. My responsibilities grew far beyond the scope of my job description but I was gaining valuable experience. This was in part due to my training and (I almost hate to admit it) my ability to do paperwork and get through red tape. I often ended up at the Area Office conducting staff meetings, participating in hiring interviews, developing work schedules and conducting training of various sorts. In my spare time I was assigned the responsibility of producing the Area's first required Operations Plan and Facilities Maintenance Program. This definitely was not Wildlife Management!

About this time in my career I picked up the moniker "c2" (Cee Two). The origin of this nickname was the result of a paperwork snafu that needed corrective action. When paperwork came across my desk for review or signature I would initial it with "CC" (Carl Chavez) to indicate that I had read the document. Subsequently I would receive another copy of this initialed document back on my desk because the "CC" was interpreted to mean that I wanted a (carbon) copy of the paperwork for my own files. This duplication of paperwork was unnecessary so I began initialing all documents with "c2". The nickname seemed to stick with me and I was known as "Cee Two" or "Cee Squared" from then on.

TALE OF A SEA MONSTER

The Pt. Mugu Area was the beach playground for millions of Los Angeles residents. Leo Carrillo SB was easily recognizable to many because it was the setting for many TV commercials and Hollywood movies. It was also widely known as an outstanding area for the surfing set. Pt. Mugu SRA, on the other hand, seven miles further up the coast was especially enjoyed by those who wanted to have a campsite right on the beach sands south of Pt. Mugu Rock. Within this setting an innumerable number of humorous, strange, and tragic incidents were bound to happen.

It is not busy on this winter day in January 1970. I'm on duty with a partner, new Park Ranger Bob Walker. The telephone at the Sycamore Canyon Campground rings and I answer. It is an excited citizen who lives in a beach house just north of the North Beach parking lot at Leo Carrillo SB. "There's some kind of sea monster washed up on the beach in front of my house and I think it's still alive" I'm told. He proceeds to describe this "thing". I humor him a bit but his call has a ring of truth to it even if what he describes does not sound like anything I'm familiar with.

More out of curiosity than anything else, Bob and I decide to drive down and check it out. Sure enough, there is something down there on the beach and it does look like a sea monster. Let me try and to describe it. It is obviously an eel-like fish of some kind, about 15'-20' long. It has smooth silvery reflective skin and it is compressed laterally. The eyes are large and it has a round ugly mouth with no teeth that I can see. The most prominent feature about it is the red dorsal fin that runs the entire length of the body from head to tail. On top of its head is another bright red "plume-like" crest and from below its chin are two long streaming antennae that are also bright red. They are actually pelvic fins that terminate in yellow diamond shaped oar-like features. I've never seen anything like it before. It is alive, though barely so, and it seems to be missing a portion of it's tail where it is cleanly sliced off. Humm...

Bob and I drove to the Leo Carrillo office and tried to find some reference to this strange creature in our limited natural history library. No luck, so I decide to call Marineland of the Pacific, a well known and recognized marine research center located at Pacific Palisades. When I described the fish there is immediate interest on the part of the person I am talking to. He advises me that he will call me right back after he does a little quick research of his own based on the description I had given him. About half an hour later he did call back and I was told that he would be right up to collect the specimen. The biologist thought that it was an Oarfish (*Regalecus glesne*).

When he arrived in a pickup truck about an hour later, and we proceeded down to the spot where the fish lay. It took several us to lift and carry the 200+ pound creature to the truck. Later I was to learn that the Oarfish, sometimes also called a RoosterFish, usually lives at depths below 1000' and are extremely rare to find. At the time, this was only the second specimen to have been recovered on the West Coast. This specimen can still be seen on display at the Los Angeles Museum of Natural History.

Who knows, one of these days I may get a telephone call saying that a mermaid has come ashore. I do know that I won't dismiss it as a crank call until I check it out!

TRAGEDY

I suppose that in our line of work one should expect to be faced with emergencies. We were trained in first aid, CPR, cliff rescue, fire fighting, search and rescue, criminal investigation, etc. Over the course of my 33 years as a park ranger I was involved in many such incidents. Fortunately, the outcome was most often positive, sometimes even humorous, in a morbid sort of way. Take for instance the time I responded to a vehicle accident on the Pacific Coast Highway behind the park office at Leo Carrillo. What made this accident unique was not that there was a death involved with the car crash, but that it resulted in the nude body of a dead man lying in the roadway. As fate would have it, the poor soul lying "baring his all" on the center divider of US Highway 1 already had a head start on his way to his Maker. He was in the process of being transported by a hearse that was involved in the accident and had come flying out of the vehicle on impact. As luck would have it, there were no serious injuries involved.

What I have found is that one does not forget those instances in which one attempts to do the right thing and still is not successful. That is what happened to me while I was assigned to Pt. Mugu SRA. Because the following incident was the **first** serious first aid situation that I was involved in, I remember it well.

On this hot summer day I was on duty at the Sycamore Canyon kiosk taking a break from my patrol duties. As you would expect on a day like this the beaches up and down the coast were very busy. We had a lifeguard on duty at our own beach, at the mouth of Sycamore Canyon. I had radio communications with him via one of our "lunchbox" Motorola radios. North of this beach we had another two miles of unguarded beach where campsites were later to be built. Beyond that area and out of our jurisdiction was Pt. Mugu Rock with its rocky shoreline and a small pocket beach that was only exposed at lower tides.

I was in the contact station when a vehicle came racing in and the occupants said there had been a drowning in the vicinity of Mugu Rock. I immediately called for the lifeguard and we raced to the scene in our patrol vehicle. I will never forget the sight that greeted us when we got out of the vehicle. A crowd had gathered on the side of the roadway looking down upon the small strip of sandy beach below. Lying on the beach were two individuals-not moving. **Everyone was just standing there doing nothing!** We had no choice; we had to do something as all eyes fell upon us to take some action. The lifeguard (whose name now escapes me) and I immediately went down to the beach and began CPR. One of the victims was a woman to whom the lifeguard went. I went to what turned out to be the woman's 8-year-old daughter and also began CPR.

To this day, I am not sure how long we continued to perform CPR on the victims. I know it was long enough for fire and rescue units to arrive from the Oxnard area several miles away. I continued CPR until the ambulance arrived to transport the victims. It was obvious to us when we began the CPR that it was to be a futile effort but **we had to do something** while the crowd watched and the family of the victims was nearby.

In the aftermath of the event we learned that the little girl and her sister had been wading at the shore's edge when a "sleeper wave" caught them and took them out to sea. Their mother and father rushed in to rescue them, only to be carried out to sea also. Two unknown persons who were surfing in the area utilized their surfboards and managed to rescue the father and one daughter. Sometime later they went back out into the ocean and recovered the two victims. We do not know how much time elapsed after that before we were contacted and finally arrived on the scene.

For many days after that event I could hardly move. The effort of bending over the victim for so long and performing the CPR, coupled with the adrenaline rush caused my back to seize up. It took a long time to recover. I don't think the psychological effect of that day ever really left me.

WITHOUT RESERVATIONS

Today in a technological computer world of news and information, on-line shopping and instant ticket purchasing for events, theaters and the like, we have come to take for granted the reserving of campsites days, weeks, months or even a year in advance as the norm. In the late 1960's that was not the case. The California Department of Parks and Recreation was the first park system in the nation to introduce advanced reservations to the general public. It was a unique concept, and not unlike many new ideas, the acceptance of making a reservation in advance of your stay for the freedom to relax on a weekend or vacation in a campground had not quite caught on.

A fledgling reservation system was first introduced for San Simeon Hearst Castle tours in 1968 but it was not expanded to include campsite reservations until a year or two later. Prior to a reservation system all campsites were available on a first-come, first-serve basis. The result of this, especially at our Southern California beach units, was an orderly chaos. Each day, around noon, a "roll call" was taken to see who of the would-be campers would be lucky enough to get a campsite. Often many of these folks had been waiting (some would say slumming) outside the park entrance for several days in the hope of getting in. Planning a vacation under those circumstances was not very conducive to relaxation and often-frayed nerves of all concerned would boil over into confrontations resulting in fisticuffs.

When the Department finally established it's first reservation system it was a park ranger's worst nightmare. Trying to keep track of reserved campsites **and** accounting for the camp fees **plus** accounting for the additional reservation fee proved no easy task. What made the procedure so difficult in the first place was that we had no computers at the parks to track the reservations. We had to rely on a cumbersome worksheet. Secondly, reservations could be made one of three ways. They could be made directly with the reservation contractor (who I believe was called Compu-Ticket), they could be made by mail to the newly established Department Reservation Section in Sacramento, or finally, they could be made in person at the park unit. This of course meant that the park staff assigned to the check station at the campground was having to keep track of reserved campsites from all of these points of sale not only by date but also by the type of campsite desired. This latter requirement was critical because all campsites are not alike and only certain types of camping equipment would fit in particular campsites. For example, it would be impossible to put a 35-foot trailer in a walk-in tent site.

On top of this there was the accounting problem. Each unit was required to prepare a Report of Collections for all fees collected during a specific period of time. Depending on the amount collected, that was usually done weekly. Now we were asked not only to account for **reservation fees** at the time the reservation was made, but also account for the **camp fee** for the time the reservation was made. For example if a reservation was made on May 7th for a stay that was to begin July 4th, you had to account separately for the reservation fee portion on a May Report of Collections and the camp fee portion on a Report of Collection that wouldn't be made up until two months down the road in July. Again, all of this was done without the aid of computers.

I vividly remember on one occasion when a ranger at Leo Carrillo State Beach was having difficulty and telephoned me one day and asked me to come down to try to help him figure out his Report of Collections. It seems he had been working non-stop for two or three day's straight trying to reconcile his accounting without success. It was obvious when I got there to help that he had been looking at the same figures in various combinations for so long that he couldn't begin to unravel the mess. He was almost in tears from frustration. It took me about 4 hours to get within .25¢ of the correct amount, at which point I told him to just record it as an overage or shortage and be done with it!

As if the accounting wasn't enough of a problem, sometime in mid-summer of 1970, probably near the Fourth of July holiday, Compu-Ticket went bankrupt! In a scramble to keep the reservation system going, the Department decided to continue on its own until a new contract could be issued. The number of reservations that were made at the park increased dramatically and with it so did our problems. At a park like Pt. Mugu all we had for an "office" was the 4' x 8' entrance station kiosk at the Big Sycamore Campground. From this tiny building we were expected to process the reservation requests as well as carry on our normal activities providing information and checking campers in and out. The amount of cash we handled in that little check station rose dramatically too. The little kiosk had sliding windows on both the entrance and exit side of the building. If the ranger or park aid inadvertently left both windows open at the same time when the off shore sea breeze was blowing strongly we would have registration cards, reservations requests, and hundreds of dollars blowing out of the kiosk down the entrance road. It was my first real experience with the direct affects of "ballooning run-away inflation". This happened on more than one occasion as staff scrambled to collect the run-away dollars and registration cards. Finally, I had my wife, Margaret, fabricate two clear vinyl pocket holders we could place over the non-sliding windows to hold the registration/reservations cards. Now at least, we had only to chase down the money "blowing in the wind".

Eventually the reservation system was refined and became a model for several other state's park systems. Compu-Ticket eventually gave way to Ticketron and later Mistix, as the system continually improved and the public began to accept, and indeed expect, this service. It was with some reservations that many of us may have initially accepted the idea but I can now say that we accept it without reservation.

SO YOU WANT TO BE IN MOVIES

Leo Carrillo State Beach, with its close proximity to Hollywood and Malibu was, and still is, a magnet for the motion picture and advertising industry. In the late 1960's I often was assigned to prepare and monitor filming permits. Anyone who has worked around the filming industry knows how difficult this can be. There is some part of "**No**" they just don't seem to understand. It is standard practice that a "**No**" is never a final "**No**" when dealing with some of these people even if they are committing a "**No-No!**" Nevertheless, interaction with production people, actors, and "Movie Stars" was always interesting work. Sometimes it was difficult to understand why they bothered to come to the park for filming. A prime example of this was a television commercial that was made at Leo Carrillo one day-and I mean the entire day.

I had issued a permit for the filming of a short **Alka-Selzer** Commercial. The script called for someone off camera to drop a tablet in a glass of water so it would fizz. That was all there was to it. I presumed voices would later be added to tout the benefits of the product. The producers of the commercial wanted the filming to be done outside. I can't even remember where in the park they wanted to do the shooting. That became irrelevant on the Saturday morning when they showed up to film the commercial because it was raining. I met with the filming people and asked if they would like to reschedule the shoot for another time. No, they wanted to go ahead with it anyway **indoors**. "Okay, what do you have in mind?" They decided that if we would move our vehicles out of the two-stall garage that was attached to the office they could work there. We moved the vehicles out of the stalls and the film crew (lots of them) scurried about setting up a table and all the necessary lighting and reflectors.

I watched for the next several hours as a person dropped one tablet after another into a glass of water as the camera rolled. Eventually, they must have gotten the lighting and camera angle they desired because they left smiling happily as the sun set over the Pacific. Why they had needed to come to the park to film in a garage is beyond me. No wonder advertising increases the price of products!

Then I thought about it a little more. Perhaps the chief reason they liked to film in California State Parks is that it is **cheap** for them to do so. Sure they would cover the Department's expenses and perhaps make a donation of some equipment now and then but they never were charged for the privilege of utilizing some of the best scenery and shooting locations in the world.

The rational for this was that if we charged the movie studios a fee we would drive them away to other states and countries to do their filming and that would hurt California's economy. To be sure the filming industry does have a huge economic impact in the areas where they make their movies and commercials. I think it is unlikely that they would leave in droves because right next door to our state parks, the National Park Service in the Santa

Monica Mountains was charging them to film in areas of their jurisdiction. Beside how many other locations in the world have a Pt. Lobos, Burney Falls, or Humboldt Redwoods? So much for my soap box tirade.

I did have the chance to meet some movie stars and other celebrities including Raquel Welch, Ann Margaret, (and wasn't that Elvis driving down the Pacific Coast Highway?) among others. The nicest and most friendly actor I talked with was Eddie Albert. He truly seemed interested in my work, but perhaps it was his acting abilities that convinced me. In any event he seemed in no rush to get away. I think we enjoyed each other's company, though today he surely would have no recollection of our conversation, which was more about conservation than filming.

At Pt. Mugu I encountered a rather strange incident involving a well-known star of a television series. Over the course of several weeks I kept getting complaints from our maintenance staff that one of the trash bins in the day-use picnic area was continually being filled by someone who was driving into the park at night and dropping off large quantities of household trash and yard clippings. This would leave little space for the legitimate park user to empty their refuse.

I decided to check out the problem and became a "Dumpster Diver" sifting through the trash until I found several items with a name, address and telephone number on it. I recognized the name as that of a television personality whose address was in Malibu Beach. I decided to try and telephone the man. The number I had found must have been a private unlisted number because, much to my surprise, I got through right away and this individual answered the phone. I explained to him who I was, how I got his telephone number, and why I was calling. He was actually very polite and apologetic. He said he would see that the practice stopped. I later got a letter from him explaining that a yard service employee, instead of taking the trash to a proper disposal site, had tried to cut corners and save his own business expenses by dropping trash off in the park. He told me the person was no longer in his employment. I was impressed by this unexpected show of class. I had not seen this attention to detail in most "Stars" that I had been around.

After leaving the Pt. Mugu Area I continued to have sporadic interaction with the filming industry. Throughout my park career I conducted numerous "local" spots on news reports or travel related television shows. I'm afraid that my stardom faded quickly after reaching a peak in 1973 at Morro Bay SP. I was part of a cast of three being filmed for a local Los Angeles children's show entitled "Domingo". The program was geared toward Hispanic children exploring future career possibilities. My costars were two marionettes, one of which was a little boy, and the other a Donkey. Some of my staff said there were actually three dummies on the set and accused me of being the "Jackass" trying to upstage the Donkey.

Years later, as Manager of The Eel River District, I was again involved in the serious business of major productions when George Lucas began filming portions of "Return of the Jedi" in Humboldt Redwoods and Grizzly Creek Redwoods State Parks. At Humboldt Redwoods, I authorized the film crew that was shooting in Federation Grove to spray a green fiber mixture onto the entrance road to conceal the pavement. In this beautiful natural setting of ferns and redwood trees, even more greenery in the form of potted ferns and forest duff was brought in to enhance the work of Mother Nature. The action scenes of a "space scooter" chase can be seen as they race through the redwood grove.

My last involvement with the filming industry occurred during Stephen Speilberg's filming of "Jurassic Park" at Patrick's Point and Prairie Creek Redwoods State Parks in 1997. In this instance I was working in Headquarters in Sacramento. The Department had some concerns that the filming activity might cause some resource damage in the parks. State Park Director Donald

Murphy asked me to meet with Mr. Speilberg to share the concern and request that Mr. Speilberg telephone him with some assurance that no harm would come to park resources.

Getting close to a high profile film director such as Mr. Speilberg is no easy task. I arrived at Prairie Creek SP with message in hand. The first thing I noticed was that I could hardly see the famous film director. He was somewhere in the middle of a group of 10-12 people who seemed to fawn and trip over his every word as he walked about. The entire mass of people moved with him as one, vying for his attention. After the group's third location stop I had only made it as far as speaking with one of the assistant directors who snootily advised me that Mr. Speilberg was a busy man. Much too busy to speak or meet with me!

I decided I was getting no where fast and would have to make a preemptive strike and burst right into the middle of the group. I picked a moment when the people barrier dispersed somewhat as every body began to board the bus for the ride to the next stop. I explained to Mr. Speilberg the purpose of my visit. He told the others to board the bus and we walked away together to talk about our issues under the canopy of the "Big Tree" at Prairie Creek. As our conversation ended I handed him the Director's business card which had the Department's Mission Statement printed on the back of it. Mr. Speilberg had given me his full attention and was most gracious. He boarded the bus and I followed in my vehicle as we drove to the next stop. As I was getting out of my car, Mr. Speilberg called and walked over to me. He said that on the ride down he had read the Department's Mission Statement to everybody on the bus and had impressed on them the need to tread lightly and care for the park resources. He told me he would telephone the Director when he got back to Los Angeles. He was a man of his word.

It is always fun for me, even today, to watch movies and commercials not so much for their content, but rather to see where the filming was done and if I am familiar with the location. I think what I miss most about filming is the catering service. The film industry knows how to feed its crews and those of us park film "groupies" who are there to insure that your resources are protected. We were well fed too.

TRANSITION

I had been in the Pt. Mugu Area for a little over three years and felt I had met most of my short-term career goals at that location. Earlier in the year of 1970 I had taken and passed the promotional State Park Ranger II examination and was resting comfortably in the 14th rank on the promotional list. It was now only a matter of time for the opportune moment and assignments to present themselves to seek greener pastures and perhaps head back up north to those parts of California where I really wanted to live and work.

The Department had recently completed another round of fine tuning reorganization that entailed establishing "Intake Areas" for the new classification of State Park Ranger Trainee that was about to enter our ranks. The idea behind this was to set up seven or eight training areas throughout the State where all newly hired rangers would report to work to complete their first year of probation. Interspersed with the on-the-job training at the Intake Area there would be classroom training at the recently establish William Penn Mott, Jr. Training Center. One of the Trainee Intake Areas that was to be established was in the San Luis Obispo Coast Area (SLOCA) on the Central California coast.

One day, while attending a District-wide facilities maintenance meeting on the program I had been putting together for our Area, I was approached by Chuck Lyden of our Sacramento Headquarters Office. He had been recently appointed the new Area Manager for SLOCA and would be reporting soon to his new assignment. After the meeting he called me aside (what had I done wrong?) and much to my surprise and relief he asked me "right out of the blue" if I would like to move up north and be a part of the training program at SLOCA. The plan, he said, was first to immediately transfer me as a State Park Ranger I to Pismo SB. Once the incumbent Supervising Ranger II, Al Ulm, promoted out and I was reachable on the promotional list I would move into the Supervising Ranger position he was vacating at Morro Bay SP. I figured that the skids were greased and so without hesitation I said "Sure".

Of course there had been no discussion of a pending move with Margaret about this turn of events. All of this was happening a day or two before Christmas so you can guess that a move at this time had been the last thing on our minds. That night I broke the news to the family, the family now including the addition of a son, Christopher, born in February of that year. I told them that I had a special surprise Christmas present to share with them. "What's that?" Margaret asked. I replied "We're moving". Again, as only Margaret can so succinctly state the obvious she asked the two most important questions. "When and where?" The answer: **"Next week and North!"**

PT. MUGU SKETCHES

FOLLOW THE PATH NORTH

We actually moved on New Year's Eve, December 31, 1970, to Pismo Beach SB and took up residence in the nearby community of Grover City about one mile from the park. Pismo Beach had two campgrounds, Oceano Campground where the park office and shops were located, and a mile up the coast, the North Beach Campground. The ranger staff consisted of myself, one other Ranger I, the Supervising Ranger, a Seasonal Ranger and a recently hired Ranger Trainee. Our primary responsibility was to patrol the many miles of beach from the Pismo Beach Pier south to the Guadalupe River where it entered the ocean

Pismo Beach was famous for the tasty Pismo Clams that could be dug up in the shallow waters of the wide, gently sloping beach. At low tide, thousand of people would come to gather these delicacies. The beach was also unique in that at low tide, standard vehicles could drive on the hard packed sand. Off-road vehicles and other 4WHD's could also operate in the major dune complex near Oso Flaco Lake and the "Pipeline". However, with the arrival of the dune buggies and 4WHD vehicles the clientele utilizing the beach began to change. No longer was it just leisurely groups of sportsmen driving out to find their favorite spot in pursuit of their quarry. Now the driving began to take on a test of speed and driving skill on the beach and in the dunes.

The early 1970's were an age of questioning authority and testing the limits. We were feeling the effects of this as enforcement problems increased in many of the parks. Further up the coast, at Pfeiffer Big Sur SP the rangers there were already trained and authorized to carry firearms as they interacted with the "Hippie" counter culture that had flocked to their area. Limits were also tested at Pismo Beach, but in a different way, especially on major holidays or when there was an extremely low tide. In those early years, camping was allowed basically anywhere on the beach or dunes south of Arroyo Grande Creek. That meant that over seven miles of beach or dunes could be used for camping in tents, trailers, campers, and motor homes with **no public sanitary facilities** services available for upwards of 4000 campsites. Under those circumstance it was inevitable that all of the problems associated with any community would surface and have to be dealt with by the park staff. The reality of this chaotic scene was even captured in a two-page photo layout in the September 3, 1971, issue of Life Magazine showing an aerial view of this "Happening." Pismo Beach SB is where I received my on-the-job field training in law enforcement. It was a part of the ranger experience I did not seek, but learned quickly out of necessity.

"SIGN HERE PLEASE"

In the four years I had been a Park Ranger I had received very little formal law enforcement training. Two weeks at the Riverside Policy Academy was the extent of it.

In my two previous assignments, first at Bodie and then at Pt. Mugu I had probably not written more than half a dozen citations for minor offenses. At Pismo SB on my first busy weekend I went through two ticket books. Most of these citations were written for serious life endangering violations of the law concerning driving too fast, drinking while driving or more likely a combination of the two offenses while drag racing down the crowded beach where the posted speed limit was 15 mph. It was not uncommon for the ranger staff to ask violators to " sign here please" on several hundred citations written over a holiday weekend.

Holiday periods such as Spring Break, Memorial Day, or Fourth of July weekends required that we provide extended coverage. Generally this meant that two of us were on duty on the beach for the day shift and two for the night shift. Occasionally our staffing was supplemented with rangers brought in from other units to assist. Our primary patrol vehicle was a specially equipped, Code 3 (red lights and siren) Myers Manx Dune Buggy. It was the only one of its kind in service at the time that was operated by the State. The "Manx" had a fiberglass body mounted on a reinforced frame and powered by a VW engine. It was also equipped with special "J" brakes that allowed us to spin and turn in a tight radius. It was essential to have this vehicle in operation at all times in order not only to keep pace with the renegade drivers, but also to respond to emergencies in the sand dunes. Training and learning to operate the Manx was mostly by trial and error after an initial briefing on the "Do's and Don'ts". One was deemed "graduated" and ready to solo once one had passed a "Final Examination" that consisted of driving the Manx down into the bottom of a circular sand bowl in the dunes with steeply sloping sides. If you could get out of that predicament you were ready to go it alone. The only way to succeed was to go faster and faster around the bowl as centrifugal force held the vehicle against the steep walls of the bowl and allowed you to maneuver up and out of the depression. I don't know that it was too safe of an exercise, but it sure was fun!

In any event the worst time of all for beach patrol was during the holiday periods when the high tide would come in and compress all the activity into a narrow space between the incoming tide and the sand dunes. This produced a situation where hundreds, if not thousands, of vehicles were driving in, around, and through campsites. Also interspersed among this vehicle traffic were the pedestrians making their way to the water and horse riders from the nearby stables galloping along the beach.

On one weekend, "Rookie" Ranger Jim Hart and I were on duty together when in the course of one hour during a not untypical holiday weekend the following occurred. First we received a call of a serious accident in the sand dunes which proved to be a fatality. We handled that situation until additional help arrived and we were free to respond to another radio call for assistance of a young woman who had fallen off a runaway horse. After providing first aid for the young lady we had to abandon the search for her horse when we received yet another call to respond to a person in distress. It turned out that it was a person in the surf who had had a fatal heart attack while in the water seeking his limit of Pismo clams. We retrieved the body from the surf and needless to say, besides being wet and tired we were emotionally spent and ready for a respite that we could not take.

Believe it or not, the description of that hour above was not out of the ordinary. Usually, after a holiday or low tide weekend, one of us would be assigned to go to the local hospital to gather information on the accidents that had occurred during that period. Except in the instance of a fatality, we simply did not have the time to make out the necessary accident reports for the "routine" accidents when they occurred. It was the job of another Ranger to check the hundreds of citations written each weekend and take them to the local court. There was another memorable incident that I recall during one wild weekend on the beach. I was on patrol alone in the park's dune buggy working to keep the traffic speed down. I had already written a couple of citations for speeds in excess of 50mph that involved two modified dune buggies racing recklessly down the crowded beach through the heavy traffic. My adrenaline level was just returning to normal when I spotted two unusual vehicles, side by side, a little way further down the beach. As I approached from behind I noticed that they appeared to be Army vehicles of some type. I counted about a dozen people in and hanging out of one of the vehicles and a lesser number on the other vehicle. It turned out that they were war surplus personnel carriers that someone had brought to the beach as their "toys". I could hear the engines rev up as the drivers prepared to race each other down the beach. I turned on my red light but it went unnoticed as they raced away. I then turned on my siren and managed to pull them over to issue citations.

I felt pretty smug when I got on the radio afterwards to announce I had cited two "tanks", a first at Pismo Beach. I was only to be outdone an hour later when Ranger Rodger Kellogg issued a citation to a helicopter pilot who had decided to land his aircraft in the middle of "our circus." I should say something about Rodger, my other patrol partner at Pismo. Many who knew him would think he was a pretty tough ranger who loved the law enforcement duties of the job. They would be right because he was very good at that aspect of our work, and he had the instinct for finding trouble that needed our attention. Rodger's degree in Criminal Justice had honed his instincts for this line of work. Many a time, just prior to our returning to the park office after patrolling the beach in our Manx, Rodger would say "Carl, let's take one more turn of the beach". That meant that we would make another sweep down and back the entire length of the beach looking for trouble – which we usually found!

Rodger had a kind streak hidden in the sometime gruff manner of his. He also had a secret that he shared with me one day while we were on patrol. Behind the sand dunes, in low-lying wet areas, there were many stands and thickets of willow that grew profusely. We drove deep into the dunes toward one of these thickets and parked the vehicle.

There was no evidence of anything special or different about this stand of willows. It was like any other in the vicinity. Rodger followed a trace of a trail into the willows that could have been made by some small animal and I followed. We emerged into a clearing in the center of this thicket and were met by a large man. This was "Bert".

Bert was of Swedish decent and had lived here for many years! He was somewhat of a Bohemian type, a loner, and perhaps suffered from some physical and mental health problems. On the other hand, he was very creative and resourceful. He had built a rather substantial shanty from driftwood that served as his home. A hand dug well supplied water and he had a ditch system to irrigate a small garden plot for vegetables.

All of this "development" had been done on State Park Property and it was strictly illegal. Nevertheless, Rodger had befriended this harmless individual to the extent of assisting him occasionally with shopping and obtaining prescription medicines when Bert was ill. I saw no reason to change the status quo on this situation.

I learned many years later, after Bert passed away, that he had left Rodger what little he had to give as a small token of gratitude for the kindness Rodger had shown him.

DOG ON A LEASH

Despite our enforcement activities, we still had not received the required training necessary to be issued firearms. To be sure, I was beginning to feel the need of one but there was an instance at our North Beach Campground when I was glad I was not armed.

Rodger and I were, as usual, on beach patrol when we received a radio transmission of a problem concerning a dog at our North Beach Campground. We responded immediately and as we entered the campground, the park aide on duty informed us that a City of Pismo Beach police unit had gone in ahead of us a few minutes earlier and the aide thought he had heard a gun shot fired.

We proceeded to the indicated campsite and indeed found a Pismo Police Department vehicle in the campsite parking stall with two obviously distressed officers nearby. As I got out of our vehicle, one of the officers (the one holding a shotgun!) immediately said to me "I had to do it, didn't I?" I didn't know what he was talking about but I did notice he was sweating profusely even on this cool foggy, overcast day. Behind the police officers, under a trailer, was a German Shepherd dog, still attached to a leash tied to the trailer. The dog was howling in pain and it's barking had attracted a large crowd that was obviously angry at the police officer who held the shotgun.

I could tell by now that the dog had been shot by the police officer and was severely wounded. We had to calm the situation or things would surely get worse. I asked someone if they could get me a blanket, which I gingerly threw over the dog to cover him completely and obscure the bloody scene from the public. I hadn't expected it, but it also had the effect of calming down the dog so that it's pitiful howling was reduced to a tolerable whimper.

The owners of the dog were nowhere to be found. They apparently had left their dog tied to the trailer and walked on down to the beach. Later, another person had also decided to go to the beach. Unfortunately, instead of going around the campsite where the dog was tied up, he had attempted to walk through the campsite. The dog, in defense of his territory, had immediately trapped the "trespasser" against the trailer. This person was not bitten, but he was held at bay by the dog.

It was at this point that some member of the public had called the police department and they responded. A major mistake was made by the officers when they drove their vehicle into the campsite and entered the "territory" that the dog was protecting. Instinctively, the officer had fired the shotgun at the dog when its attention was diverted from the camper to himself. How the officer failed to kill the dog at such close range, or even more importantly, failed to hit anyone else in the full campground was beyond me.

Now, even the man who the dog had pinned against the trailer was mad at the police officer. When I asked the officer if he had called Animal Control he told me he had not yet done so. We immediately made the call and began dispersing the crowd. About this time the owner of the dog and his family returned to the campsite. You can imagine their reaction as we once again had a near riot on our hands. I finally convinced the police officers to leave and that had the effect of quieting down the crowd.

The animal control people finally did arrive and took the dog to a veterinary clinic. Pellets from the shotgun had creased the top of the dog's head and wounded him in the hindquarters. We learned later that the dog had survived. We never did learn if the police officer did.

AT LAST, WILDLIFE MANAGEMENT!

To be sure, ranger life at Pismo SB wasn't all law enforcement, accidents and incidents. We had many opportunities for interpretive activities with the local schools and provided campfire programs and nature walks for the park visitors. One of the major interpretive attractions was the presence of Monarch butterflies that wintered in the North Beach Campground eucalyptus grove. Another major activity involved a dune restoration project that required planting iceplant and dune grasses to stabilize the sand. Unfortunately, that project was instituted with non-native plant species, which, I'm sure, many years later generated a project to replace them with native plant species. In the early days, even a resource based agency like Department of Parks and Recreation wasn't always in step with the environmental movement.

I'm not certain, but I believe that most of my classmates in the Wildlife Management program at Humboldt State College actually went into that worthy field of endeavor. I know that a couple of my peers did embark on successful careers as National Park Service Rangers. I was the only one from the Class of 1966 that entered the California State Park System.

Quite frankly, little of my academic training was directly related to the work I was doing. My knowledge of natural history, of course, was helpful when conducting nature walks, campfire programs or explaining natural systems to school groups. I did not, however, actually conduct wildlife management studies, surveys, or any other actual fieldwork. Up to this point in my wildlife management career I had only murdered one Sage Hen at Bodie, captured a rabid fox at Leo Carrillo and found one rare fish at Pt. Mugu. Now at Pismo Beach, of all places, I would get my chance for real wildlife management and it would not be with a clam, but a beaver (Castor canadensis).

Adjacent to the Oceano Campground at Pismo is a freshwater lagoon. The campground road separates some of the campsites from the lagoon and continues on to the employee housing area and park maintenance yard. Just prior to reaching the housing area the road goes over a pair of three-foot diameter culverts. It was apparent that a beaver was working in the lagoon and damming up the culverts each night. This nocturnal activity resulted in a nightly mini-flood of the roadway since the lagoon could no longer drain properly.

You might ask, "How did a beaver get in the lagoon?" Well, it wasn't easy. It seems that back in the mid 1960's, Park Ranger John Bollinger received a report of a beaver in the surf off the beach opposite the campground. The beaver had apparently floated down Arroyo Grande Creek and out to sea. John rescued the critter from the ocean waves by capturing it in a garbage can and transported it back to the campground about a mile away where it was released into the lagoon.

Ranger Hart, a "wannabe" Cowboy/Mountain Man, had some experience trapping and I had had **theoretical** experience trapping. In any event, Jim and I decided we would rid the park of the problem and capture the beaver and take it back up toward Lopez Lake from whence it must have come.

We borrowed a live trap from Fish & Game and went to work. Sure enough we got the beaver right away and transported it out of the area. A funny thing, though, the next night the culverts were blocked again. Twelve or thirteen beaver later we had finally succeeded in keeping the culverts clear. All we could figure is that the original beaver that was put in the lagoon must have been a pregnant female and things progressed from there. Five or six years later when I moved to Plumas-Eureka State Park I would once again put my four years of college training in wildlife management to good use. At Plumas-Eureka we were also kept busy trapping another half dozen of my "loyal opposition" that were busy clogging the domestic water ditches in the park - dam them!

"WE BEST CLAM UP"

Ranger led Campfire Programs are a tradition in National and State parks. Prior to the advent of sophisticated sound systems, lapse dissolve slide projectors, drop down screens and remote controls, park rangers actually talked to the public. At the Oceano Campground we had a relatively small informal campfire center. It was situated in a sandy, bowl-like amphitheater in the sand dunes adjacent to the campground.

As a change of pace, Ranger Hart and I decided to take a break from the rigors of law enforcement on the "Pismo Beach Speedway" and conduct an old fashioned campfire program. We chose as our topic "How to Dig

Pismo Clams", a pleasant change from "How fast can this Dune Buggy race down the beach". The premise of the program was that Jim was a novice clam digger who knew nothing about the proper way to dig clams. I, as the seasoned Pro, would be ever so helpful in correcting and critiquing Jim's technique. Topics we would cover included, water safety, legal size and limits, how to properly replace undersize clams and the natural history of the Pismo Clam.

Prior to the campers arriving for the program, Jim and I "salted" the sand at center stage with clamshells of various sizes that we buried. We then left for dinner and agreed to meet back at the campfire center before the program began. As we left, Jim asked how would he be able to find the clams in the dark, with only the light of the campfire. I told him not to worry that I would mark the spots where the clams were buried so they would be easy for him to find.

After dinner, I got to the campfire center first and proceeded to mark the location of the clams with some red pieces of yarn. Jim arrived just as campers were taking their seats on the rustic benches so I had no time to point out the location of the pieces of yarn.

We began the campfire warm up with our usual bad song leading. Neither Jim nor I could carry a tune, much less lift a note! When it came time for our little demonstration skit and got to the point where Jim was to prod with his pitchfork into the sand to locate the clams, we immediately ran into trouble. Jim could not find the clams, and I was doing everything I could think of to stall and just "wing it" as Jim continued his futile search for the clams. The audience was having a great time laughing at our ineptness. I think they thought that our misfortune was part of the program.

The Rookie Ranger finally did manage to hit pay dirt after I not so discreetly kicked away sand to expose some of the clams. It was only after the program that I found out that Jim was colorblind and could not see the red yarn I had used to mark the spots where the clams were buried!

A LITTLE FURTHER NORTH

My stay at Pismo SB did not last long, only eight months though at times it seemed like a lifetime! Al Ulm, the Supervising Ranger at Morro Bay SP had moved on so with the vacancy created by his promotion it now seemed likely that I would be moving too. But first I needed a vacation. I had told my patrol partner, Rodger, of our vacation plans and where I could be reached if my Ranger II promotion should come up while I was away. As it turned out I learned of my promotion when we made a rest stop at San Luis Reservoir SRA in the Central Valley and found a message from Rodger waiting for me. I immediately called him and he was kind enough to make my moving arrangements while we continued on our vacation. Upon our return from vacation a moving van was waiting for us to take us to our new assignment just up the road in Morro Bay. It was September 1, 1971.

PISMO SKETCHES

RENAISSANCE RANGERS

After a four- year hiatus we were once again living in State housing at Morro Bay State Park. The house was one of two, "standard" state park residences located behind the shop complex near the campground. My next door neighbor was Ranger John Myers, the very person I had replaced when we had started at Bodie SHP. Now I was his supervisor, but I was smart enough to know that I could learn a lot from this experienced "Old Time" Ranger.

It really was a very tranquil, idyllic setting and a wonderful place to live. The quaint little town of Morro Bay with it's picturesque harbor and fishing fleet, the bay itself, and nearby Morro Rock dominating the scene offered a prospect more in keeping with the lifestyle I had envisioned for our family. The visitor clientele and the pace of activity on this assignment was sure to be different and more to my liking than what I had experienced at Pismo SB.

My duties as the Supervising Ranger for this section of the San Luis Obispo Coast Area (SLOCA) encompassed a much wider range of activities than I had encountered at Pismo SB. In truth, many parts of the job were similar to my job as a Ranger I in the Pt. Mugu Area. I had operational responsibility for three primary parks and a couple of smaller sub-units. Central to my operation was Morro Bay SP. Seven miles across the bay and down coast was Montana de Oro SP and a couple of miles north of Morro Bay was Atascadero SB. All of these units have camping facilities, though Morro Bay has the most development and includes a golf course, boat marina, and natural history museum.

Most of the campground operations were adequately handled by a competent staff of park aides and seasonal rangers. Our permanent ranger staff was comprised of myself, as Supervising Ranger, and two other Ranger I's. All of us were hard pressed and spread too thinly to meet all of the demands required for supervision, administration, patrol, interpretation, and training required for the job. The one break we got was that duties of the park naturalist, assigned to the museum, and the duties of the maintenance crew were under the direction of other Area staff supervisors, so these positions were not my direct responsibility.

Since our most recent reorganization there had been an on-going discussion and debate within the Department as to what the role of today's State Park Ranger should be. Much of the debate concerned our role as peace officers, whether all park rangers would be armed, and whether we would be specialist or generalist.

TRAINEE TRIBULATIONS

Almost immediately after I arrived in Morro Bay they came. The "new breed" of ranger designated "Ranger Trainee". They were the wave of the future, all college graduates, idealistic, motivated, and for the most part, a great pool of talent that today is the heart and soul of the Department of Parks and Recreation. Unfortunately, not all of those who came to SLOCA fit that description.

Since SLOCA had been designated as a Ranger Trainee "Intake Area" it seemed like our staffing problems would be over. They came in groups of three or four over a period of months until I had 12 - 14 assigned to my units. When I say assigned to my units I'm not entirely correct. Officially, the Ranger Trainees were under the direct supervision and training of the Area's Chief Ranger who worked out of the Area Office located at Camp San Luis about ten miles way. He, however, resided in the park at Morro Bay. In the case of the Ranger Trainees, I was back in my role as "Pseudo Supervisor".

I found myself dealing with the worst scheduling nightmares I had ever encountered before or since the Ranger Trainee program was established. On some days I would have twelve trainees on duty, the next day I might have 4, then **zero**, then half a dozen. Part of the reason for this was that over the course of a year the various Trainee Groups were required periodically to attend formal training at the Mott Training Center (MTC) for periods of one to several weeks at a time.

In addition to the formal training at the MTC each group of trainees was supposed to be working its way through planned on-the-job training experiences that were part of what was a coordinated effort between the Intake Area and the MTC. It was the responsibility of the Area Training Officer to see that that was done. It was not up to me!

The outcome of this fragmented arrangement did not make for a smooth operation in the SLOCA Intake

Area. Other Intake Areas around the state had much more success, in part, due to a more structured program and perhaps better ranger candidates. In our case, only about half of the original 14 Ranger Trainees from our groups were with DPR two years later and today only four of those are still with DPR in leadership positions.

I knew that there was a problem with the program and attempted to pass my concerns on up the line. I didn't have much success. Things finally came to a head late (too late) in the program when the Ranger Trainees, themselves, "revolted" and marched over to the Area Manager's residence for an impromptu meeting one evening to express their concerns about the lack of coordinated training efforts in the Area. I was unaware of this meeting so you can imagine my surprise when the next morning, Area Manager Chuck Lyden drove to my office at the Morro Bay check station and asked, no, told me, to get in his car and take a ride with him.

He told me about the Trainees meeting with him the night before and said based on that meeting he was going to make some drastic changes. Fortunately, or unfortunately depending on one's viewpoint, they all concerned me. He told me the program wasn't working out very well under the lack of direction from the Area Office. Chuck wanted me, in addition to my regular duties, to take over the direct supervision and training of the Ranger Trainees starting immediately - like today. I was to implement a more structured program. My thought was "Wow", someone has finally seen the light and perhaps I would be doing what I thought I had originally been promoted to Morro Bay to do. After a two-hour drive and conversation, Chuck brought me back to my office in Morro Bay. As I got out of his vehicle he said one more thing. "Incidentally Carl, we are having some problems with the Natural History Museum operations also and I would like you to take over supervision of the Naturalist too". Sure, no problem!

I did restructure the program and was able to inject some of the required experiences into the program as well as a few other extras. For example, I conducted cliff rescue training on Morro Rock, introducing the trainee to the basics. I established required campfire programs and nature hikes. I planned rotational assignment to Pismo SB for exposure to more stressful enforcement situations and scheduled each trainee for public contact duty at the Natural History Museum. For the trainee's facilities maintenance experiences requirement, I had them, under the direction of Ranger Bob Addkison, construct a new campfire center that was very much needed. But in the end, I must confess it was too little, too late, for many of them.

During this time it seems that the questions concerning the role of rangers was answered. State Park rangers would remain generalists. That is we would continue to conduct interpretive programs such as nature hikes and campfire programs as well as be trained in the full range of enforcement duties. There would be no separate, specialized classification of "park police", "naturalist", or "park ranger" as was done in the National Park Service. We would be "Renaissance Rangers" and do it all!

COPS & ROBBERS

Before we could "do it all" and become fully sworn peace officers, all of the Ranger Trainees and incumbent rangers were required to complete 540 hours of certified law enforcement training at one of several locations across the state. In our case we were sent to the Modesto Junior College Criminal Justice Center (MCJTC) for five weeks of intensive training to receive our POST (Peace Officer Standards and Training) Certification. The training included all aspects of arrest and seizure, criminal investigation, defensive tactics, firearms, etc. All of the Ranger Trainees who were hired at this time knew of the law enforcement requirements as part of their job description. For those of us who were hired prior to the Trainee Program this was a **new requirement.** It was a difficult transition for some of the "Old Timers".

Our Basic Peace Officer Class was one of two other classes attending the MCJC classes at this time. The other classes were comprised of cadets and current police officers from other law enforcement jurisdictions as well as students attending the Junior College to obtain their certificate in the hope of being hired by a police agency. The training was conducted in a military manner. That is to say that it was very regimented with room and bed checks, "yes sir, no sir", will a quarter bounce off the made up bed, etc. That style or method of teaching did not set well with those of us who "like the outdoors and enjoy people." We ignored the demerit slips and frustrated our overseers. For example, they were at a loss at what to do about Rangers John J. and Harry M. who, upon returning from a weekend duck hunting trip, were busy cleaning their freshly killed quarry in the communal restroom.

Perhaps the most bizarre incident that occurred during our six weeks of training was not a lapse on the part of the students but rather a mistake made by one of our instructors. I do not remember the details of the class, only that the instructor was an FBI Agent. He was impressing upon us that a peace officer never gives up his weapon willingly no matter what the circumstances. He had removed his firearm from a concealed shoulder holster, perhaps for dramatic effect, to make his point. Instead of returning the gun to his holster he nonchalantly placed it on the shelf of the podium he was standing behind. None of us noticed this at the time. When the class was over the Agent left. After a short break the next instructor came in as we took our seats and he began his lecture. Suddenly he stopped, reached for something on the shelf of the podium and pulled out the previous instructor's loaded gun. Holding it gingerly between his fingers he asked: "Whose gun is this?" We all gasped as we realized the weapon belonged to the FBI Agent. The very same Agent who told us never to give up your weapon! A few minutes later the classroom door opened and the FBI Agent stuck his head in through the doorway. The instructor behind the podium held up the gun and said to the FBI Agent: "Did you forget something?" as the Agent sheepishly retrieved it.

I think what was even more frustrating for those in charge of the program was that we performed so well in the aspects of training that really mattered. Our test scores **always** exceeded those of the other groups. I'm sure our college education had a lot to do with that. In the end, the MCJTC officials gave up on the petty stuff and accepted us as we were.

In addition to our initial Peace Officer training we were required to have periodic refresher and update training as well mandatory quarterly defensive tactics and firearms qualifications. One other requirement that all of us had to take part in was an "Emergency Vehicle Operations Course (EVOC). This was training I could have used in 1970 when we were chasing the "crazies" on Pismo Beach, but instead, received in 1986 when I was driving nothing faster than my desk in the Area Office at Humboldt Redwoods.

When the time came for me to attend EVOC training I was accompanied by State Park Ranger Gary McLaughlin, the unit ranger at Standish-Hickey SRA. Gary and I drove to Chico and checked in at nearby Butte College for the two-day course that was to be conducted by instructors from the California Highway Patrol. We were the only park rangers in a class that was comprised primarily of law enforcement officers from various county sheriff departments.

After several hours of classroom instruction we began the actual training that was supposed to hone our operating skills, especially when driving under "Code 3" driving conditions when red lights, siren, radio and adrenaline are all going at full blast. First we had some fun skidding around on wet pavement and learning to recognize the rumbling and shaking that foretold of the skid to come. Next we went to a safety cone course to learn how to conduct controlled panic stops and lane changes (OOPS! I didn't mean to hit that baby carriage with the doll in it) and also practiced high speed driving in reverse. On the panic stop training I don't think that I endeared myself to one of the CHP instructors who was injured while I was driving. I hadn't noticed that the instructor had failed to buckle his seat belt so that when I slammed on the breaks he was thrust forward into the shotgun rack and sliced his hand on one of the steel upright bars of the gun rack. It was a bloody mess reminiscent of the Cuyamaca "Chain Saw Massacre" you will read of later in this story. Actually I think the Officer was a little chagrined at his own failure to "Buckle Up," and there were no repercussions over the accident. Except for that incident it was all great fun, and by the end of the day Gary and I were feeling quite good about the class.

The next day the class was shifted from Butte College out to the EVOC training site at the Butte County Airport. On a twisting looping course a gravel roadway had been laid out. The circuit course was surrounded by plowed fallow fields that in the early dawn were frozen and could easily be walked or driven upon should one go off of the roadway. After practice, each of us was expected to "graduate" by making an error free circuit of the course within a specified qualifying time period. So it was, with red lights flashing, sirens wailing and instructor at our side, that we began this part of the training.

Time after time, student after student, we began testing our newly learned skills. Time after time, student after student, many us went skidding off the roadway and out into the fields. Fortunately we were using older, worn out vehicles for this part of the training since there was evidence that some of these cars had rolled over on previous training exercises. As lunch approached we began our qualification tests. Some of the students impressed the CHP instructors with their driving prowess by passing immediately - unfortunately I was not one of them.

When it actually came time for the lunch break I still hadn't completed a circuit of the course without skidding out into the field. The instructors asked for volunteers to stay with the vehicles while everyone else went to lunch. I told the CHP Officers that Gary and I would stay provided we could practice while they were gone. They agreed to this and just told me to "be careful".

Once the rest of the class was gone and out of sight I jumped into one of the vehicles and with obsessive determination put the "pedal to the metal". I did it! I made a complete error free trip around the course within the required time limit. That was the good news. The bad news was, of course, that it didn't count because no one had seen me do it, not even Gary who was busily munching away on his lunch in one of the parked vehicles removed (probably for his safety) from the scene.

I was so pleased with myself that I went to Gary and told him to come over and watch me do it again. It was so easy "once you got the hang of it". Gary came over to watch his Area Manager perform at utmost efficiency. Just as I had done minutes earlier I whipped around the course with great speed and confidence. Now, with the finish line in sight what is that distant rumbling and shaking of the steering wheel I was beginning to hear and feel? Yikes! My heart raced as I proceed to "lose it" and skidded off the gravel roadway and out onto the once frozen field. The vehicle quickly lurched to a stop after only going about 20 feet off of the roadway. No problem, I'll just back out of here back onto the roadway.

There was a problem. It was no longer a freezing morning. It was now a warm afternoon and the heat of the day had thawed out the frozen field turning it into a muddy quagmire. All four wheels of my vehicle had broken through the previously frozen crust of the soil and were now buried in the mud. As I went about surveying the situation all I could hear was Gary rolling with laughter about my predicament. His laughter was infectious and soon I too was laughing so hard that tears were streaming down my cheeks. Gary went over to get another vehicle to see if we could somehow, with its help, get my car unstuck from this muddy mess. Almost immediately we got the second vehicle stuck and the two white vehicles were now a chocolate brown in color. This only made us laugh more as I said to Gary, "What else could go wrong?" That's when Gary pointed behind me and I stopped laughing.

What I saw when I turned around were flames shooting out from under my vehicle. Apparently the heat from the catalytic converter had ignited the dry grasses under the car! I began scooping up mud and slinging it under the car until I had extinguished the fire. Gary, of course, was enjoying every minute of this demonstration of Management expertise. Eventually we did get both cars out of the field and parked them in line with the other vehicles before the class returned from lunch. It was easily recognizable which cars we had been driving for practice since there was no nearby car wash to wash away my sins. The CHP Officers took one look at my muddy uniform, shook their heads and took me out on the course once again. I passed with flying colors (brown).

Even though **all** rangers were now POST certified and qualified to carry firearms, the Department was still uncomfortable with the idea of **all** rangers **actually carrying weapons**. Previously I mentioned that a **few** rangers in parks such as Big Sur SP and Folsom Lake SRA had been trained and authorized to carry weapons before the rest of us complete our training. A rather strange comprised was reached.

The day did come when, back in Morro Bay, we were issued our first weapons. They were .38 cal. Dan Wesson Specials - obviously a cheap, low bid, revolver. Later we were to receive our more reliable .38cal. Smith & Wesson revolver. The State Park arms races went on from there to a stainless steel Smith & Wesson revolver and eventually to the currently authorized 9mm automatic pistols, shotguns, AR-15's, howitzers, A-bombs – you get the picture!

The problem was that when initially issued our Peace Officer Protective Equipment (POPE) we were not allowed to wear it! This gear consisted of our weapon, handcuffs, Mace and baton that had to be carried with us at all times while on duty **in a briefcase or bowling ball bag.** If one opted for the bowling bag it would seem to give new meaning to **strike** force! This seemed ludicrous to us, as any peace officer knows you can not pick the time or place you will need your weapon for self defense or to protect others.

The craziness of the restrictive policy was clearly demonstrated one night at Morro Bay in what thankfully turned out to be a humorous episode. The Morro Bay Museum of Natural History had a security protection system that was linked up directly with the Morro Bay Police Department. When the silent burglar alarm went off the City Police would receive the warning. There were often false alarms. It was standard procedure for the police to notify me when the alarm went off so I could go up and check on the situation. They too usually sent one of their officers to check.

On this night around 2:00 am I received a call and was told an officer was enroute to the museum to check it out. I was requested to respond as back up. I quickly dressed and grabbed my brief case and drove the short distance to the museum. The Morro Bay PD officer's car was parked near the entrance but no one was around. I immediately popped open my brief case only to find that I had the wrong briefcase! It was apparent I would be able to " red-tape" the bad guy into custody if need be because I had picked up my administrative brief case and my weapon was still snugly in bed at home in the other brief case.

Oh well, I thought. It was probably another false alarm so I proceeded up the walkway. Fortunately there was enough light so that I could see the Morro Bay Officer coming towards me with his gun drawn. I quickly identified myself and he told me he had found nothing unusual and assumed it was a false alarm. I reset the alarm system and returned home. The next morning I went back to the museum for a closer inspection in the daylight to see if there was any evidence of an attempted break in. When I looked closely at the emergency exit door at the rear of the museum's auditorium I noticed six widely spaced dents in the steel door. On the walkway between the door and a rocky slope were the remains of several spent bullets that had ricocheted off the steel door. Whoever had done this did not have his gun in a brief case! Eventually the firearm policy was revised.

BETWEEN A ROCK AND A HARD PLACE

Dominating the scene at the entrance to the harbor at Morro Bay is the remnant of an ancient volcano. At 576' high, Morro Rock must look much as it did in 1542 when Spanish explorer Juan Rodriquez Cabrillo named it. There are few places along Estero Bay where "The Rock" can not be seen. It is one of a string of volcanic plugs that stretch inland from Morro Bay to San Luis Obispo. It was a magnet to Cabrillo and it remains an attraction to tourists today.

In the early 1970's, it was also an attraction to the few remaining Peregrine Falcons in California. There were only two nesting pair and six others known in all of the State. A pair was nesting on Morro Rock when I arrived in 1971. The Rock, encompassing some 62 acres is a designated a State Historic Landmark. Climbing on the Rock and/or disturbing the birds is strictly prohibited. Nevertheless, it was an attractive challenge to many people who were unaware that disturbing the nesting falcons would hinder breeding or that they could be placing themselves in danger by climbing Morro Rock.

There are steep cliffs and gullies dropping off onto a parking lot and roadway on one side of the rock while on the other side the cliffs drop straight down into the Pacific Ocean. To the unwary climber a trip to the top can appear deceptively easy. Actually near the top of the massive rock are the remains of stairs and handrails that people once used to climb to the top for the magnificent view up and down the coast. Assuming one is successful in finding one of the easier routes to the top, it is the descent that poses the greater problem. Most often the folks who illegally climb to the summit fail to return exactly the same way. Consequently, the trip back down can be extremely dangerous. The descent can lead into a blind chute where it is easy to become stuck, or worse yet, fall to the rocks or ocean below.

When I transferred to Morro Bay SP from Pismo SB, the crew at Morro Bay was making more body recoveries than rescues. They were doing a good job with what they had. That is, self-taught knowledge and experience, but little formal rescue training or proper equipment. In 1971, we were finally able to get authorization to attend formal mountain rescue training at Sequoia National Park. It was excellent training provided by our National Park counterparts. Based upon the training I wrote a Morro Rock Rescue Plan and was successful in obtaining all of the necessary climbing gear needed to effect safer rescues. It was the first formal cliff rescue training in the Department. Later, cliff rescue training became commonplace along the southern California beach parks. Even after our training however, body recovery was more common than rescue, but at least the rescuers weren't exposed to the degree of danger they had been previously. The saddest case of a death occurred when a newly wed couple on honeymoon, stopped at Morro Rock. The groom of only a few days, climbed the rock in front of his bride and slipped, plunging to his death before her eyes.

We had to be prepared for such events, so I set up a training program with the Ranger Trainees. It was great fun to rig up in climbing gear and practice the Stokes

Litter maneuvering, belaying, and general use of ropes and knots. Once when conducting training at a location that was clearly visible from the roadway, a large crowd gathered to watch. I was "on belay", that is holding the safety rope in the event of a fall, for the person who was making a controlled descent and also practicing falling. At some point, Peter Van Coop, the Ranger Trainee on the line, leaned back to far and completely flipped over. My view of him from my sitting position above was a set of Vibram boot soles, as he hung helplessly upside down. It really was a very funny sight and I was having a good laugh. As soon as the other Trainees realized that Pete really wasn't in much danger they joined in on the laugh at Pete's expense. The crowd below must have really wondered what was going on. Pete asked what he should do and I could give him no answer because I had never experienced this event before. Since Pete had a hard-hat on I finally decided to just slowly lower him down to the ground about 15'- 20' below while he swayed back and forth. Once he was on the ground we could hear the crowd below as the sound of their cheers drifted up to us high on the precipitous slope of Morro Rock. Pete had certainly been between a rock and a hard place!

MAINTENANCE MISCHIEF

Around 1970 the department reorganized and split the ranger ranks into Visitor Services and Maintenance Services in order to improve efficiency. This change was looked upon suspiciously by some and applauded by others. The specialization of duties resulted in conflicts of authority between the two sections. I'm sad to say that some "turf battles" resulting from this division did nothing to advance the Department's mission in serving the public and protecting our natural resources.

At Morro Bay, as Supervising Ranger for three parks (Morro Bay SP, Atascadero SB, and Montana de Oro SP), I was a reluctant participant in the "politics" of sorting out these differences and trying to maintain a sense of civility. In some instances the problem was a petty nuisance. For example, at Morro Bay the maintenance staff became very possessive of "their" supplies and equipment. This was understandable to some degree because the ranger staff did not always return borrowed items in the condition they had found them. On the other hand, the reaction of the maintenance staff was to lock up **all** supplies so that visitor services staff had no access for necessary or emergency items.

On one occasion we had a ranger on night patrol duty all alone. In those days there was no 24-hr radio dispatch, no backup ranger on duty, or any maintenance personnel scheduled to work after dark. What should happen but when the patrol ranger made a circuit through the campground, several campers stopped him to report there was no toilet paper in one of the restrooms. When the ranger checked he found there was a crisis of sorts to be sure and there was no more toilet paper in the storage closet of the restroom. In order to rectify the situation, Ranger John returned to the shop complex to obtain additional toilet paper from the storage area. The problem was that the Maintenance Supervisor had placed a new lock on the door so that Visitor Service employees could not open it. In total frustration, Ranger John took an ax to the lock and broke it. "Flushed" with success he restocked the restroom facility with toilet paper. Needless to say the proverbial "S--- hit the fan" the next morning as the Maintenance Supervisor and I worked to sort out the problem so that we didn't have a reoccurrence of that situation.

Speaking of reoccurrence, we did have a more serious conflict on another occasion. This time it took place at Montana de Oro State Park. Back in 1970 the old ranch house at Spooner's Cove was not much in use. Today it serves as a visitor center and office. Each spring hundreds of barn swallows would nest under the eaves of the old white ranch house. The San Luis Obispo coast area was, and remains, a spectacular location for bird watching and there is an active Audubon Society in the area. Many of the members of Audubon Society and other nature lovers in general would come to Montana de Oro for bird watching activities. The nesting swallows were one of the main attractions as the baby chicks could often be seen poking their heads out of the nests. The swallow nest constructed of mud would of course stain the sides of the building. The muddy streaks, along with their bird droppings must have been a thing of beauty to the birds but only looked dirty to the Maintenance Supervisor and the maintenance crew responsible for the cleanliness of the structure.

Unbeknownst to Visitor Services staff, or for that matter anyone in our Area Office, maintenance crews had taken a high-pressure pump and sprayed the building, washing all the nests away and onto the ground! It was a natural and public relations disaster of the first degree with hundreds of dead baby birds strewn upon the ground and their panicked parents fluttering about. We first learned of what happened from angry park visitors, but you didn't have to be there to be angry. The story made front-page news in local newspapers so that the whole county was up in arms. There was no excuse for this action. As impossible as it is to believe, **the same thing happened the following year**! I still am at a loss to explain how or why it could happen again without adverse action being taken against the guilty party.

One other situation occurred while I was at Morro Bay that demonstrates the depth of the problem in understanding between Visitor Services and Maintenance Services. That involved the building of a campfire center for evening programs. When I first arrived in Morro Bay there was no formal campfire program area where slide shows or movies might be shown as part of the regular interpretive activities. The museum generally wasn't available in the evening and it did not have the feel of a traditional campfire program setting with the park ranger.

By this time I was in charge of the Ranger Trainees for the Area. As part of Trainees On-the-Job Training they were supposed to be involved in some maintenance project. I drew up plans for a campfire center and received the okay from the Area Manager Lyden to proceed with the Trainees doing the work under the direction of Ranger Bob Addkison. Bob was a first class electrician so the campfire center was wired for remote lights, projector and sound. In hindsight, the location I had selected for the campfire center perhaps was not the best. It was adjacent to the campground but also within shouting distance of the residence of the Maintenance Supervisor who complained to me that the noise from the campfire center would disrupt his after work-activities. I did not agree since my house was even closer to the campfire center than his and I did not expect any noise problem. Imagine my surprise after I returned from a long weekend to find that the maintenance staff had suddenly decided to construct a loading ramp right next to the campfire center and completed the work while I was away. The ramp was not only an unsightly intrusion on the campfire center, but also, a safety hazard, as it would undoubtedly attract youngsters as a play spot. The likelihood of a person falling was real danger and the placing of this facility where it was served as an attractive nuisance.

What was done, was done and since the timing of the loading ramp was such that it coincided with the "Inaugural" first campfire program there was not much I could do about it except one thing. I invited the Area Manager to the first campfire program to inspect the finished campfire center and view the first program. Over 200 campers came to that first program which was considerably more than any previous programs given at the park. I pointed out to the Area Manager the danger posed by the new adjacent ramp and while I was not successful in getting it removed the maintenance staff did have to return and install safety rails all around it. It's funny, but in all the time I was at Morro Bay I never saw that ramp utilized - perhaps it was used after I left to haul away ill feelings.

Despite the sometimes rough start of the maintenance "profession" in the California State Park System it has grown and matured into an outstanding program. As I said before, in its infancy almost all of the maintenance staff came from the splitting up of the existing Park Ranger and Park Attendant classifications. Later, as the years progressed, maintenance staffing grew and evolved with the addition of employees hired specifically for the maintenance positions. At this point in the Department's history I am proud to say that some of our finest Park Superintendent's have come up through the maintenance ranks and succeeded at the highest management levels within the Department. I guess a little mischief paid off!

BIRDS, BEES, CLAMS & CATS

In 1971-73 there were some advantages to living in a park in state housing. Certainly at Morro Bay SP there was the economic benefit of reduced rent for a house that was located in such beautiful surroundings. There were/are also downsides to living in a park. For one thing, you are always on duty and it is difficult to get away from the job unless you do in fact get away. Once the public knows or learns where your house is you are fair game – "after all the taxpayer pays my salary" (I think the entire State Park budget is something like 1/10th of 1% or less of the entire State Budget). I cannot tell you how many times park visitors have walked right into my home unannounced without knocking, often at dinner, to ask sometimes inane questions. You learn to live with it.

Despite the inconveniences and intrusion, the intangible benefits of raising a family in a park setting are wonderful. Our experience at Morro Bay may offer a glimpse of this life.

Many times after dinner and work the family would go for a walk through the campground and up the golf course fairway that extended from the bottom of the slope near the museum road to the tee area for that hole at the top of a hill. Often we pulled Abby and Chris in a wagon on this trek. Once at the top we turned the kids loose as they careened, at full speed, down the slope. I'm sure the golf course groundskeepers would have had a fit if they had ever seen us at our sport. We were never caught.

Some evenings we also walked to the boat marina and mud flats located below the Natural History Museum. It was in this area that we were introduced to Geoduck clams (pronounced Gooey Duck). Geoducks are a large (6"-8"), rather grotesque Bi-valves, with a neck that can extend up to 18". During low tide we would trek out through the mud flats to the clam beds where we would attempt to extract the clams from the mud. This required digging a hole, often several feet deep, in a race to capture the clam before it retracted it's neck (siphon) and burrowed deeper into the mud. It was a messy business because often we lay on our stomachs in the incoming tide in our attempts to grab our quarry. If we were successful we were rewarded with a tasty delicacy. We also were able to gather Gaper, Horseneck and Washington clams and the occasional oyster.

Our children had the opportunity, up close and personal, to learn much about the bird life of the area. Morro Bay is situated on the Pacific Coast Flyway and is a wintering area for many waterfowl and a nesting area for many other birds. Black Brandt, Canadian Geese, and both Great Blue Herons and Black-crowned Night Herons and Hummingbirds being the most notable. On Morro Rock, as I mentioned earlier, we also had one of the few nesting pairs of Peregrine Falcons on the West Coast at the time.

The main heron rookery was located just north of the museum in a grove of Eucalyptus trees. When the young birds were ready to fledge, they would often end up on the ground and be picked up by park visitors who were attempting to "save" them. Of course if the young birds had been left where they were, the parent birds would have continued to care for them until they could care for themselves and fly out of harm's way.

Once park visitors discovered and knew where our house was, it instantly turned into wildlife rescue center, whether we liked it or not. The public would bring the birds to our house for care. Most common were the young Black-crowned Night Herons who, quite frankly, were ugly, awkward looking birds. We taught the kids to force feed them dog food or any other concoction that might be suggested. While it was not a pretty sight, it did prove successful. At other times we assisted in the care of ducks, blue jays, hummingbirds and the occasional raptor.

Because our residence was located so near the campground I was often the first one called out to respond to "emergencies" that at times were a little unusual if not interesting. Take for instance the time an agitated camper came to my door to complain about a swarm of bees in his campsite. I went out to investigate and sure enough, hanging from a tree branch next to his campsite was a large mass of bees suspended about 18″ from the branch much like a Sugar Pine cone. Now I knew little about apiary science, but I did know you were supposed to capture the queen bee that was hidden somewhere in that mass of bees hanging from that branch in order to control the them. I figured that I could capture the whole swarm at once by placing a plastic bag underneath them and cutting off the branch. The bees in no way appeared aggressive as they hung from there,

I returned home and decided that I should make some sort of beekeeper outfit for my protection just to be on the safe side before I attempted to remove the bees. For this purpose I put on my chest-high fishing waders, borrowed a large hat from Margaret, some netting and gloves. I was quite the fashion statement! When I returned to the campsite the bees were gone! I was quickly informed by a contingent of helpful campers that the swarm had moved to another campsite. Indeed they had. They were now amassed on a campsite number post and would have to be scraped off of the post. Gingerly I did this to the cheers of my audience.

"Hummmm", I thought after this successful venture, "maybe I can get some honey out of this effort". With that in mind I took the bees home with me. One of the seasonal rangers loaned me a beehive and I put the swarm in it to await my golden harvest. Most of the bees either died or left and my experiment failed. Later I was to learn that we had a bee expert on staff. A young Cal Poly student, on the maintenance crew, was majoring in apiary science at the college just down the road from us. If only I had known.

Like many families, we too, had our own menagerie of pets over the years as we moved from park to park. At Morro Bay that list included fish, snakes, African finches, hamsters, and a cat named "Scamper". Scamper was a large female housecat of unknown pedigree. One day Abby decide to play house and dress Scamper in one of her doll's white, frilly lacy slips. Scamper did not like this and proceeded to scamper right out of the house. She did not return. I searched for the next two days and nights to no avail. Finally, on the third night, we heard a ruckus of two cats fighting, or more likely, courting, but still Scamper did not return home.

The next morning I noticed, under the bushes, near the park entrance station the shape of a cat laying still. Upon investigation I saw that it was a huge tomcat. It was dead! In some respects this was good news for our family since it wasn't Scamper. That evening we heard a mournful meowing and scratching at the front door. Upon opening the door, what sight should greet us but a disheveled Scamper, still wearing her white (but stained), frilly slip all askew! Our wayward cat had returned home at last.

Eight weeks later, Scamper gave birth to two kittens. To this day I would swear that the old tomcat I had found dead under the bushes had died with a smile on his face.

We had lived at Morro Bay for almost two years when my first opportunity for the next series of promotional examinations came up. The test that was given consisted of a written portion and an oral interview. In this instance the same written test was to be used for both the State Park Ranger III and the Manager I & II promotional list but separate oral interviews would be conducted. The oral interviews were scheduled a month apart.

The first interview was for the SPR III position. This classification was most often utilized as the Chief Ranger in a larger Area while the classification of Manager I or II was used as the Manager of a medium sized Area.

At the Ranger III interview, I was asked by Jack Knight, Chief of Park Operations, "Why do you want to be a Chief Ranger?" I responded "I want to be a Chief Ranger because...". A month later I was back for the Manager interview. Much to my surprise, Jack was again on the interview panel. This time he asked, "Why do you want to be an Area Manager?" Again I responded that "I wanted to be an Area Manager because...". "Wait a minute" Jack replied. "I thought that last month you said you wanted to be a Chief Ranger". To this day I can not remember how I responded to this last question because I became so flustered. I would sure love to listen to the tape recording of that interview to see how I did in fact reply.

My answers must have been okay because I ended up reachable on both hiring lists. It was decision time again for the family as offers began to come in for positions from both lists. I walked up to the Museum overlooking the bay to ponder my decision. I thought about how much we loved this area but I still felt that it was a natural progression for my career development to accept a Chief Ranger position. It was time to move on again.

MORRO BAY SKETCHES

Carl S. Chavez

BACK TO THE BEGINNING

On New Years Day, 1971, after we had moved north from Pt. Mugu SRA to Pismo SB, I vowed never to return to an assignment in Southern California. It was not my cup of tea. Ever since climbing aboard that Greyhound bus and setting off to college, I had fallen in love with a part of California that I knew was for me. But people change. I had changed.

My parents and several of my sisters still resided in the San Diego area where I had grown up. It was only occasionally on infrequent family visits that they were able to interact with our children. Abby and Chris really didn't know their grandparents or aunts that well, so I thought it would be good for them to have closer extended family contact. That opportunity came when I received an offer to promote to Chief Ranger in the Montane Area.

The Montane Area is in the eastern mountains of San Diego County and is comprised of two State Parks. The two parks are Cuyamaca Rancho SP and Palomar Mountain SP. I was already very familiar with both parks. I had even attended 6th grade school camp at Palomar and participated in many hiking and camping activities at Cuyamaca when I was in Boy Scouts. I was able to rationalize that I really wasn't breaking my vow to never take an assignment in Southern California again because this assignment wasn't really like Southern California was supposed to be. It was more like the Sierra Nevada being transported south. I accepted the position. We were going back to where it all began-only 45 miles from my boyhood home. Never say never!

PROBATION

We moved from Morro Bay to Cuyamaca the second week of September and I reported for duty on September 12, 1973. It was a rather strange move in that we moved from our standard house in Morro Bay to another standard house in Cuyamaca. The only difference was that one house was the mirror image of the other. It was an easy job for the moving company personnel to place our furnishings. The house was in a great location, situated as it was in the Paso Picacho area, near the gate and road leading up to the fire lookout on 7,000' Cuyamaca Peak.

Cuyamaca Rancho SP, at the time, comprised 20,000 acres of forests, oak-woodland, chaparral, and meadowland. State Highway 79 and the Sweetwater River bisect the park. There are major campground facilities at Paso Picacho near the summit of Highway 79 and at Green Valley Fall a little further south. Midway between was the Park Headquarters and museum in the old Dyar Ranch House, and a San Diego County School Camp situated behind the headquarters.. Other facilities included Boy Scout and Girl Scout camps, horse camps, trail camps and miles and miles of hiking trails. It is truly a prime recreational area in Southern California.

Palomar Mountain SP, on the other hand, is a much smaller more intimate unit located not far from the famous Palomar Mountain Telescope Observatory and about 40 miles from Park Headquarters. It too had a school camp, the one I had attended in my youth, a fishing pond and some great campsites.

As Chief Ranger I would be responsible for the operation of the two units and supervision of the ranger staff. The staff included, for the most part, a mature and experienced group of rangers that in truth needed very little supervision. This was a welcome change from my Morro Bay experience. One of the rangers assigned to Palomar Mountain SP was the very same Jim Hart that I had worked with at Pismo Beach.

When one is promoted to a new position in the State Park System he/she is subjected to a 6-month probationary period to "prove" capable of doing the assigned job. I found my probation unique in that it was nearly completely performed in *abstentia*.

My first day on the job in the Montane Area consisted of meeting with the Area Manager, Glenn Jones, and touring the parks with him. He gave me a quick rundown of what was expected of me, some background on the personnel and employee dynamics of the Area and two specific assignments. Then he told me that he was leaving the **next day** for his two months of peace officer training and then an extended two months of vacation after that. The two assignments he gave me were to complete the Area's Operation Plan and the Area Budget for the next budget cycle. The Operations Plan assignment didn't bother me since I had been so heavily involved in completed plans for both the Point Mugu and San Luis Obispo Areas. I had not, however, been responsible for an entire Area budget so that was to be a new experience. I relied heavily on our Maintenance Supervisor Sam Bitting and Secretary Nona Rikansrud to complete those assignments in time along with assistance from the ranger staff. Meanwhile, the first probationary review period and then the second passed with no documentation of how I was doing. I didn't give it much thought or concern, however, because I knew that if the reports were not completed in a timely fashion I would pass probation by default. Nevertheless, I felt a little like I had a ball and chain tethering me in place until I had officially passed my probationary period. I didn't know if I would get a "thumbs up" or "thumbs" down report". Imagine my surprise when I received through the mail from Area Manager Jones a final probationary report with a note asking me to fill it out on myself and return it to him for his signature. That was the easiest probation period I ever passed! I had gained my freedom.

Glenn eventually promoted to a position in our Sacramento Headquarters and was replaced by a new Area Manager. The new manager was Jim Geary, who was transferring from Point Mugu Area. We had come full circle, as Jim had been my Area Manager when I had worked at Pt. Mugu. This time I would have the chance to break him in to a new assignment.

SEX IN THE '70's, (A TITILLATING TALE)

Many of California's state parks are located relatively close to nearby metropolitan centers. Cuyamaca Rancho SP was only one hour driving time from downtown San Diego and even less than that from the East County. The potential is always present, at any park, for all situations that might be encountered in a large urban area to be brought into the park environment. At Cuyamaca, more so than most parks I have worked in, it seemed that the park visitor often forgot to pack their inhibitions and leave their secret desires in the bedroom at home! In truth, Cuyamaca was not Sin City. At every park in which I worked, with the exception of Bodie (maybe it was too "frigid!"), I unexpectedly encountered visitor's engaging in sexual behavior of one sort or another. Usually I was as surprised as those I stumbled across engaged in this often very public, but human, display of activity.

It would take too long to go into some of the situations I encountered at other parks. Some were as innocent as merely "skinny dipping" and other times much more animated. For example the couple that had the ultimate *coitus interuptus* when a large redwood tree branch fell on their car and trapped them inside. On another occasion I came upon a couple on the beach lost in passion. The man said to me "Do you mind, this is my wife!" I responded "Do you mind, this beach is closed!" The most common of all comprising situations occurred when I would walk into a campsite for fee collection purposes and interrupt "work in progress". Of course this could be at any hour of the day or night. I soon learned to look and if necessary make a hasty retreat, before asking "can I help you?" It goes on and on from there

Perhaps I remember the incidents at Cuyamaca more vividly because they occurred at the end of the era of "Free Love" in the early and mid 1970's and what I saw was just an expression of those times. Let's start with a simple "skinny dipping" situation and proceed from there. It is the summer of 1974.

I often worked the day shift on Saturdays at Cuyamaca and enjoyed the chance to get out of the office and away from the administrative paperwork. I was patrolling in the vicinity of Green Valley Falls where the Sweetwater River flows over rocky boulders to create the falls for which the area is named. The river continues another mile or two further down stream to a series of beaver dams and ponds before leaving the park on its course to the Pacific Ocean. Beyond the campground and a locked gate, a fire road leads to the ponds. Park visitors can follow a river trail to the same area.

I drove to the beaver pond area where I parked my vehicle and got out to walk the short remaining distance to the first pond. As I got nearer I heard a faint, but rhythmic, slapping of the water. I had never heard a beaver slap it's tail in this manner before. Whoops! There standing face to face in the water was a young couple "in their birthday suits" enjoying nature. At first I didn't see anyone else around so I decided to leave. The couple was obviously unaware of my presence. I turned to leave when my eyes caught a glint of sunlight flashed from some bushes on the other side of the pond. The flash of light had come from the reflection off of the lens of a camera as a person hidden in the bushes took photographs of the scene before us.

I circled around the pond and walked up undetected behind the photographer. I must say I took pleasure in startling him when I interrupted his photographic activity. We had a brief conversation and I asked if I could see his camera. Sheepishly he complied and handed it to me. It was a fine 35mm with telephoto lens. As I inspected the camera I "inadvertently" opened it and exposed all the film inside and suggested to our photographer that he be on his way. I was surprised, when without argument; he left and walked off on his way further downstream along the trail. I then decided it best I contact the couple and advise them what had happened. While I discreetly moved away they came out of the water and dressed, all the while explaining to me that they were a newly married couple. "No problem" I said. I even gave them a ride back to the campground and away from the creep who had been sneaking photos of them.

Later that evening, while at home, I received a call that a park visitor had been injured on the trail **below the beaver ponds.** An alarm bell went off in my head as I drove to the area. It seems our friend, the photographer, had taken a fall in a gorge further down the canyon and broken not only his leg, but also his camera. It took four of us to carry him out on a stretcher to where a helicopter could land and transport him to the hospital. In the process I ruined a pair of boots from walking in the water to retrieve the injured photographer from the stream where he lay. I had little sympathy for him as I felt justice had been served.

Sometimes things get a little more complex as Ranger Jimmie "Tex" Ritter and I discovered while on patrol on one particularly fine spring day. Tex was a very competent ranger and student of human nature. He was later to become a very good and well liked manger in his own right. He had "been around the block" and I had no problem with him taking the lead on this patrol or the situation that we encountered that afternoon.

It was a very busy weekend with a lot of people out and about in the park. As we approached a large turnout and parking area along Highway 79, north of the Green Valley Campground, we notice a vehicle parked off the roadway on the hillside adjacent to the parking lot. The driver had driven past the parking lot barriers and abandoned the car where it now sat. Gasoline was leaking from the gas tank cap due to the steep angle in which the car had been parked. It was a clear violation that warranted a citation. The occupant(s) of the vehicle were not around but there were lots of families with their children enjoying the area and preparing to walk further up the slope. After we questions a few of the other park visitors we established that, a couple acting a little strangely, had wandered up the hill from the vehicle.

Tex and I proceeded up the hill ahead of a group that was preparing to take a hike in same direction we were headed. As we walked up the grassy slope into the trees we began to notice a trail of belongings. Here a high heel shoe, there a scarf, ahead a champagne glass, a blouse, even more clothing, two towels and finally at the end of the trail two individuals, both stark naked laying on a blanket sound asleep. We had been gathering up the items as we went further into the woods. It appeared we might have a major problem on our hands.

I write the following, not because I want to sound bigoted, but because the scene before us presented a situation that stood out for its contrast. The woman was a

Caucasian of very, very pale completion. Her gentleman friend was a very, very dark skinned African American. We could hear the sound of voices drifting our way as people made their way up the hill.

Picking up the towels and the clothes we had gathered, Tex walked over to the sleeping couple. I stayed behind to stop the other families and hikers coming up the hill if necessary. As Tex reached the couple he tapped the man on the shoulder and, gingerly holding the towels between finger and thumb, handed them to the man and suggested that they might get dressed as quickly as possible before others stumbled across the scene. With that Tex returned to my location as the couple dressed.

It was obvious that the couple had been drinking but we did not feel the driver was intoxicated, though I could not say the same for the "lady". This guy may have been the most cooperative person we ever encountered when it came time to sign the citation. All he wanted was to get out of there. The party was over!

Finally there is a most difficult story to relate in a "G" rated narrative. It is another day, another weekend. There are several state park houses located throughout the park. One of these was the house that Tex lived in with his family, including several children. Across the roadway from Tex's home in the vicinity of the Horse Camp also lived Sam, the Maintenance Supervisor, and his family. It was not unusual for the children (known within the "Park Family" as "Park Brats") to ride their bikes on the less traveled interior park road that led to the Group Horse Camp or the Stonewall Mine Area.

I was driving along this road when I saw one of Sam's boys and one of Tex's boys together on their bicycles headed in the same direction as I was. I waved to the boys as I passed by. Further ahead I could see a car parked on the wrong side of the road with its emergency flashers blinking.

I was probably a mile ahead of the boys on the bicycles when I stopped in front of the vehicle with the blinking lights. I could see a driver sitting behind the steering wheel with a smile and look of ecstasy on his face, which seemed strange under the circumstances. The window on the passenger side was rolled down as I approached from that side and leaned in to ask, "Can I help you". I stopped in mid-sentence as I realized the driver's female companion was on the floor directly in front of him. Her head, in moments of passion, had hit the emergency flasher button on the steering column and turned them on!

I could see the boys on their bike getting closer. Perhaps, against my better judgment, because I could tell that alcohol was involved, I hurried to get the couple on their way and out of the park in order to keep innocent eyes from observing this scene. I did in fact get the people out of there in time and as the boys peddled by my parked vehicle I smiled nonchalantly and waved to them again. Another bullet, or perhaps, but not likely, Cupid's arrow dodged!

A BUSMAN'S HOLIDAY

All was not work and no play in the Montane Area. On my days off, if we didn't have shopping to do in town, we were usually off to hike the many trails in the park, climb Stonewall Peak, visit friends and relatives, or take short overnight camping trips to the adjacent Anza-Borrego Desert State Park. Our vacations too were usually taken on trips to other state or national parks. On one occasion during the spring my son Chris and I went to the desert for an overnight outing and had a great time. It was warm and we found a wonderful primitive campsite amongst some sheltering boulders. In the evening around our campfire we noticed little Kangaroo mice poking their noses out of crevices in a search for crumbs. We found they would become very bold if we offered them a tidbit. So bold in fact that they would eat out of our gloved hands. Chris loved this!

When we returned home, Chris was quick to gleefully tell his sister of the great time we had "playing" with the mice. It really had been a fun trip so I told Margaret and Abby that we could go back again the next weekend so they too could enjoy the experience.

Everything was packed for the camping trip the Friday morning we were to leave so that we could depart as soon as I got off work. On that day, however, an unexpectedly severe cold storm arrived, accompanied by strong winds that dumped several inches of snow in the park. The snowstorm caught a group of Boy Scouts unprepared as they hiked along the trail from Anza-Borrego Desert SP to the Paso Picacho campground in Cuyamaca.

I was in my office at Park Headquarters when I got the call from the Park Aide on duty in the check station that a Boy Scout was in trouble and in need of immediate assistance. I drove "Code 3" to the check station and was directed to a large Travelall type vehicle. Inside was a young scout in obvious distress. He was shivering violently and having difficulty breathing as he lay in a sleeping bag in the back of the vehicle. I quickly determined he was hypothermic and about the same time he quit breathing. I immediately began CPR and revived him and then climbed into the sleeping bag to warm him up.

A short- time later an ambulance that had been previously called arrived and the attendants took out the gurney, made a quick check of vitals, attached an IV and started to load the patient onto the gurney. I was holding the young man's head and shoulders while bent over inside the vehicle. The two attendants had his lower extremities and were pulling him onto the gurney. I thought I was going to drop him because they were moving so fast and I had to **step down** from the back of the vehicle while I still held the boy. In doing so I stepped right onto an icy patch of frozen ground. I heard and felt my ankle make an unnatural sound and movement but did not drop the lad.

The ambulance left and I walked gingerly back to my vehicle and drove back to my office. The pain in my ankle was severe, but manageable. I wrapped the swollen ankle in an Ace bandage and figured I would tough it out.

By the time I got home after work the ankle was really swollen and Margaret did not think we should go on the trip, but I convinced her I would be okay if she would just do the driving. I did not want to disappoint the kids. We clambered aboard the VW van and headed down the mountain to the desert. In our stay at Cuyamaca we had acquired a Brittany Spaniel named "Cinnamon" as a family pet and she accompanied us on this adventure.

We arrived at the chosen primitive campsite, where Chris and I had previously camped, only to find it already occupied. In the gathering darkness we found another site but it had no rock shelter or mice. There were strong cold winds sweeping down from the Laguna Mountains to add to our disappointment. We made the best of it as we set up our camp. The plan was for Chris and Margaret to sleep in the van while Abby and I pitched a small backpack tent for our quarters. We left it to Cinnamon to make her own choice of which accommodation she preferred.

Quite frankly we were pretty cold and miserable. It was not turning out to be the camping trip we had hoped for. With little to do we turned in early to get out of the cold wind since building a campfire was out of the question. I don't know about the others, but I slept fitfully as my ankle throbbed from pain. I thought I had been asleep for hours but when I checked my watch it was only 9:00pm! "Now what?" It was Cinnamon at our tent flap whining to get in the tent! Apparently Margaret had let her out of the van to relieve herself. Upon opening the tent flap there stood our foul looking and smelling dog. She had found some excrement to roll in and now wanted to come into our tent. This adventure was quickly turning into what was later to be regarded in the family as the **"Chavez Trip from Hell"**. I got out of my sleeping bag and hobbled out of the tent and awoke Margaret. This was a dry campsite and we had only the limited supply of water we brought with us with which to clean up the dog (ugh). We did the best we could with what we had. Could things get any worse? Sure.

My ankle was killing me as I went back to bed. I awoke again about 3:00am when I could stand the pain no longer. I turned on my flashlight and rolled up my pant leg to have a look. It was not a pretty sight. My whole leg was swollen from ankle to knee and was purple in color. My injury was worse than I thought. Surprise, surprise. We (read Margaret) decided we best throw in the towel, tents, kids, and dog into the van and beat a path for home. There was little protest with this course of action even at this early hour.

The next afternoon Margaret took me to see a doctor who placed my foot in a cast after determining I had torn ligaments in my right ankle. I went to work on Monday but to this day my ankle still bothers me. It really was not much of a "Busman's Holiday"

THIN WALLS

We were only in the Montane Area about one and a half years when opportunities to transfer into Area Manager positions began to surface. At this point in my career I now felt ready to take on that kind of assignment. I was still on the Manger promotional list so it was not a problem to take a higher-level management assignment or transfer laterally into a smaller Area operation as a park manager.

I chose to do the latter when it appeared a vacancy was to open in the Mt. San Jacinto Area. That was a beautiful area near Idyllwild that included the San Jacinto SP and San Jacinto Wilderness Area. Much like Cuyamaca and Palomar the area did not fit the stereotypical image one thinks of as Southern California. Mt. San Jacinto is one of the few true wilderness areas in the State Park System and it has a feel much more like the

Sierra Nevada that I loved so much. The Area Manager position at Mt. San Jacinto was to be vacated by the incumbent who was transferring to Plumas-Eureka State Park, one of my dream parks that I had asked to be transferred to previously when I was forced to leave Bodie nine years previous.

In any event, I accepted the State Park Manager I position for the San Jacinto Area and prepared the family for another move. At this same time, preparations for a District 6 Area Manager's Meeting were underway. District 6 was comprised of all of the Park Areas in the southern part of the State.

Normally, as a Chief Ranger, I would not attend these meeting except in the absence of my own Area Manager. Because my move to San Jacinto appeared imminent, however, Montane Area Manger Geary telephoned his supervisor, District 6 Superintendent Jim Whitehead, to ask if I should attend the meeting. It was not that I was eavesdropping, but my office was next door to Jim's and the walls between the office were very thin. I could hear Jim's end of the telephone conversation that seemed to indicate that I should not go to the meeting because the current Manger at San Jacinto wasn't going to move after all. Evidently his wife had refused to move again. I can't say that I was disappointed with this news because I quickly saw that an opportunity was near at hand.

In fact, once I deduced that the position at Plumas-Eureka was still open I was ecstatic. There was no doubt in my mind that the family would rather transfer to Plumas-Eureka Area than to Mt. San Jacinto. I mulled over what to do next to take advantage of the situation and the important bit of information I had gleaned from behind that thin wall. I decided to wait until Jim left the office. I then proceeded to telephone our "Manpower Utilization" section in Sacramento and talk to Dick Brock, the person in charge, whom I knew well from our Peace Officer training time together at Modesto J.C. I told him that I understood that Plumas-Eureka was vacant again and I would take it. Dick Brock's response was "******, how could you know about that, I just learned of it a few minutes ago myself!" Then he laughed and said "The job's yours". No interview, no nothing, just go ahead and move-again. My tenure in the Montane Area ended on May 14, 1975.

There is a sad addendum to this story as a result of the terrible "Cedar Fire" of October 2003 that destroyed so much of the Cuyamaca Rancho State Park. One of the structures to fall victim to the flames was the old Dyar Ranch House that was constructed in 1923 and had served as the park headquarters since the state first acquired the property in 1933. All that remained after the flames had consumed most of the building were the thick exterior stone walls. The interior walls, ceiling, and floors that had served me so well were engulfed in flames and collapsed into the basement. A few of my memories are in those ashes.

DYAR RANCH HOUSE

CUYAMACA SKETCHES

A SECRET PLACE

Although I had been to Plumas-Eureka State Park (PESP) only once before, it felt like we were going home. That first visit was in September 1967. The visit to the park had made a lasting impression on me. Perhaps it was the pet deer that lay on the floor at the feet of the Park Supervisor as we visited with him in his house. More likely it was because of the beauty of the area with the forest, streams (fly fishing!), lakes, and rich gold mining history of the area. It was the kind of park I had dreamed about as a kid. On that visit I knew I would be back someday. This was the day.

The drive from Cuyamaca to PESP was memorable for what did not happen. We drove up Interstate 5 in the Central Valley in our trusty VW van. We were loaded to the gills with kids, dog, cat, houseplants, and other items that the commercial moving van, which was following, could not legally transport. At one brief rest stop in Button Willow, our dog, Cinnamon thought it would be a great idea to chase after one of the jackrabbits that frequented the area. The last sight and sound of her we had was as she went yapping, ears a flapping, over a rise into the desert-like scrub country in pursuit of her quarry. We thought she was lost for good after two hours of fruitless searching and we were heart sick at the thought of leaving her. Just when we had given up all hope and prepared to leave she returned panting, tongue hanging out, smiling and tail wagging with a look that said, "Boy was that fun, I needed a run". With our family now reunited we continued on our journey north.

I hadn't been interviewed for the manager job at PESP anymore than I had been for the position at Bodie or Pt. Mugu. I got the job by pure luck, being at the right place at the right time. For that reason I felt that when we got to Stockton where the District Office Headquarters was located we should drop in to meet my new bosses. When we arrived at the office, Ted Wilson, the District Superintendent, and the other key members of the staff were in a meeting. I told the secretary who I was and asked her to relay to those attending the meeting that I was reporting in on my way to my new assignment. I figured someone would at least come out of the meeting to welcome me. When the secretary returned she informed me that was not to be the case. I worried that this was an ominous start to a new job. Gee, wouldn't "They" be a little bit curious about who the new Manager was? Oh, well if they didn't care I didn't care to hang around either. We drove up Highway 80 to Truckee, turned north driving for one hour on Highway 89 to Graeagle and then headed five miles up the mountain on County Road A-14 to Johnsville. We had arrived. We were home. It was almost too good to be true!

Invariably when one mentions Plumas-Eureka the immediate response is something like "I've been there.

Isn't that it in the redwoods somewhere up the coast north of San Francisco?" Even our moving van crew thought that they would be driving nearly the length of California from San Diego to the city of Eureka. I straightened that out in a hurry before they left Cuyamaca.

Plumas-Eureka State Park is a small 5000-acre park located in the northern Sierra Nevada Range. Surrounded all around by Plumas National Forest lands it is also one of the major gateways to the Lakes Basin Recreation Area and the nearby Pacific Crest Trail. It is only about one hour driving time northwest of Reno, Nevada. The park surrounds the small, former gold mining town of Johnsville and ranges in elevation of 4700' at Park Headquarters to 7,447' at the top of Eureka Peak. In the late 1880's, millions of dollars worth of gold was extracted by hardrock mining methods from the rich gold veins of Eureka Peak. The 5-story Mohawk Stamp Mill where the gold ore was crushed for processing is the most noticeable structure remaining of those glory days. PESP is also thought to be the birthplace of downhill ski racing in the United States. In the early days, miners, many of whom were from Scandinavian countries and were familiar with skis, would often ride in ore buckets up the mountain on an aerial tramway and ski back down on the heavy longboard skis that were in use in those days. The Park Headquarters, which also serves as a museum, was once the miner's boarding house. The park also has a beautiful 67-unit campground along Jamison Creek and is the only State Park in California to have a downhill ski operation in winter, modest though it may be. It is a Paradise of a Park that in the 1970's was still one of California's best-kept secrets. A throw back to the "Good 'Ol Days" of camping, not even well known to many employees of State Parks, much less the general public. It was our "Secret Place".

It was to this, one of the smallest "Area" operations in the California State Park System that I had come. Like Bodie, there was only one other full-time Ranger on staff, but unlike Bodie, there was also a full-time Maintenance worker. Remarkably, this small park operation, just like the larger park I had I left, also had three seasonal rangers, and ten park aides. Later I was able to supplement that staffing with 5-7 "free" employees hired through various federal, state, and local county programs. I couldn't believe my good fortune as I whispered the words "Over staffed" to myself. Man, I was in Fat City and I planned to make the best of it.

COMMUNITY RELATIONS

Johnsville, as I said before is, a landlocked in-holding, surrounded by the park. Two of the park's three employee residences are located in the town, having been purchased by the State from the previous owners. "Our" house had been purchased from Ora White, who was also the mail delivery person for our rural route. Many of the houses in Johnsville were rehabilitated historic structures that now served as summer homes. In fact in 1975, the year we arrived there were only seven year-round residences occupied, and that included the two park employee's houses. In the summer, however, Johnsville would experience a population boom with the number of residents numbering as "many" as 35-40 people. For a town this small it was interesting and telling to note that we should have both a former and a current State Senator living part-time in Johnsville. Local zoning ordinances prohibited any commercial activities in Johnsville with the exception of a fine restaurant, "The Iron Door", which pre-dated the ordinance. Today, Johnsville has many more year round residents. A number of new homes have been built and others restored in keeping with the historic architectural style of the town.

We loved our place. It was a large 3-story house with two floors situated above the two-stall garage. The entire front living room, facing east, had windows, which in winter were a godsend for light and warmth. The only downside to the house was that the steep roof sloped in such a manner that snow sliding off the roof would accumulate in front of the garage doors. It was sometimes so deep that anyone, and that often included our son Chris, could walk up the drift and look in through the living room windows, two stories above the roadway.

Upon arriving at Plumas Eureka I felt it important to establish good community relations, as it was obvious that I would have to work closely with the citizens of Johnsville, Graeagle and other surrounding communities of Plumas County. One way I could accomplished this was by establishing a local Park Cooperative Association which not only helped the park develop interpretive programs and provided additional revenue sources, but just as importantly, brought park staff in contact with the locals in a positive manner that focused upon mutually agreed goals. Too often, in the past, the contact with locals had occurred only when there was an issue in dispute.

The formation of the Plumas Eureka State Park Association (PESPA) was no easy task. Cooperative Associations in California State Parks were still in their infancy since establishment of the first ones in parks along the Central Coast. There was a blur and indistinct separation of powers and duties between the early associations and parks. It was difficult to determine when one was a volunteer, employee, or an association member, to say nothing of keeping the financial records separate.

The other problem was the laborious, bureaucratic paperwork procedures that needed to be accomplished to form a non-profit organization. Fortunately, on that front we had the models to follow from those associations that had first broken this new ground. From them we copied and borrowed *shamelessly* in order to "cross the "*t*'s" and dot the "*i's*" on the necessary documents. I had assigned Ranger Ken Leigh the task of wading through all the "Red Tape" which he did admirably leading to the establishment of PESPA in 1977.

My job in the establishment of PESPA was to create the spark and interest for such an organization and recruit board members and general membership to make it a viable organization. As I was later to do at Humboldt Redwoods State Park in forming a new association there, I utilized what I considered a "Fail Proof" formula. I quickly identified individuals who were leaders in the community and sought their support in order to provide leadership and direction for our fledgling organization. Our first Board of Directors consisted of Harvey W., Graeagle town developer, Jack R., instructor at the Feather River Preparatory School, Michael Y., Feather River College Forestry Instructor and his wife Sally, Larry and Pat F., Johnsville Residents, Ed B., local historian and last but not least, Terry S., Editor of the local Feather River Bulletin newspaper in Quincy. Each of these individuals brought different interests and talents to PESPA that laid the foundation for the success and growth of the organization that continues today. They also each brought $5 to put into the hat we passed around as our initial membership dues to start us down the road to financial independence!

We organized community pot luck dinners and showed nature films in the museum for a "Saturday Night at the Movies" diversion to break the monotony of winter nights since radio and television reception was so poor (our time in Johnsville pre-dated cable and satellite service). It also helped to hire some of the college kids who resided with their families in Johnsville as part of our summer work crew. Later, when water service to town became an all time-consuming issue for both the park and residents of Johnsville I knew my efforts had paid dividends.

Today at the PESP there is also a very fine Docent Program that is an outgrowth of the Plumas-Eureka Interpretive Association that I founded in 1977. Since 1988, one of the outstanding programs that the docents conduct are demonstrations of a blacksmith at work during "Living History Days" which are conducted throughout the summer. Volunteer blacksmiths, in period costume, fire up the forge, pump the bellows and get to work. Items such as candle holders, dinner gongs and children's rings are made and sold to park visitors. It is an excellent program, but it isn't the first blacksmith demonstration at the park.

In 1975 the park's blacksmith shop was a static display of questionable authenticity and unexplained equipment. The huge, hand-made leather bellows were not functional. With the help of our Sacramento Headquarters Interpretive Section, I was able to get the bellows repaired and working. Still none of us on staff knew much about the blacksmith trade. I decided to take a chance. I placed an advertisement in the local newspaper requesting the services of a skilled blacksmith to come and explain the equipment and demonstrate its use. I got one response from an old, retired blacksmith who lived in Chester, about 90 miles north of the park. I talked to Karl on the telephone and I learned he was from the "Old Country"(Germany) where he had practiced his trade before coming to America to continue crafting. Karl was willing to come to the park to share his knowledge and set up the blacksmith shop, as it should be. I was very excited about the prospect of this happening until he asked "How much will I be paid?" Apparently he had misunderstood the newspaper advertisement. I had wanted a volunteer since I had no means to pay for the service I was requesting.

I explained this problem to Karl and (without consulting with my wife) offered to give him free room and board at our house in Johnsville if he agreed to come. It would be fun I assured him. Karl agreed to this arrangement with a stay arranged for the first two days in August. Margaret was not impressed with my negotiating skills. It was not her idea of fun inviting a total stranger into the house for two nights. When Karl showed up at the house we found him to be friendly but very loud, demanding and opinionated. I think the kids were a little intimidated by him and Abby, to say the least, was upset because she had to give up her room for the two nights. I survived the scorn of my family and moved ahead with the plan.

Karl did, in fact, do a good job of putting the blacksmith shop in order. He fired up the forge and the smell of coal smoke filled the air. That, along with the sound of hammer and anvil, made the Mohawk Stamp Mill site come alive again. Visitors flocked to the demonstration then, as they do today, to watch the fascinating demonstration. When Karl left he gave us a rustic, but very functional, iron triangle that we used to call the family to dinner. We were not able to continue the blacksmith program in subsequent years. That was left for the Docents and their "Living History Days" to develop into the fine program it has become - **but we were first!**

For now, on my first day in the office, there was still five feet of snow on the ground and I had to look no further than the parking area next to my office to see an old friend - a Tucker SnoCat. I could not tell if this was the same one we had in Bodie. Probably it was not, but it was just the same type and still very familiar. One of the first things I did using the SnoCat was take the local USFS snow survey team up to the "Eureka Bowl" on the slopes of Eureka Peak to conduct their monthly snow survey. The measurements are taken at two elevations. To give you some idea of the snow depths in May when we arrived at our new assignment they are recorded here.

Eureka Lake transect (elevation 6300')   75"
Eureka Bowl transect (elevation 6800')   108"

By all indications we had missed an above average winter arriving as we did in the spring, but the snow was melting fast and the campground would soon be open. We were not to experience another winter like the one we had just missed for two more years. The winters of 1975 -1976 and 1976-77 were drought years. Despite this the Ski Hill was able to operate each winter and served to unite the community and the local kids who benefited from the ski program run by schools. We were even able to work with Phil Intorf from the local Ski Club to have a Pomo Ski Lift installed, which believe it or not, was an upgrade over the previous rope tow. Unfortunately, due to poor snow conditions and deteriorating equipment the Ski Hill has received little use in recent years. Perhaps it is just as well so we can keep it our little secret.

Yes indeed, not many folks, including some State Park employees in other parts of California, knew then or now of our little Shangri-La in the Sierra - **and that was and is just fine with us!**

A PLAGUE ON US

A member of the community I was soon to meet was **Bubonic Plague**. The plague or "Black Death" as it was known in the Middle Ages, is transmitted by fleas carried on rodents such as ground squirrels and chipmunks. It is known to be indigenous to the Sierra Nevada but for many years there had been few cases of individuals contracting the disease in California.

I had never met my immediate supervisor, Assistant Superintendent Bob Hewitt, in person. We had had infrequent telephone conversations, but until he came up for a meeting on June 5th, three weeks after I had reported to my new assignment, he was a mystery voice at the other end of the telephone line. I did not see Bob again at the park until he and District Superintendent Ted Wilson made a return visit to PESP on October 17th. You can imagine my embarrassment as we drove to our house for lunch when my dog, Cinnamon, came charging up the steep bank from the creek with a squirrel in her mouth and crossed in front of our car.

Dogs in a State Park are supposed to be on a leash and, of course, wildlife is supposed to be protected. I mumbled something about "At least we're not in the park" (We were in Johnsville) and said I thought I'd better have the squirrel checked for bubonic plague. I sent the animal to the Vector Control Section of the State Health Department for testing. The results came back positive but there was no immediate repercussion of the incident and no one came down with the Black Death – not even my dog Cinnamon (It must have been the flea collar!).

The repercussions of the October incident did not occur until nine months later on June 25, 1976. It was the beginning of our busiest period of the year with the 4th of July weekend about to start. The campground was full to bursting at the seams when I went home after work that Friday evening. I was confident that all was in readiness for the holiday. I was at home in bed at 11:00pm when the telephone rang and I answered. The call was from a woman in the San Francisco Bay area. She said, "I have campsite reservations for this weekend. Is it true that the campground is closed?" I answered, perhaps a little too officiously, "Of course it's not closed. This is 4th of July week". "Then why is the evening news here in the Bay Area reporting that it is closed because a little girl has contracted bubonic plague and is in the hospital?" She went on to say that it was reported that the girl had been staying in a campsite at the Upper Jamison Creek Campground when she was bitten by a flea and contracted the disease. It was also reported that the State Health Department had closed the campground. I was stunned by this news to say the least.

What could I do about this most unwelcome revelation, especially at this hour of the night? I needed to confirm the information the women had given me. I had been positive that all campsites had been reserved, if not occupied, when I left work. Our night patrol ranger, Paul Quandt, had reported nothing unusual. Over the next several hours I made numerous telephone calls. I called the television station and was informed that they had received the news from the hospital where the little girl had been taken. I tried calling the State Health Department. I got a recording to call back during business hours. I called the Center for Disease Control in Atlanta with no luck. I figured things would just have to wait until morning before I could do anything about what I was sure would be a developing crisis and media nightmare.

First thing in the morning I met with park staff and told them what had happened the previous night and to stand by for further developments. After several hours on the telephone I determined that the State Heath Department had indeed announced to the world that the Upper Jamison Campground, at Plumas Eureka State Park was closed due to bubonic plague. They had told everybody **except** us! By now the telephone was ringing off the hook. I received many calls from distraught campers with reservations who wanted to know our status. There were also telephone calls and interviews with radio, television and newspapers from all over the west.

When I at last was able to reach the proper authority in State Health I informed him that the campground was not closed and that, in fact, we had a full campground. Then he asked if I was going to close the campground. My response was "Are you ordering me to close it?" I explained that I would not close the campground unless ordered to do so by the appropriate authority. He responded by saying he was not ordering me to close the campground, only **recommending** that I close it." It was obvious that this gentleman did not like the prospect any more than I did, of evacuating and disappointing hundreds of holiday campers. He suggested that I contact the Plumas County Health Department for an order to close the campground. I conferred with our District and Sacramento

Headquarters staff who confirmed that we should only close if so ordered. When I talked to Plumas County authorities they also declined to issue a closing order. It was a classic case of "finger pointing" and "passing the buck". I finally decided to called State Health again and try a bluff. I informed State Health that since no agency wanted to issue a legal closure order it was obvious that the situation wasn't serious enough to warrant an evacuation. That did the trick and I received the closure order within an hour.

The immediate problem was now back in our lap. I briefed the staff on what to say and we all fanned out into the campground in order to contact everybody. There was concern, for the most part, but no panic on the part of the campers. As one would expect we talked to a lot of disappointed people, but few were actually angry about this turn of events. We had made arrangements for most of those campers with confirmed reservations to be assigned to overflow areas in State Parks around Lake Tahoe and Donner Lake. Others we directed to nearby USFS campsites. Within a few hours the campground was deserted but for a few exceptions where the occupants were out and about on a hike or day trip. Ironically the last of these to leave, was very angry about this inconvenient displacement. He turned out to be a veterinarian camping with his family who "pooh-poohed" the fear of bubonic plague as media hype. I was surprised that a veterinarian, of all people, wouldn't have a better understanding of the dangers involved with the public's exposure to bubonic plague.

The next day a contingent of State Health Department personnel from Vector Control arrived in full force to begin trapping and testing animals for plague. Using simple live traps, squirrels, chipmunks and an occasional mouse or wood rat, were caught, anesthetized, and a blood sample taken. An alarming number of animals tested positive. Park staff received training from the Vector Control people and under their supervision we began an intensive and extensive trapping and dusting program over the next two weeks. The goal was to dust the rodents with a flea powder substance that would kill the fleas, which are the carriers of the plague. After the initial two-week treatment period we finally got the okay to re-open the campground on July 14, 1976

Throughout the remainder of the summer we continued with the dusting and trapping and also instituted an interpretive and information program about the dangers of plague and how to avoid contracting it. That program continues to this day, but I must say, for the remainder of the camping season in 1976 we had fewer people sleeping directly on the ground near rodent burrows than in previous years. Unfortunately, while we were the first major outbreak of bubonic plague in the Sierra Nevada area in a long time, we were not the last. Numerous outbreaks occurred in subsequent years. And yes, the little girl survived.

RESCUE

The winter of 1978-79 brought more surprising adventures. On March 1st the snow at our weather station near Park Headquarters measured 90" on the snow stake. That was at an elevation of 5161'. There was a lot more snow higher up on the surrounding mountains.

February had also been a heavy snow month with several cold storms sweeping in unexpectedly. Avalanches are a constant cause of concern when conditions are right, i.e.: when fresh snow falls atop a layer of frozen compacted icy snow, making it prone to slipping. The steep slopes of Eureka Peak between Park Headquarters and the Upper Jamison Campground are a prime example of such a dangerous area. Evidence of numerous avalanches can be seen, where snow rushing down avalanche chutes, has taken everything in its path, leaving a jumble of trees and debris swept across the park road as far as the creek.

Portola High School is located about 15 miles from the park, and has a curriculum that includes Outdoor Education. I knew the instructor Richard Hardy, whose son Paul was in my son's class. Richard's Outdoor Education class had decided to take a winter snow hike and camping trip for a couple of days into the Lakes Basin Recreation Area. Their plan was to snowshoe in off the Gold Lake Road and swing around Mt. Elwell, roughly on the route of the Pacific Crest Trail, and intersect the Johnsville-La Porte road before coming out at Park Headquarters. A storm caught them unexpectedly and they were a day over due. Parents and school officials were, of course, concerned when I was contacted. I contacted the Plumas County Search & Rescue unit to advise them of the situation and preparations were immediately made to mount a rescue. The thought at that time was to trace the route of the group starting at Gold Lake. I offered the use of the SnoCat if needed.

The group had been out for two or three days when the storm caught them. Imagine my surprise, when on February 20, 1979 at about 11:00am, as I was sitting in my office preparing to launch the rescue attempt, Richard and another student walked into the museum. They were fine and they reported that the other 10-12 students were okay also but were "trapped", for fear of avalanche danger in the canyon at a place where they had set up camp several miles further up the canyon, near McCrea Meadows. Prudently, not wanting to risk danger and expose his students more than necessary, Richard and the one student had hiked out to seek assistance for the others.

It was decided we would have to avoid the direct route to McCrea meadows via the La Porte Road. . It was too dangerous for the rescuers and the steep snow slopes made it impossible for either the SnoCat or snowmobiles to transverse the avalanche areas. By now we had gathered a rescue force which included another snow vehicle, a Thiokol "Sprite", operated by the California Department of Water Resources as well as several snowmobiles operated by volunteers from Plumas County Search & Rescue.

The route to the students would take us up to Eureka Ridge and around Eureka Peak then back down to McCrea Meadows. We started out with the snowmobiles in the lead and the Thiokol and SnoCat following. It was very difficult traveling through the deep snow. I'm sure it was up to 15' deep in some locations. There were no roads or landmarks that could be easily discerned and it took us several hours to reach the ridge. In fact, the Thiokol was unable to make it to the top but I managed to keep the SnoCat plodding right along to the top of the ridge. When the Water Resources vehicle could go no further we had it stand by where it was in order to serve as a shuttle for the students when and if we got them out.

By now darkness had descended upon us, making the going even tougher. At last we reached a point where I felt I could not safely take the SnoCat any farther because of the steep angle of the slope and avalanche danger. I would wait here, on the backside of Eureka Peak, while the snowmobile crews went on to McCrea Meadow. They reached the students all right and began shuttling them back to where I was waiting. The students walked across the last bit of dangerous avalanche slope to the SnoCat. Now the snowmobiles began coming across. All of them made it safely across except for one. An avalanche broke loose and swept a rider and machine down the slope. Fortunately, the snowmobile operator escaped unharmed and was not buried by the avalanche. His machine, however, was temporarily lost and not recovered until later in the spring.

We loaded all the students on to the SnoCat and drove back to where we had left the Thiokol, transferring some of them to that vehicle for the trip back. Everybody was safely back in Johnsville at 2:00am on February 21, 1979. It had been a long day with a successful rescue and a happy ending!

A BLOCK OF ICE

To be sure, winter at Plumas-Eureka in general was not nearly as difficult as what we had experienced in Bodie. But things did get interesting in December 1978 when a severe storm struck bringing with it temperatures that dropped to zero at night and never rose above freezing during the day for a period of a week. The worst of it was that electric power was also off for that week.

My concern was keeping the pipes in our house and in the museum from freezing and keeping the family warm as best we could. I never gave a thought to the Park's surplus California Division of Forestry (CDF) fire truck that was kept on the ready in a rented garage a few houses down the street from our place. The garage had no insulation; in fact the walls of the structure were shingled with flattened metal tin cans. Once we had insulated the interior and placed a small portable heater inside we felt secure that the truck could remain fully loaded with it's 500 gallons of water, ready for use, without fear of freezing. As an added touch to our "Fire House" I had added a red light outside above the garage door. Johnsville once again had a Red Light District. Of course without electrical power the light above the door of the garage was off. I was outside on our front porch shoveling snow when the power finally did come back on. I looked down the street and noticed the red light was back on. My God, the fire truck! I had forgotten all about it.

I ran down the street and opened the garage door. What an awful sight I did behold. The fire truck looked like one big icicle with beautiful "beards" of ice hanging down from every brass fitting and much of the water in the 500 gallon tank frozen! The truck engine, which of course had antifreeze in it, was okay. I was sure that it was going to cost thousands of dollars to repair the damage that was done. What would the town's Senator, who had arranged for the acquisition of the fire truck, and my boss think about this catastrophe? More importantly, what was I going to do about it?

I decided the first thing to do was thaw the damn truck out. I had our Maintenance Man, Terry Hurd, drive the truck down to Marshall Gold Discovery SHP in Coloma. I followed Terry as we descended to the warmer foothills of the Sacramento Valley. Water streamed from the truck from all of the leaks. It looked more like a fireboat spewing water going down the highway than it did a fire truck.

After talking with Kenneth MacLaurin, a Maintenance Worker II at Marshall Gold, Terry and I returned home. The next week Ken, bless his heart, telephoned me and said that though the damage was indeed severe he thought he could get it fixed cheaply. He knew someone at the CDF repair facility in Davis who he had contacted. They had a truck just like ours that had been totaled in a head on collision. Apparently at this CDF facility they also did training and were willing to replace the fittings on our truck with those from their damaged one as a training exercise. Cost to us was minimal, less than $200! I never did tell our District Office about this incident until long after I had moved on to a new assignment. For that I'm sorry. But I had dodged yet another bullet. And for that I was not sorry!

It is only recently that I learned from Bob Macomber, retired Superintendent of the Sierra District, that all of my work to save the fire truck was for naught. As it turned out the truck suffered the same fate a second time when it was not winterized or stored properly. All of the fittings were again frozen and ruined. This time there was no luck in getting the repairs made at a likely cost of thousands of dollars. The fire truck was surveyed and relegated to the junkyard and a smaller fire unit was acquired for fire protection.

FAMILY FUN

We had lived in state park residences at Bodie, Morro Bay and Cuyamaca prior to settling in at our Johnsville home at Plumas-Eureka. Each of the previous locations had much to offer and we enjoyed those family experiences. However, none of the previous locations so closely matched our family interests, as did life in Johnsville.

The four years we were at Plumas-Eureka were the formative years that shaped our children's lives. They are the most cherished and memorable years of my life in parks. Why is this so? Perhaps an account of major areas of interest or activity about each Chavez family member will help to illustrate why we loved this place so much.

You might say that I'm a "fishing fool" and am totally addicted to "stalking the wily trout" in the streams and lakes of Plumas County. To do this I needed to go no further than step out my front door, cross the street, and go down a steep bank to Jamison Creek. I know the creek like the back of my hand, from it's upper reaches below Raney Falls to its terminus as it enters the Middle Fork of the Feather River. I have fished the entire length of the stream many times, trusty fly rod in hand. I have caught and released thousands of rainbow trout and a fewer number of brown trout in Jamison Creek in the course of four years. In the summer, it wasn't uncommon to fish a portion of the stream three, four or even five times a week in addition to fishing on my days off. I would race home, gather my fishing gear, my dog, and my son and be off. Many an evening we would return to a cold dinner, much to the disgust of wife and daughter, who had given up on us in the gathering darkness.

What I enjoyed most about fishing Jamison Creek was that I grew to **know** individual trout. If I hooked and lost a particular fish or if I saw one that I could not tease to strike my fly I could always come back the next day for another try. I'm sure I caught the same fish on more than one occasion. Most often I fished the steep gorges at either end of the creek, where few other fishermen ventured and wild trout remained. I would come home all beaten and battered from rock hopping, cliff climbing, slips, and falls. On more than one occasion I returned with a broken fly rod. Margaret said my fly fishing technique was akin to a "contact sport" so thrashed did I return home.

The fish "tail" I would like to relate did not occur on Jamison Creek, but rather in an adjacent drainage on the other side of a ridge from PESP. One day I noticed a fisherman in the museum parking lot holding a stringer of nice fish. I went outside to admire his catch and found that he had a limit of 14"-16" Lake Trout. These were not normal Lake Trout because they were long and skinny with big heads and big tails, almost eel-like. He told me that he had caught them in Fraizer Creek. Fraizer Creek flows out of Gold Lake, over 176'-high Fraizer Falls into a steep, almost inaccessible gorge - my kind of fishing!

On my day off, I decided to try my luck in Fraizer Creek. Starting at a point below the waterfall, my son Chris, nephew Tony and I, along with Cinnamon the dog, were dropped off on the Old Gold Lake Road near the falls. Down through the thick manzanita brush and rocky cliffs we plunged, taking about half an hour to reach the creek. Our fishing was successful. We caught plenty of fish. Just like those fish caught by the fisherman who had told me of this place, all of the fish were skinny and had large heads and tails. It was obvious they had been washed out of Gold Lake and ended up in the creek where there was insufficient food to sustain them. We fished and hiked our way out to the roadway about three or four miles farther downstream. It was a successful outing.

A few days later, Mike Merkle, a retired park employee that I had known for many years, came up to the park for a visit. I told him about the great fishing we had experienced. He became excited about the prospect of catching some of those Lake Trout too. I reminded him, however, of the difficulty in reaching the stream. He seemed unconcerned and thought he would give it a try.

Several days later Mike accosted me at work. He was madder than a wet hen (or rooster). He asked "How could you play such a cruel trick on me? There was no water in the creek!" Mike had made the difficult hike down (and back up) to the creek only to find it dry! I couldn't believe him. I assured him that I had not been joking and there had been water in the creek only a few days earlier. He left in a huff.

On my next day off, back we went to Fraizer Creek to check out Mike's story. Sure enough, there were only a few scattered pools in the rocky creek bed. Fraizer Falls, which had been thundering down from the cliffs above, a week earlier was now only a trickle of its former majesty. What water did make it to the bottom was seeping below the rocky creek bed, only to surface a mile farther down the creek.

I later learned that there was a small check dam at the outlet of Gold Lake that could be opened or closed as necessary to control the lake level and stream flow. Apparently the gate had been closed shortly after our fishing trip and Mike had seen the results of that action. I telephoned him to tell him of my findings. We are still friends today.

Margaret's life in Johnsville, while not nearly as physical, was no less as pleasurable but sometimes hectic. One of the few downsides to living in Johnsville was that there was no school bus service from our home to transport the children to elementary school, 15 miles away in Portola. That meant that everyday Margaret had to drive five miles to the bus stop at the bottom of the hill in Mohawk and back, not once but three times a day because of different bus schedules. It is a nice drive, but sometimes tricky in winter. Eventually, things improved when the school district agreed to pay mileage and Margaret started working as a Teacher's Aide and could then drive the kids to school. Only once, in four years, was she unable to get down the hill because the road hadn't been plowed after a snowstorm. On that day the entire family took the day off and skied the 5 miles down the road, catching a ride on the county snowplow with Guido Maddalena for the return trip up the hill home.

In winter, skiing was a major activity for Margaret, if not directly, at least indirectly. She often went crosscounty skiing with her friend and neighbor Pat. They made regular treks to the campground and back. It was beautiful winter wonderland after a fresh snow and great fun to be the first to leave tracks. The Plumas Ski Cub, a local non-profit organization, operated the Park's downhill ski concession. It was pretty much a volunteer operation and Margaret was one of the volunteers in the "lodge".

The Ski Club, weather and snow conditions permitting, usually operated on Wednesdays, weekends and holidays. On Saturdays, the Plumas Unified School District ran a program instructing youngsters on ski technique and safety. It was a terrific program that has since, due to budget constraints, gone by the wayside. In any event, our kids learned to ski through the program. Margaret's volunteer efforts earned free ski time for the kids and they took full advantage of it.

When Margaret wasn't playing "bus driver" or "Ski Mom" and truly had time of her own to relax, she enjoyed a quieter time of reading, quilting and sewing.

She also did some complicated Macramé work. It was a good life. There were also moonlight walks up the road to the Ski Hill parking lot over pristine falling snow or on clear starry nights when the muffled sound of footsteps shuffling in the snow and your own frosted and labored breathing could be heard. The town was ours with no traffic over the unplowed road to disturb us.

One winter the family decided to build an igloo next to our house after I deemed that the snow was in perfect condition to undertake such a project. Never having built an igloo we enlisted the help of our houseguests, Seasonal Ranger Jay Headley and his family. Unless one is an Eskimo or has previously built an igloo it is harder to do than it looks. We managed to get a good start but could never seem to get the knack of enclosing the top properly. Nevertheless, once we did succeed in making a sort of dome top we stepped back to survey our masterpiece. It was not a pretty sight. The igloo was more of a modern art masterpiece than a symmetrical dome. On the other hand it was functional and quite large since it kept growing in height as we struggled to finish the roof.

About the time we had finished with our igloo, a local reporter for the Feather River Bulletin newspaper happened by. Since the igloo was right next to the road it could not be missed. It must surely have been a slow news day because the reporter immediately stopped and interviewed all of us (well, mainly the kids) and took photographs of the Chavez Igloo with kids and dogs in and about the structure. A large photograph was to grace the front page of the newspaper's next edition when it came out. We were fortunate to have cold weather for an extended period of time so that the igloo remained in place and functional for several weeks after it was completed. It was a great family playhouse for a while and a greater attraction to those who drove up to Johnsville that winter.

Abigail was our cowgirl. She loved all animals, and like many preadolescent girls, she especially loved horses. At the Cuyamaca Horse Camp there was a volunteer Campground Host who befriended her. Vern was a crusty wrangler who seemed to be from another era. He was the one who introduced her to horseback riding. She also often helped care and feed Missy, the Cuyamaca patrol horse that was stabled near our house.

When we moved to Plumas-Eureka, Abigail, certainly, missed "her" horses. The void was somewhat filled with the arrival of "Desi", a Golden Retriever and Guide Dog for the Blind puppy, which Abby was to raise as a 4-H project. This was the first puppy to be raised in Plumas County for Guide Dogs for the Blind of San Rafael. Desi was to be one of four guide dogs that Abby raised over the next few years.

Not having a horse, Abby did the next best thing she could think of - she made one. Somehow she managed to create a huge papier-mâché horse head that she placed over our oversize mailbox. It was big enough to mount and "ride" which she did often until the mail carrier made her take it down. Finally in the summer of 1978 Abby's dream came true. After hanging around the local stable in Mohawk, and making herself useful, the stable owner took pity and invited her to come and help on a regular basis. True, the job was non-paying but she was working with real horses. The stable was located at the bottom of the hill, across from the school bus stop, which, of course, meant more driving for Margaret. Initially Abby starting out cleaning stables and grooming horses but, she quickly advanced to being "Tail-end Charley" on conducted trail rides, eventually leading them. She became good at what she did and won a Blue Ribbon in riding competition at the Plumas County Fair. For her efforts, the operators of the stable offered to give her a horse and tack as final compensation. Unfortunately we had no place to keep a horse. As disappointed, as she was, other opportunities were to come later - but the dream started here.

Our son Christopher was five years old when we moved to Johnsville. He was introduced to fly fishing at an early age as you have already read. Today he is an accomplished fly fisherman and has carried his love of that sport into the classroom where he is an elementary teacher. For many years now his classes have worked with Trout Unlimited in studying and raising steelhead and salmon from eggs in aquaria and releasing the fish into local streams and rivers in the Sacramento area.

But from 1975-1979 much of Chris' life centered on his bicycle and the freedom that mode of transportation can give a kid. He had learned to ride a bike at Cuyamaca, but the terrain of that park and the location and traffic where we lived were not conducive to the safety of a small child on a bicycle. That was not a major problem at Johnsville. The ground was basically flat in and around Johnsville and all the way to the campground that was located a little over a mile, past the museum, down the road from our house. Chris was quick to make friends with the children of Seasonal Ranger Jay Headley who came up each summer from Southern California. Chris also often met the children of campers who were staying in the park and one summer he had his older cousin, Tony, to ride and fish with him too.

We acquired a speedometer/odometer for Chris' bicycle at some point, because like young boys everywhere on a bike, he wanted to see how far and fast he could go. It was not the speed that amazed us, however, but rather the number of miles he put on that bike in just one summer. He tells me it was 600 miles that first summer alone. Sometimes he was up and down the road between our house and the campground three or four times a day. Who knows what he was really up to?

The four years we lived in Johnsville was also a period of considerable construction in town. Several individuals and contractors were building new homes in the area. The friendly young men on the construction crews, their dogs, and their equipment were an endless source of fascination for a young boy. Chris became a friend with all the workers and their pets, riding his bicycle to the most current construction site and spending many hours "supervising" their efforts. I guess Jeff, Al, John, Dave and the others didn't mind his company, as we never received any complaints. We did receive lots of progress reports and gossip from Chris.

His other passion after fishing and biking became skiing. Our first winter in Johnsville, even before the Ski Hill was in operation he had constructed his own ski run adjacent to the house. Style and safety were not the concern of a 6-year-old on skis. Speed and ski jumping were! His mother and I cringed as we looked out the window and watched him hurtle down the slope of the lawn, seemingly out of control, toward one of his ski jump snow mounds to a sometimes-successful landing.

There were more traditional activities for a young boy to participate in also. Chris joined the local Graeagle Little League Team and did well. To me these activities, however, seemed more like diversions. Real life was up in the park and in Johnsville. These are the times we all remember!

Eventually, we were to move on from Plumas-Eureka State Park and the community of Johnsville, but we were really never to leave it.

CLAIM JUMPERS

My assignment at Plumas-Eureka State Park was the third park in which I had worked with a gold mining history. Bodie, of course, was well known for its productive mines and notorious boomtown history. Within Cuyamaca Rancho State Park there was the Stonewall Mine, which was one of the more productive gold mines in Southern California for a short time. The gold mines of Plumas-Eureka, including Jamison Mine, though not as productive as Bodie were nevertheless producing gold into the early 1900's. There was, and still is, gold in them "thar" hills and in and around streams of Plumas-Eureka State Park.

Today gold mining activity in the park is restricted to minor recreational and interpretive gold panning, where a few traces of gold, or more likely mercury, left over from the smelting process can be found in Big Jamison or Little Jamison Creeks. In the 1970's, however, there were still some semi-active mining claims both upstream and downstream from the park on U.S. Forest Service property. The Forest Service was in the process of shutting down most of the claims and demolishing the ramshackle structures that were usually associated with them.

Downstream, near the old town site of Jamison City there was an old placer miner named Lew who came every summer to try to strike it rich. Lew had lost an eye and wore a pirate-like patch over it. He had a pet dog named Sue and the worst looking Army surplus jeep I have ever seen. Everyone in the park and Johnsville knew the old prospector as "One-Eyed Lew and Sierra Sue". He was quick to show anyone that asked his vial of gold, panned from Jamison Creek. I could never ascertain if that vial displayed the work of one day, one week, a year, or several years' effort. He once gave me a ride from his cabin up the steep jeep trail to the cemetery in Johnsville. I thought for sure that the jeep would never make it up the steep ravine. It seemed certain that at any moment as we lurched our way uphill we would roll back down the steep incline and pitch over the cliff into the creek below. Somehow we arrived safely at the cemetery, not for burial but as surviving commuters.

Either Lew or his jeep eventually became too old and decrepit to make the trip down to the creek and so the mining claim was abandoned and washed away. At least Lew was a friendly miner who was fun to be around. There were others I met that were not so friendly and seemed to think they were still living in the "Old Shoot'em Up West."

My son Chris, nephew Tony, and I were on one occasion fishing in the Upper Gorge of Jamison Creek. We drove to the campground, parked the car and began fishing our way upstream beyond the park's western boundary. The gorge is very spectacular with a series of beautiful waterfalls in a half-mile stretch of the stream. Above one area that I called "Five Pools Falls" we worked our way further upstream, rock-hopping in the creek, until we emerged along the shallower, vegetated banks in an area just outside the park boundary on U.S. Forest Service property. The area was well know for it's nice isolated campsite and the mine tunnel that burrowed into a nearby rock formation.

As we emerged from the willows, alders and cow parsnip that lined the bank we burst out of the cover into a clearing where a man was leaning over a suction dredge working in the creek. Upon hearing us he immediately stood up and pulled a revolver from his hip holster and pointed it at the kids and me. This guy really did think he was living in the 1880's. He told us to put our hands up, which was not necessary since we all instinctively had done that as soon as we saw the gun.

This fellow could see that we had fishing poles in our hands but he never lowered the weapon. He said we were "claim jumping" and trespassing on his mining operations. I pointed out to him very, very politely, that we were only fishing and I didn't think we were trespassing as we were on Forest Service land. My main concern was to get away from this nut before he raised the stakes. I finally told him we would turn around and leave and he allowed us to do so without ever lowering the gun. Talk about ruining a fishing trip!

I knew that the my counterpart with the U.S. Forest Service, District Ranger Clint Tripp, was in the process of removing illegal mining operations, so once back at park headquarters I immediately telephoned him about this incident. Clint said he would meet me immediately to take care of the situation. I went home, got in uniform and armed myself with my service revolver. When Clint arrived, we drove up the Johnsville-La Porte road to the miner's camp. Imagine his surprise when we again met, this time on even terms. I took great pleasure in disarming him. Mr. "Quickdraw" did not have any of the required paperwork for the mining operations so Clint was able to shut down the operation and move him back into the real world. That is the last placer miner I ever saw on Upper Jamison Creek. Things just didn't pan out for him.

"WEATHER" OR NOT

Everyone seems to talk about the weather whether one is a meteorologist or not. Certainly when on a family camping vacation the weather is of utmost concern especially if the family is tent camping. That was the case in October 1977 as the Chavez family embarked on yet another "busman's holiday" vacation.

This time we were going to explore the Four Corners region of the Southwest with stops at Canyon De Chelly, Mesa Verde, and Chaco Canyon before traveling on to see relatives living in other parts of New Mexico. We had a wonderful, memorable trip that was a great learning experience for our children. Most of the time we stayed in either U.S. Forest Service or National Park campgrounds. On these camping trips I was always on the lookout for "new" ideas that I might introduced into my own park, in this case, Plumas-Eureka State Park.

On this occasion I was able to make a "discovery" that I "stole" or "borrowed" which in turn has spread into other California State Parks since I brought the idea back to California. We were camped at Chaco Canyon Cultural Natural Historic Park in the northwestern part of New Mexico and had gone in to take a look at the park visitor center/museum. Upon leaving the museum I noticed a rock suspended by a rope from three sticks tied in tripod fashion near the entrance. I had taken little notice of it when we first entered the building, but now my curiosity got the better of me so I wandered over to take a look at this "thing". As I approached it I could not figure out what purpose it served until I noticed the neatly lettered signed mounted on it that read "THE WEATHER PROPHET ROCK". Following is the wording on the sign that described the purpose of the "Weather Rock":

THE WEATHER PROPHET ROCK

This rock is the perfect weather indicator, it never fails. It is more accurate than your local weatherman. This rock is the living word and it is 100% correct. This is how it works.

A dry rock means fair weather
A wet rock means it's raining
A dusty rock means a dust storm
A swaying means the wind is blowing
A shadow under the rock means the sun is shining
If the rock is jumping up and down, an earthquake is upon us
A white rock means there is a snowstorm
Most beautiful of all, though the rock is not attached to its existence - it doesn't mind which of the above is occurring.

After reading the sign and looking at this contraption I called Margaret and the kids over to take a look at it. Their response to the Weather Rock was the same as mine in eliciting a belly laugh. At first I gave it no further thought as we walked away to our vehicle in the parking lot. The further we got away from the Weather Rock and the closer we got to our car the more I did think about that damn rock on a rope. By the time we reached our old VW van I had decided that that Weather Rock was indeed something unique. I scrambled around for paper and pencil in the cluttered van and walked back to the Weather Rock to copy the wording as written.

Weeks later, back at Plumas-Eureka State Park, I found in my notes of our vacation trip the scrap of paper with the Weather Rock words on it and decided to make my own specimen to place outside of the entrance of our park museum. Constructing the replica Weather Rock was no problem at all, but I wanted the sign to put on the tripod to look a little better than my poor printing abilities could muster did. I used a Leroy Lettering Set to make the first sign. I was not too adept at utilizing this draftsman's tool and it seemed to take me forever to get a finished product that would pass the public's scrutiny. I covered the sign with contact paper and placed it outside. It was an immediate success and what's more, it worked. Right after I put it up the rock turned white and sure enough we had snow!

The Weather Rock I constructed at Plumas-Eureka remained in place for many years after I had moved on to Humboldt Redwoods. At Humboldt Redwoods I built another Weather Rock that also was placed in front of the Visitor Center there. That Weather Rock is the one that had the distinction of having the suspended rock fall to the ground during the major Humboldt County earthquake of 1983, serving as of further proof of the amazing accuracy of this friend of all weather watchers.

Many years later when I returned to Plumas-Eureka State Park I was surprised, but should not have been, to see that my Leroy Lettering sign had been replaced by a professionally made metal sign. Granted it was more readable, but I think the Weather Rock lost some of its humble heritage with that metal sign. I guess that metal sign is now in stock in the Department's sign inventory because there is now a metal sign on the Weather Rock at Humboldt Redwoods and on a new Weather Rock that is in place in front of the museum at Donner Memorial State Park. The Weather Rock became so popular that copies of the text were sold at the both the Plumas-Eureka and Humboldt Redwoods visitor centers. Today, where the Weather Rock may be found you can get

a picture postcard. It would not surprise me to learn that
Weather Rocks are popping up in other parks throughout
the California State Park System.

TAKING A CHANCE

Anyway you looked at it, the Plumas-Eureka Area
was a small operation. It consisted of one park (PESP)
and a staff of three. Our nearest State Park neighbor
was the Sierra Area. That operation included, Donner
Memorial State Park, the parks around Lake Tahoe, as
well as Grover Hot Springs and Bodie.

We were blissfully independent, which usually
worked to our advantage, but sometimes it would have
been nice to have the additional resources, equipment,
and manpower that a larger Area operation had to offer.
Rather than give up our independence, we vowed to
make do with what we had. To illustrate the point I offer
the following account.

In the summer of 1975 an individual came into
the museum and inquired if the park might be interested
in acquiring a small operating stamp mill to put on
display for demonstration purposes. A stamp mill is the
machinery that is used to crush gold ore in preparation
for smelting. I was indeed interested in obtaining the
stamp mill. The donor said it was ours, all we had to do
was get it and haul it away. The mill, known as the
Bushman Stamp Mill was located about 35 miles away
in a remote area northwest of Quincy.

Maintenance Man Al Thomas and I drove to the
site and inspected the donation. All of the major
components of the mill were there, stamps, hopper,
flywheel, etc. It was definitely worth salvaging. The
problem was that it was on the other side of dry creek
bed. The only way across the creek was over a rickety,
dilapidated, broken down wooden bridge. The bridge was
about ten feet above the creek bed and the only
equipment we had available that we felt we could use for

dismantling and transporting the heavy mill back to the Park was an old Ford tractor and a 2-ton stakeside truck. We had no way of moving the tractor but to drive it down Highway 70 to the site.

In September, after the rush of the tourist season was over, I decided it was time to move it. We probably put more hours on the Ford tractor just driving it to and from the mill than we normally would put on it in several months. When we finally arrived at the mill location with the tractor it was decision time again. Did we dare take the tractor across the rickety old bridge? I said, "go for it". This time I hedged my bet by insisting we first shore up the old bridge with timbers we found lying about. The tractor would be carrying considerably more than its' own weight when it crossed the bridge.

I sketched the stamp mill and numbered the parts before we dismantled it. Once back at the park we would have to reassemble the structure utilizing new replacement timbers. It was necessary to make several trips back and forth across the bridge in order to get all the parts into the truck. We held our breath as the tractor crossed and re-crossed the bridge. The bridge creaked and groaned as it swayed back and forth under the combined weight of the tractor and its load. We managed to load all the parts on the truck and drive the tractor the 35 miles back home. We had taken a chance and succeeded!

During my tenure at PESP we were not able to put the Bushman Mill back together. That was left to the staff to do in 1986. Now if you go up to the park and take a walk amongst the historic structure you will find the fully restored Bushman Mill in place. The only part missing is how it got there!

ACCOMPLISMENTS

I have never worked in a park before or since where I felt such a sense of accomplishment as I did at Plumas-Eureka SP. In the winter of 1978-79, however, as I sat at my desk with very little to do I began to have doubts and reservations about remaining here. Yes it was a beautiful park. Yes, I had had great park experiences here. Yes, it was the best place I had ever lived. Yes it was even where I would want to retire. But when I asked myself "would the next few years be a challenge for me and allow my career to advance", the resounding answer to that question was **"NO"**

That, coupled with the fact I seemed to have developed a "love/hate" relationship with the District Office in Stockton, seemed to indicate that perhaps I should move on. On the one hand, I loved the independence and freedom of having no one looking over my shoulder. I was rarely checked up on and usually it was me that initiated any contact with the District Office. Sometimes weeks would go by without any communication with my supervisors. I felt like a very small fish in a big pond.

This was best demonstrated by the time that I once took a two-week vacation. Earlier in the year I had been asked to submit my vacation request months in advance of actually taking it. I did as requested and received approval for the dates I had chosen. When I was ready go on vacation I decided that since I had prior approval I would say nothing about leaving. This would surely show "Them" how important I was to the operation of the park. I was sure that upon my return there would be some consternation about not telling my supervisor of my planned absence. When I returned from the vacation two weeks later, much to my consternation, the staff told me there had been no contact with the District Office. I telephoned District, only to learn **they didn't even know that I had been gone!** So much for my importance.

That is when I decided to sit down and write a list of what I considered were the major accomplishments that I had been responsible for in the nearly four years I had been at Plumas-Eureka State Park. Four years was, after all, longer than any previous assignment I had ever worked. The list was extensive. A partial list looked something like this:

Established Interpretive Association
Constructed the parks first permanent campfire center
Constructed fisherman's and museum trails
Established "Living Forest" Self-Guided Nature Trail
Developed PESP Teacher's Aid Kit
Constructed Madora Lake Nature Trail
Constructed Madora Lake Parking Area and restroom
Developed Jamison Creek Picnic Area and restroom
Constructed new restroom at Eureka Lake
Developed "Little Theater" in Assay Office
Re-shingled and re-sided 5-story Mohawk Mill
Re-shingled and painted all Jamison Mine structures
Developed and signed two cross-country ski trails
Fenced and paved museum parking lot
Acquired Bushman Stamp Mill
Restored horse drawn hearse
Refurbished Blacksmith Shop and bellows repaired
Increased all Interpretive Programs by 200%
Supervised and managed water system developments
Supervised and managed museum foundation project
Budgeted for modern new shop complex
Budgeted moving seasonal housing from Historic Zone
Budgeted for initial Morarity House historic studies.

It was a list I felt I could be proud of. Then I heard a sound of a car coming up the hill below the museum. I went outside into the parking lot and realized that whoever was driving that vehicle was not coming to the museum. In fact, no one had come to the museum all day. At Bodie, I had expected no visitors in winter. At

Plumas-Eureka I had hoped for more winter visitors and activity but they did not often come. It was then that I realized that the pace had become too slow for me in winter to feel productive. Vowing to come back some day, I now knew it was time to move again. This was not going to be an easy "sale" to the family.

I was again on a Managerial promotional list and thought it was time to make a career move, but it was going to take someplace special to make me do so. Then the "someplace special" vacancy occurred. The Dyerville Area, in Humboldt County, had a vacancy. The Dyerville Area was comprised of the largest Redwood Park in the State Park System, Humboldt Redwoods SP and a second unit, Grizzly Creek Redwoods SP, which is about the size of PESP.

This time I had a fairly in-depth interview. The telephone interview with Carl "Andy" Anderson left me confident that I would get the position. I had known and worked with Andy off and on throughout my entire career. He was my mentor and I knew I would enjoy working with him again. If I was confident, I wasn't so confident that my family would be as happy about a promotion and move as I was - and they weren't. Sometimes you just have to do what you have to do. My tour of duty at Plumas-Eureka State Park officially ended on April 30, 1979. It had been a most memorable experience. I left with a sense of accomplishment knowing that I would be back someday.

PLUMAS-EUREKA SKETCHES

AMONGST GIANTS

My son Chris and I left for Humboldt Redwoods in advance of Margaret and Abby to check things out and find out where we would be living in the park. We drove across on Highway 299 from Redding to the coast. Once again I had come full circle, this time to Arcata and my alma mater of Humboldt State University. We continued south on Highway 101 to Eureka and the District Office at Fort Humboldt State Historic Park. My new boss, Allan "Tiny" Philbrook, was in a meeting and could not come out to see me. Starting a new job with this kind of greeting was getting old. As Yogi Berra says, "It's *deja vu* all over again." In any event, there was a welcoming face in Assistant Superintendent Anderson who warmly greeted us. He was quick to reiterate the marching orders that we had discussed during the telephone interview. As Area Manager for the Dyerville Area my first charge was to establish better public relations with the surrounding communities.

I distinctly remember the chills and the hair on the back of my neck prickling as we approached the north end of Humboldt Redwoods State Park (HRSP) and the famous Avenue of the Giants. I thought, "I'm going to be responsible for the largest redwood park in the State Park System and the largest single stand of virgin redwood forest in the world!" It was a humbling experience. For me this was going to be a quantum leap from one of the smallest parks in the Department to one of the largest.

We located our new home, adjacent to the Burlington Campground and Park Headquarters, a mile south of the small community Weott. Margaret and Abby were soon to follow and all of us were pleasantly surprised with the housing arrangement. We were to reside in the "Chapman House" once belonging to a park neighbor. It was situated in an apple orchard across from the Burlington Campground and within walking distance of the park office. A small creek separated us from the campground with access by a small footbridge. Towering coastal redwoods that also lined the long driveway leading to the house from the Avenue of the Giants surrounded the entire open area of the orchard, where the house was situated. May in the redwoods was simply beautiful.

Humboldt Redwoods is a large park. It is 50,000 acres of redwood forest, grassland prairie, mixed conifer and deciduous forest. The Rockefeller Forest is the area of the park with the largest single stand of old growth redwood forest remaining in the world. It is truly magnificent. The South Fork of the Eel River (Hooray, fishing!) runs the length of the park and a major tributary, Bull Creek, drains the interior of the park and Rockefeller Forest. This was going to be fun!

Grizzly Creek is the second unit in the Dyerville Area and it is located about 45 miles northeast of the Area Office. I had never been to Grizzly Creek before but that was soon to change. Andy had told me to meet him at the Grizzly Creek office first thing in the morning on my first day on the job. He did not say why it was so important that I should be there. Upon arriving at Grizzly Creek I entered the office to find Andy and another park employee. Andy introduced me to this individual and told me that he had just transferred to Grizzly Creek and this was also his first day on the job. The purpose of the meeting was to hold a Corrective Interview with this employee and he wanted me there so I would be aware of the situation should further problems develop. A discussion between Andy and the employee ensued. Darned if I could tell what the transgression had been that warranted the employee's transfer to Grizzly Creek. At the end of the interview Andy asked me if I had any questions. I did. I asked, "What did he do?" Let us just say that I was stunned by the answer I received. The allegation was of a sexual nature and I couldn't believe the employee hadn't been fired. Later, Andy said, "Your eyes got as big as saucers." I am happy to say we had no re-occurrence of the problem and the employee proved to be a productive worker.

I must say again, that I wondered if I would ever have a "normal" beginning to a new assignment. I was getting tired of these dramatics every time I moved.

A "TINY" TALE

I first met "Tiny" some time in the spring of 1973 when I was living in Morro Bay. Of course I had heard of him, everyone had. Allan, or "Tiny" as he was better known, was not so little. He was a big, bear of a man. He was also the District 1 Superintendent in the Eureka office.

The occasion of our first meeting was not business but pleasure. In March of 1973, our State Park Ranger's Association (CSPRA) was holding its annual conference. I was assisting, Rodger, my former Pismo Beach patrol partner, with some of the preparations for the Conference. There would be rangers from all over the State coming to this event. Many of them were friends and acquaintances that would opt to stay in the campground rather than the motel accommodations that were available.

It was some of these folks that Margaret and I decided to invite over to our house for a little social gathering. In preparation for the party I had been saving up the Geoduck clams that I had dug from the bay over the past few months. We would make a pot of clam chowder to go along with the wine and cheese and Margaret's freshly baked bread. We told our friends about the party when they arrived and many came over to visit and socialize. You may recall that at this time we lived in a small, standard two bedroom State house in the park at Morro Bay.

Soon the house was overflowing with guests as the word got out about a "Clam Feed" over at the Chavez'. Margaret kept adding milk, potatoes and any other good stuff she could find to throw into the kettle until we had at least five gallons of clam chowder. About this time the doorbell rang.

I opened the door and there stood before me this giant of a man. Instinctively I knew who he was, having heard many stories of this living legend in State Parks. Tiny stuck out his hand for a handshake and introduced himself and then asked, "Is this where the party is?" When I said, "Yes, come on in" he turned around and waved to a group of 15-20 people who were standing outside our front gate and yelled, "This is it, come on in we're all invited!" The gathering got so crowded that it spilled out into the front yard. I don't know if everyone who was there got their fill of clam chowder, but at least they got a sampling. And as usually happens at any park gathering, other food magically materialized so no one went away hungry, least of all Tiny! That was my first introduction to Tiny.

I did not meet Tiny again until six years later in 1979. This time it was a work related meeting. He was my boss when I was appointed Area Manager of the Dyerville Area. His assistant, Andy, had actually conducted the interview and; with Tiny's approval, had selected me for the position. When my son Chris and I had stopped by Tiny's Eureka Office we had not been able to see him because he was in a meeting. Now, two weeks later he was coming to see me.

Tiny arrived as scheduled and came into my office. After pleasantries were exchanged he sat down and said to me, "I want you to sit there and listen to me". I sat, and I listened for about 45 minutes of uninterrupted speech. What I thought was to be my welcoming charge as the new Manager at Dyerville, turned out to be Tiny's life story. He told me of his growing up in the Central Valley. I believe he also said something about his early work with school buses, his career in the Army, and of course his family and park career. I honestly did not know what to make of it. For sure Tiny had enjoyed a colorful, productive and successful life.

He then asked me if I had any questions or comments. "Well, no but let me tell you about myself" I answered. I then began for the next half-hour, to tell Tiny about my life and career, much of what you have already read here. Of course I left out those things that might have tarnished my image, but you get the picture.

One of the other things that Tiny liked to do besides talk about himself was to really enjoy the after work hours camaraderie of a relaxing evening with those around him. It did not matter if you were a lowly park aide, a Ranger I or District Superintendent. If you wanted to have fun you were made welcome. Of course it wouldn't hurt if you knew how to play a little poker. After a day of training at Asilomar or a particularly long business meeting, Tiny liked nothing better than to start up a poker game, imbibe in a bit of "rot gut" and savor a stogie. He was a down to earth kind of guy.

Tiny and I got along fine. Perhaps it was the hospitality and clam chowder of years earlier that he fondly remembered. In any event, periodically, Tiny and his wife, Marie, would drive down to Humboldt Redwoods just to "get away from it all" and ask me to drive them out to the Rockefeller Forest. On one such occasion he telephoned me from Eureka and said that he and Marie would be down in an hour because he wanted to "inspect" the Grasshopper Peak CDF Fire Lookout. There really wasn't much to inspect since the lookout wasn't even staffed. It was obvious, and he told me so, that he just wanted to get "out in the field" again to see how things were. I could relate to that and so I gladly chauffeured Tiny and Marie up to the peak. On the way up in the park sedan I managed to hit a rock and knock the muffler off of the vehicle. That didn't phase Tiny one bit and in fact may only have served to open the door to stories of his vehicle exploits earlier in his career. With the car sounding much like a teenager's "hot rod" we continued to roar up the mountain road until we reached the summit lookout. The silence was deafening and most welcome as we stood there and surveyed the greatest redwood forest in the world stretching out below us. That is what Tiny had really come to see. It made ones heart swell with pride to know that we were stewards of a great park. Later, as I really came to know Mr. Philbrook, I learned that he may have been "Tiny" but he had the biggest heart of them all!

HRIA

So, my first day had started with an issue of alleged impropriety of sexual relations. My second day, and for several years after, were to deal with community relations. It seemed that to a greater or lesser degree, depending upon whom you talk to, a wall had been built up between park staff and members of the community. It was "Them" versus "Us." It was up to me to try and turn things around.

In order to do that I decided to do what had worked at Plumas-Eureka and develop a community support group of volunteers to run a Cooperative Association for the park. One of the first things that struck me when I walked through the front door of the Headquarters Office building was a complete lack of a place to meet the public and provide information. I couldn't believe that a park of this stature did not have a museum or nature center to meet and greet the visiting public and assist them in the enjoyment of such a prime resource. I decided we would form the Humboldt Redwoods Interpretive Association and we, the park and the community together, would build a Visitor Center (VC).

I started working at HRSP on May 1,1979. On May 29th we held the first organizational meeting of the association. On October 19th we were officially incorporated as a non-profit cooperative association. On February 22, 1980 we started work on the VC and finally on August 10,1980 we opened the Visitor Center for business. I often ask, "How did we do that so fast?"

In order to tell how it happened I must back up for a minute. My first month or two, after the initial incident at Grizzly Creek, I felt that I wasn't an Area Manager, but rather a "Father Confessor" or Marriage Counselor. The Dyerville Area had a large staff and about 20 State owned houses that were rented by park employees. Almost everyone on the staff resided in a

State residence. I became the *de facto* mayor of our "Park Family". Whether I wanted them or not I received complaints, problems and issues, often of a personal nature, concerning family disputes. Again, this was not something I had been taught to deal with in my HSC Wildlife classes. Shortly after my arrival, I received a call on my day off from the wife of an employee saying she was moving out and taking everything in the house with her. I hardly knew the lady and here she was telling me because she, "thought she should tell someone" (did she think to tell her husband?). The end result of this family dispute is that the park ended up with a vacant house in an ideal location for a visitor center.

Now back to the story. I recruited some local folks that I thought we could work with. One of the most important being a writer for a local newspaper. I figured that if we could get her on the Board of Directors we would have plenty of free publicity. It worked and we did! Though the Board of Directors initially included several employee spouses we were eventually successful in bringing in true community members to the Board and into the general membership of the newly formed Humboldt Redwoods Interpretive Association (HRIA)

HRIA initially had an almost non-existent budget. At our first meeting we passed a hat around to raise seed money just as we had at Plumas-Eureka but it was obvious that a $5.00 membership fee alone would not result in a visitor center. Somehow I had to figure out a way to utilize other resources to get the job done. The first thing I decided was to tell no one further up the "Chain of Command' what we were up to. I knew that if I did that I would run into endless obstacles of red tape. Besides, hadn't Andy already given me tacit approval to cement community relations? Building this visitor center was part of that process.

Once Residence #7 was vacated, a core group of off-duty park employees, their spouses, student interns from HSU, and a few community members proceeded to tear down walls and convert the building into a museum/visitor center. I told the group that as long as we built a visitor center that was worthy of the name and it was something that State Parks could be proud of, I would take any heat from above. We were fortunate, in that we had a lumber mill operation in the park which produced rough redwood and fir lumber (more about that later). I "borrowed" materials from the mill for use in the renovation. I was able to obtain $5,000 from the Save the Redwoods League (more about that later too), and I "temporarily reassigned some maintenance staff to assist on the project. Lastly, I assigned Chief Ranger Ted Reinhardt the task of overseeing the project and purchasing items "discreetly" (no more about that now or later!)

I did indeed take a little heat from the Manager of Facilities Maintenance in Sacramento Headquarters when he learned of the extent of our little "Bootleg" project. He was especially upset when he learned that we had re-roofed the entire structure without authorization. He demanded to know where I got all the shakes and how did I pay for them. I never did tell him since "I" never did buy them. Ted did all the purchasing by splitting Sub-Purchase Orders instead of shakes and shingles!

Fortunately, prior to my run in with Headquarters and at a point where the project had taken on a life of its own to the point of no return, I had finally taken the prudent step of telephoning Andy in Eureka. I invited him down to the park to see the surprise I had in store for him. Andy was delighted with the "work in progress" and was totally supportive of our efforts. That support was needed to call the "Headquarters Dogs" off our case. Sometimes brash enthusiasm does succeed over red tape bureaucracy. The end result was indeed a visitor center worthy of the State Park System.

Meanwhile, our spouses were busy too doing their part. Margaret, Jeanne Reinhardt, Jeannie Ash, and

Brigett Young quickly learned the art of silk screening and began producing T-shirts for sale at the VC. The shirts were designed by seasonal employee Dusty O'Neill-Knight and featured a logo with a redwood tree growing out of a hiking boot. They proved to be so popular that it was difficult to keep them in stock even when the Ladies went into full production in the Park's Recreation Hall. Those T-shirts, along with book sales, became one of the Associations chief sources of income in the first year of operation.

The year after opening we added a nature center room and expanded the sales area. The following year we added a deck, outdoor BBQ, office annex and storage room. Later, in 1986, a theater/auditorium room was added, and finally an outdoor self guided nature trail/garden and paved parking area. Most of the construction costs for these expansion projects were at minimal cost to the park or the HRIA as the California Conservation Corps provided the labor to do most of the work under our supervision. In later years our Region Headquarters began referring to the Visitor Center as "Carl's Winchester House - North." In 1999, at the 20th anniversary of the HRIA a fourth room, housing the Kellogg Log (Truck) was added. Today, the Humboldt Redwoods Visitor Center has over 80,000 visitors annually and an operating budget of over $350,000. Not bad for passing the hat!

In the end, however, the Visitor Center is nothing more than a structure, and we built a wonderful structure. More importantly we succeeded in bringing the community into the Park Family. Today there are almost 200 Association members and 40 Docents who staff the Visitor Center and perform the duties of Campground Hosts. - a far cry from the days I often had to assign a sometimes reluctant ranger to desk duty in order to staff the VC and keep it open. Of all my accomplishments, this "Bootleg" project is the one that I take most proud in.

RIVER PIRATES

I mentioned that the South Fork of the Eel River runs the length of the park. That is not quite correct, Within the park's boundaries it flows from Sylvandale at the south end of the park past the communities of Phillipsville, Miranda, Myers Flat and Weott until it converges with the Main Eel at the Dyerville Overlook. From there the Eel continues flowing past the small communities of Redcrest, Holmes Flat, Shively, Pepperwood and on out of the park to the Pacific Ocean near Ferndale. Like any river the Eel River floods periodically. Major floods of recent time happened in 1955 and 1964. I had witnessed the effects of the '64 flood while attending HSC. During my time at HRSP there were two other severe floods that caused considerable damage to the parks in the District. One was in 1983 and three years later another in 1986. All of these floods, and to a lesser degree, any high water in the river during winter resulted in many large redwood trees falling into the river as the silty banks collapsed when the water receded. In a few years this could result in hundreds of huge redwood trees strewn along the river's edge.

Redwood trees, old growth in particular, are **very** valuable. A single tree can be worth $25,000 or more. The California State Park System is not in the business of commercially harvesting this valuable resource. It is our job to protect the resource. That is sometimes difficult when at flood the Eel river can approach flows as high as those of much larger river systems such as the Mississippi River. When that occurs we lose trees.

Park Rangers at Humboldt Redwoods had been fighting a losing battle for many years trying to prevent these fallen redwood trees from being stolen by individuals who would sell them to lumber mills in the area. The Park Rangers referred to these persons as "River Pirates." It was an apt name for them since they were stealing a resource that belonged to all Californians. As the trees fell park staff would mark them as State Property. This was usually done with a discreet metal tag that was difficult to spot and hopefully missed by the thieves. We also spray painted identifying marks of ownership on the tree trunks but they could be removed when the bark was cutaway. Additionally, the spray paint was an unsightly intrusion on the natural scene. The River Pirates generally worked under cover of darkness, coming upriver in a boat and cutting the tree at any point their chain saw could reach. Then they would float the log downstream out of the park and onto a sandbar where it could be cut up to a more manageable size. Some of the logs were as much as 10'-14' in diameter with lengths of as much as 100'.

Night patrols and stakeouts proved futile in most instances. More often we had better luck in recovering the marked logs on the sandbars before the culprits could haul them away. We seldom were able to catch the River Pirates themselves.

Prior to my arrival at HRSP there was a three person, portable saw mill operation underway adjacent to our Albee Creek Campground in the area know as Bull Creek Basin. It was in that area, that those logs the park did salvage would be taken and placed in the log deck for future use as needed. It was against the law to sell lumber from the mill. A difficult decision had to be made. Should we continue to "allow" the River Pirates to take this valuable resource, or would it be better for our crews to salvage the logs before the River Pirates got to them.

I proposed that since they were a State Park resource then it was logical that State Parks salvage them, **not for sale**, but for use throughout the State Park System. We figured we could salvage the logs, store them in our log deck, and have our lumber mill crew cut the lumber for shipment to state parks throughout California. The receiving parks could reimburse the lumber mill operation for transportation of the lumber to the destination. We received approval to go ahead with this plan and it worked.

Twice over a period of several years we issued salvage contracts to private commercial timber operators to recover the fallen trees along the river and transport them to our log deck at Albee Creek. Over a million board feet of prime old growth redwood was salvaged and milled by the park's lumber mill crew. I figured that if we couldn't catch the River Pirates, then we might as well beat them to the punch (or in this case to the lumber). After that there were slim pickings for the River Pirates for the next several years.

TREES TALES

There was a time when the redwoods were much more widespread in the Northern Hemisphere. Sixty million years ago there were over 40 species of redwoods. Today there are three. The Redwood of the Pacific Coast (*Sequoia sempervirens*) the Giant Sequoia of the Sierra (*Sequoia gigantea*) and the Dawn Redwood of China (*Metasequoia glytostroboides*). It is the remnants of the Coast Redwoods extending in a narrow belt from the California-Oregon border to Monterey County in Central California that is the heart and soul of Humboldt Redwoods State Park. Within its 53,000 acres, Humboldt Redwoods State Park contains the largest remaining single stand of virgin redwood forest in the world in the 17,000-acre Rockefeller Forest of Bull Creek and Dyerville Flats.

Throughout the park, especially along the Avenue of the Giants, stand many other beautiful old growth groves which have been preserved through the efforts and partnership of the California Department of Parks and Recreation and the Save the Redwoods League. Many of the most beautiful of these redwood groves are located at the north end of the Avenue in and around the community of Pepperwood.

Periodically, besides having to withstand the ravages of flood and fire for which the redwood is well adapted, the redwood forest can be exposed to hurricane force winds that may have the devastating result of felling these shallow rooted giants in a domino-like fashion. This is especially true around clearings and forest edges. I experienced one such windstorm when a number of trees came down across the Avenue of the Giants one night in the vicinity of Dyerville Flats. It is a frightening experience.

I received a call from the local CalTrans highway crew requesting assistance in removing a tree that had fallen across the Avenue of the Giants at the Founders Grove junction. It was a large 12' diameter tree. Our first priority was to get to the scene and block off the highway before a vehicle crashed into the tree. This had happened on more than one occasion and as you might suspect, the State has been sued more than once over such accidents.

Maintenance Worker Larry Pope and I parked our truck on the Avenue just south of the Dyerville Bridge to stop traffic there, while other staff likewise closed off the road at the Federation Grove Bridge. It was raining heavily and the wind was gusting in excess if 50 mph. CalTrans and State Park crews were working together to saw through the fallen giant and move it off the roadway with heavy equipment. Suddenly, somewhere in the surrounding forest, in a direction that could not be determined, was the sound of giant trees beginning to snap, crackle, and pop.

I had been standing outside our vehicle on the passenger side and Larry was sitting inside on the passenger seat when the sounds began building to a crescendo. You must remember that a 300'+ redwood can do a lot of damage to a person's body, even from the length of a football field away. At once people and vehicles began scurrying for shelter, but where? It was pitch dark, raining heavily and no one knew in which direction the trees were falling. It was literally every man for himself.

My instinct was to get in the vehicle, back it up, and get the hell out of there. Larry's instinct was to get out of the vehicle and run. He did not want to be crushed like a recycled soda can inside the truck. I guess he preferred to be squashed like a bug. We collided with each other as he tried to get out of the truck and I tried to get in. I finally yelled at him and pushed him into the driver's seat. He slammed the truck into reverse and we raced backwards onto the bridge behind us. The trees did come crashing down. I believe in all there were four huge redwoods that fell in several directions. At least one of them fell across the Avenue. Eventually, the mess was cleared up and the portions of the trees that fell across the Avenue that were not shattered were cut into manageable lengths and salvaged for use in the park's lumber mill operation. The remainder of the trees, as is park policy, are left to return to the soil in the course of the next several centuries. The remnants of some of these trees are still visible on along the Avenue of the Giants.

Redwood trees are slow to regenerate from seed. They do well as root or stump sprouts but those sprouting from seed and surviving the effects of flood, fire, erosion, and natural competition with surrounding seedlings and other vegetation are few. One has to be in awe when you realize how a 350' redwood tree could have possibly had its start from a seed barely larger than a gain of sand.

Since the Save the Redwoods League had been acquiring property in the Pepperwood area for the Park the land had been left fallow. The fields that had once grown vegetables were now filled with nothing more than impenetrable tangle of berry bushes and thistles. These areas were adjacent to some of the Park's finest Memorial Groves, subjecting them to the winds, which could have the damaging effects I have previously described. Because of this it was decided that we should embark upon an aggressive reforestation program to provide a measure of protection to the old growth forest with a buffer of newly planted redwoods. In 1980, with financial assistance from

SRL, we began our first plantings. We did not anticipate the uproar that it created.

Many of the local residents of Pepperwood who continued to raise vegetables to sell from their roadside stands became alarmed with our activity. Strong opposition was formed in an attempt to keep the Park from depriving them of their "right to sunlight". This based upon the premise that once the redwoods grew tall they would shade out the surrounding few remaining open parcels of land. In addition to this some individuals claimed that we were introducing trees into areas where they never had grown before. This was especially hard to believe since the entire townsite of Pepperwood is situated on a flood plain that is the most ideal location for the regeneration of redwoods. And lastly, we were accused of being a blight on the landscape and taking away the pastoral scene of sheep and vegetables growing in harmony with the redwoods. Besides didn't we have enough redwood trees already? This last argument came from some individuals whose own front yards were a shamble of abandoned cars, weeds, and dilapidated outbuildings. Things really came to a head when the publicity department of a local and powerful lumber company took out an advertisement in the local newspaper chastising the Park for removing agricultural lands from production.

I quickly called the lumber company president and pointed out to him that his own company had done the same thing a year earlier and the result of that effort was clearly visible from the adjacent freeway. He apologized, the advertisement was removed from the newspaper, and the public relations person for the lumber company was called on the carpet by the president.

The next order of business was to deal with the irate citizens of Pepperwood. A public meeting was called for. At the meeting I met with the local folks and was accompanied by Hank Saddler, a former State Park employee, now working for the SRL as their representative in Eureka. I had prepared well for what I knew would be a hostile meeting. I wasn't disappointed. The primary and final thesis of the opposition was that the trees would never grow in the area we were scheduled to plant in because they had never grown there in the first place. I had researched these claims earlier and found copies of field notes and historical photographs taken by E.P. "Percy" French. Mr. French was a well-respected forester, and in 1938, the first State Park District Superintendent in the North Coast of California. The historical photographs were especially helpful as they showed the removal of 12'-16' redwood stumps as the land was cleared for the fields that remain today. It was a situation where being prepared really paid off. The meeting ended and we proceeded with our reforestation plans.

Our initial efforts were not without problems. It was our desire to plant the trees in a random fashion in order to establish a landscape that was natural in appearance. Inmates from the High Rock Honor Camp, that was located within the park, were doing most of the planting work. We could not get the random concept through to them and no matter what we said or did the trees were planted in regular patterns or rows. The next problem we faced was keeping the 8"-12" seedlings from choking to death under the mass and tangle of weeds and berry vines. Ted and I made daily trips to the area to clear the few hardy survivors. Eventually we succeed in fine tuning our planting efforts. With the introduction of the California Conservation Corps crew as replacements for the Honor Camp workers, progress was made. Additionally, the SRL provided sufficient funding to place an on-site park employee to supervise the work.

The only other setback we faced was an internal miscommunication of facts. As the reforestation program in Pepperwood continued in each subsequent year, we refined our efforts. Initially, the redwood trees were obtained from a California Division of Forestry nursery near Santa Cruz. Little thought had been given to gene pool source and the concept of Biodiversity. Later, we changed our methods and acquired redwood tree seedlings grown from local stock. By this time in the evolution of DPR we were able to obtain assistance from the Resource Ecologists that were on staff in the Regional Offices. Dave Boyd, our Ecologist out of the Santa Rosa Headquarters, was immensely helpful in our efforts but for one major miscommunication. He had informed us that the containers, which the trees came in, were biodegradable and the seedling, container and all, could be planted in the ground. He corrected his mistake only after State Park crews had planted 10,000 seedlings. It was quite an effort to dig them up and replant the trees.

The Pepperwood reforestation program that started in 1980 continued on well into the 1990's. As additional parcels are acquired they too are planted. The program was successful, maybe too successful as considerable thinning of trees was necessary because our survival rate was so high. In May 2000, the last time I saw some of the redwood trees we had planted in the early 1980's, many of them were approaching 50′ tall. The truth is that, " When you've seen one redwood, You haven't seen enough."

BEFORE THE FALL, A LESSON LEARNED

To witness the fall of a 300′ tall redwood is awesome. As you have read, it can be a frightening experience. When it is a natural occurrence it is spellbinding and an event to be remembered. It is a different feeling when a 1,000-1,500 year old redwood falls as a result of human intervention. Then, especially in the sanctuary of a park, it can be an upsetting and sickening experience. I was witness to several natural tree falls and a participant in a few events in which the cause of the tree's demise was a chainsaw in the hand of man.

Perhaps the strangest result of a natural tree fall actually had its beginning prior to my arrival at Humboldt Redwoods. Sometime in 1978 two small redwoods, perhaps

2'-3' in diameter and a larger 5' diameter redwood fell, of natural causes, across all lanes of the U.S. 101 freeway north of the little community of Myers Flat. This happened late at night. Subsequently, three cars driving in a northbound direction crashed into the trees, severely damaging the cars and injuring the occupants. As a result of the accident, both CalTrans and State Parks were named in a lawsuit that followed. Of course, like much of the litigation that involves the State, a lengthy and drawn out investigation and legal process usually follows the incident. Often this can take years. That was the case in this instance.

An attorney from the State Attorney General's Office contacted me in 1980 to initiate a meeting to discuss the 1978 accident. When he arrived at my office at Humboldt Redwoods I was distressed to learn that one possible solution to a settlement of the case was that all redwoods trees with the potential of falling on the freeway should be cut down in order to prevent another occurrence. My first thought was, "You've got to be kidding!" – but he wasn't. The attorney wanted us to estimate the number of trees that would have to be removed, not only from the CalTrans right-of-way, but also from park property on both sides of the freeway! That would amount to a major logging operation along a 20-mile stretch of freeway and destroy thousands of old growth redwood trees. I was able to convince him of the folly of this plan without too much trouble. I could not speak for CalTrans, but I had no doubt in my mind that State Parks would never allow this to happen. At any rate I told him that an accident like this may happen occasionally, but they are few and far between. Certainly it was worth the risk to protect the integrity of the park.

I had no sooner given my spiel about the trees rarely falling, when over the Dispatch radio in the outer office we all heard the excited voice of Ranger Marla Rayburn shout, "My gosh, it just missed a car!" Marla had been on patrol, driving south on the Avenue of the Giants, when a 10′-diameter redwood had crashed down between her truck and another vehicle traveling ahead of her. This could not help my argument.

I told the attorney that we might as well adjourn the meeting and drive to the scene of this incident that had just occurred. When we arrived at the scene, there was no doubt that a tree had fallen. It was also apparent that the tree had fallen in conditions of clear weather, no wind, and no saturated soil. The tree had no apparent rot or weakness that would account for the failure. Mother Nature had just said, "Now."

I never did hear the outcome of the lawsuit. My guess is that it was settled out of court. The real winners were the thousand of old-growth redwoods that make the drive along the freeway so spectacular.

I was "snookered" and learned a hard lesson the first time I authorized a CalTrans highway crew to cut down an old-growth redwood along the Avenue of the Giants. It was not long after my arrival that I was approached by the CalTrans highway foreman who informed me that his crew needed to take down a large redwood growing at the road edge in Dimond Grove, north of Weott. CalTrans controlled a right-of-way of various widths along the length of the Avenue. The trees on the right-of way were the property of State Parks; thus our permission was needed for felling what was deemed a hazardous tree.

The tree in question was growing right at the pavement edge and it leaned inward toward the road. It was over 14′ in diameter and had a huge "Goosepen" at its base. A Goosepen is a hollow burn scar that is large enough to accommodate many geese, and was used as such by early settlers, or for that matter as a shelter for human beings. The foreman explained that his crew had been watching this particular tree for years and had taken measurements as it leaned off center. They were convinced that it would soon fall, as there was some evidence of soil movement at its base.

I went out and inspected the tree with the foreman, but he failed to convince me that there was an imminent danger of it falling. However, against my better judgment, I told him I would call the State Park Forester in the Eureka office to come down and inspect the tree. I would abide by his decision. I'm afraid that I had taken the easy way out and "passed the buck." When the Forester came down to inspect the tree he was in agreement with the CalTrans foreman. The tree must come down. That was the decision.

On the appointed day we gathered to watch this noble giant fall. The timber faller put on his climbing gear and proceeded to climb up the tree to a point about 15' above road level and the base swell of the trunk. Utilizing the largest chainsaw he had the faller began cutting. It took considerable time to saw the tree to the point where the faller yelled "Timber!" At that point he swung off the tree onto another adjacent redwood that he was roped to. We waited. Nothing happened. After perhaps ten minutes the faller swung back onto the wounded tree and soon sawdust was flying again. "Timber" – nothing happened as he again swung to the adjacent tree. Again we waited, and waited. Finally the tree faller swung back for a third try. This time he was successful as the giant began creaking and groaning and started its inexorable plunge to the forest floor.

As "My Mistake" crashed through a cathedral of towering redwoods it struck two other trees and brought both of them down with it. The two trees that came down were much smaller, "only" 5'-6' in diameter. It was a sickening sight and one that I have never forgotten. This was a tree, which in all probability, would not have fallen in our lifetime had we but left it alone.

CalTrans had a much more difficult time getting approval for the removal of any tree after that. I had established a benchmark with a hard lesson learned. It was a lesson that I impressed upon my successor when I left the redwoods.

A FLOOD OF PROBLEMS

In Humboldt County, floods are not unusual. They are a part of nature and have been happening periodically in the forests of Humboldt Redwoods for eons. The floods, in fact, are necessary to enrich the forest floor with silt deposits, which sustain the growth of these giants and occasionally are responsible for their demise. I had seen the full destructive force of a major flood in Humboldt County in 1964.

I did not experience a flood in a park until I had worked in Southern and Central California. At Point Mugu SRA in 1969 a flood devastated the Sycamore Canyon Campground and in 1973 at Morro Bay SP a flood caused considerable damage to roadways and the Chorro Willow Group Camp. Neither of these two floods could prepare me for what I experienced in the Dyerville Area flood of 1983 or the Eel River District flood of 1986.

I did have a little inkling though of what was to come during my first winter at Humboldt Redwoods SP. Our house was located in the apple orchard clearing just east of the Avenue of the Giants. It was, at most, one eighth to one quarter of a mile to the South Fork of the Eel River, directly across from our house. Often, after work, Margaret and I would take the walk down our long driveway to the Avenue and cross to the dirt road that led to the river. Near the steep bank there was a well and pump that supplied the park's water needs. During times of normal flow a great gravel bar separated the steep bank from the river. This gravel bar could be many yards wide at low flow and the river was generally placid.

I had been briefed by staff on my arrival that there was a "Flood Plan" prepared in case of emergency, which outlined procedures to be taken for evacuation and protection of Life and Property. When a real potential for flooding appeared likely, the plan called for monitoring flood warning markers that were located on the Dyerville Bridge and on a marker attached to a redwood tree slightly north of our house on the Avenue of the Giants. It also called for notifying the Area Manager when the water level reached a certain point on the Avenue marker.

It had been raining steadily for a week during one period of my first winter when I left work Friday afternoon. The forecast called for steady, sometimes heavy rain, over the weekend. The short drive from the office to my home along the Avenue did not give me a view of the river; it was too far away and not visible through the redwood trees. It so happened that on that weekend I did not leave the house to go out to the Avenue. It was warm and cozy at home with only the sound of wind and heavy rain pelting the roof.

On Sunday, Ranger Dan Ash called me at home and said we were going on flood alert. I was quite surprised. He suggested I go down to the Avenue and have a look. As I walked down my driveway toward the Avenue, things looked a little different. As I got closer they looked a lot different! Where Margaret and I once walked down the dirt road to the river there was water flowing through the undergrowth and redwood trees. The water level had almost reached the Avenue already. That meant the river had overflowed the 12'-15' bank opposite our house. Not only that, but it must mean that the river itself was now several hundred yards wide. It was not the width and depth of the water that surprised me, but rather **how fast the waters had risen**. We did not suffer any severe damage from this flood event, but it was a lesson learned, and I would never again underestimate the power of the river or how fast it could rise.

In the winter of 1982/83 I got my first real taste of a flood. We had a total of 60″ of rainfall in December and November with only two days in which rain did not fall during that period. Total rainfall for the 1982/83 year reached a record 117″ at Park Headquarters. Considerable damage was done to facilities at Humboldt

Redwoods State Park. I saw for the first time how the water level measured on the highway bridge at Dyerville, where no damage was occurring, translated into damaging flood waters miles upriver at Federation and Williams Groves where mud, silt and water rose to depths of 3'-4' on restroom walls. I also watched in amazement as whole redwood trees floated down river to serve as battering rams against anything that stood in their path. One of the most important lessons I learned is to pay more attention to the rainfall amounts to the south of us than the amount that actually fell on the park. HRSP served only as the mouth of a funnel that gathered rainfall from a much larger Eel River Basin than our own immediate drainage.

The **most important** lesson I learned from the1982/83 Flood was how **together, unselfish** and **focused** the staff became in times of crisis. The spirit of cooperation and teamwork was at an all time high during a flood event. No longer did individuals worry about matters of overtime. Petty bickering ended and conflicts between visitor services and maintenance services responsibilities were swept away with the floodwaters. Everyone pitched in to do what was needed. From my perspective as Manger of the park the job actually got easier. I no longer had to be as concerned about budgets and spending limits. Sure, we had to keep accounting records for FEMA (Federal Emergency Management Agency) to help pay the repair bills. But more importantly, from the entire staff's point of view, we had to make repairs as quickly and efficiently as we could in order to be open for business again. We had many veteran employees who had been through several floods at the park. All I had to do was insure they had the materials and equipment on hand to get the job done. I did and they did. The park was open for business in record time.

The 1982/83 Flood was only a "drop in the (rain) bucket" compared to the Flood of 1986. Now there was a real flood. Certainly not to the degree of 1955 or 1964 floods, but certainly one to write home about-if you could get the mail out. It was February, between Lincoln and Washington's birthdays. I remember that not because of the holidays, but rather because Margaret had taken our son Chris on a planned ski trip for his birthday. We were experiencing our typical winter weather, rain, more Rain and a lot of RAIN.

The floodwaters rose rapidly, especially between Richardson Grove State Park to the south of Humboldt Redwoods, all the way to the mouth of the South Fork where it empties into the main Eel River at Dyerville. Park Headquarters quickly became isolated to the north when the South Fork overflowed its banks and covered the Avenue of the Giants in the vicinity of the old town site of Weott. Farther north near the town of Rio Dell the newer of two Highway 101 bridges collapsed. This coupled with numerous slides and road slipouts effectively closed down Highway 101.

To the south of us, where I had learned to look for danger, there was an even more ominous event. Again, on Highway 101, north of our Standish-Hickey SRA a tremendous landslide occurred that completely blocked the South Fork of the Eel River. The slide became known as, "Carl's Slide" (no relation!), named so after a nearby café. The slide created a dam that backed up the river. It was not certain if the rising level of the water behind the dam would simply flow over and erode the landslide releasing the water slowly, or if the dam would burst catastrophically, sending a torrent of water rushing down river. If that were to happen many small communities would be endangered. As far as the Eel River District was concerned we were now isolated and on our own. Severe flooding and damage was occurring at Richardson Grove State Park, Benbow SR, Humboldt Redwoods and to a lessor extent at Grizzly Creek Redwoods on the Van Duzan River.

Soon reports came in that Highway 101 was closed between Garberville and Richardson Grove due to landslides. Shortly after that Supervising Ranger Joe Hardcastle, at Richardson Grove called to inform us of major damage to the park that had wiped out our newly paved Day-Use parking lot and threatened to damage additional facilities. For the time being it was up to him and the staff in the South Sector to handle their own problems and priorities. We had our hands full up north and with road closed between us we could not get there to help anyway.

We received hourly reports on "Carl's Slide" and were relieved when we finally heard that the South Fork had breached the landslide and slowly carved a path through the dam. Waters would rise again but not with the anticipated force of a dam bursting. Meanwhile, back at HRSP many parts of the Avenue of the Giants were underwater. Park crews had opened up the emergency gate on Pesula Road in order to have access to those portions of Highway 101 that were still open. It was then that we discovered another problem.

South of Park Headquarters, on Highway 101, another gigantic landslide occurred, producing a chaotic jumble of redwood trees slumping down the slope toward the Avenue and the park's "boneyard" near Williford Road. Many huge trees were still standing, swaying and leaning at all angles. Two lanes of the four-lane freeway were gone.

I called Margaret and Chris at her parent's home near Santa Rosa. They had scrapped their skiing plans because of too much snow in the mountains, and instead had obtained tickets to a basketball game in the Bay Area. But, they too were trapped and could not get to the game because of flooding at the Sonoma-Marin County line. In the meantime they were stuck where they were with no way to get back home. For that they would have to wait.

After several days, the Eel River began to recede and an assessment of damage could begin. The usual, and almost routine, flood cleanup of mud and silt in Founders Grove, Federal Grove and Williams Grove was needed. We had been fortunate at Williams Grove when a large old growth redwood had fallen between the restroom and 500 gallon propane tank barely missing them. Throughout the park we had lost hundreds of 12"x 12" x 4' redwood vehicle barriers that popped out of the ground like corks as the floodwater reached them. In the summer the river was 20-30 feet below this level. Our well pump had washout out again for the third time (You'd think we would learn). After the last flood we had moved it another 100 yards away from the riverbank. Now all of that dirt and gravel was missing, and so was the well pump.

At last, I was able to make my way south toward Benbow SRA and Richardson Grove SP. At Benbow the damage was significant but easily repairable. Much of the area at Benbow was flooded in the summer to create a lake. It is a wide expanse and the floodwaters had inundated the area but not with force. Logs and other debris were everywhere and a high-water mark halfway up the chain link fence could be seen.

We continued south on Highway 101 and were stopped by another slide. It was awesome. The slide had occurred at a highway cut above the roadway and rushed down slope with such massive force that it actually had driven tree trunks **underneath** the highway and forced large slabs of roadway to fold and accordion upwards into the air. We found our way around this barrier on a portion of old Highway 101.

When we finally reached Richardson Grove we were not prepared for what we saw. Joe had previously attempted to explain the situation to us on the telephone but that description did not do justice to the scene before us. He had been a fortunate witness to the initial destruction. A minute or two earlier and he would have been a victim of that destruction.

Joe, who lived in the park, had walked down toward the river with Ranger John Quirk to survey the situation right after a huge segment of steep hillside had slipped into the river opposite the new parking lot and the Richardson Grove Lodge. This slump, somewhat similar too, but smaller than the one up at Humboldt, had carried with it whole trees that still stood upright in the earth. As Joe and John approached the Lodge they saw a wall of water rushing **back** toward the river.

The slide, which now protruded into the river, had forced a huge tsunami-like wave all the way across the river, over the parking lot and several hundred feet farther to the lodge - a total distance of several hundred yards. There were splash marks on the Visitor Center door and fish remained on the deck and the surrounding ground. One large salmon even had a tree branch rammed down its throat by the force of the water. The area looked like a moonscape. All fences, barriers and vegetation had been swept clean as the river rushed back toward the channel. Joe and John could have been swept away too if they had been in the area just seconds earlier.

Our problems at Richardson Grove had just begun, even as the still powerful river receded. The protruding toe of the slide had forced the flow of water on a new course against the opposite bank and was slowly eroding away the opposite bank. The park's well pump was in danger here too, as was the campfire center and picnic area. Helplessly, over the next few days, we watched as first the campfire center then the picnic area tumbled into the relentless river. We were able to save the well pump. Crews at the park had a terrific battle on their hands as they tried to keep Durphy Creek from entirely filling with gravel and endangering both the Highway 101 bridge in the park and an interior park bridge as well.

I was in contact with the Region Office but just as Joe had difficulty conveying to me the magnitude of the problem at Richardson Grove, I was having difficulty conveying the problems to Regional Director Curt Mitchell. I believe he had experienced the 1964 Flood at Richardson Grove when he worked there earlier in his career. Perhaps he felt that nothing could be worse than that. I didn't know about that, but I knew it was going to take lot of money, manpower and materials to make things right in dealing with our flood.

Fortunately, in the Region Office, we had a great Maintenance Specialist in Ted Crane. Ted intuitively understood the problems in the field and told us to get to work and fix things. He would take care of the red tape, funding and dealings with FEMA. Another example, one of the best, of the teamwork I had come to expect in times of crisis. With the help of District, Region and Sacramento Headquarters staff we were able to make repairs in time for the summer season. We constructed a new campfire center, converted the remains of the Day Use Area into a Group Campground and repaired the parking lot and grounds. Later we were successful in obtaining a grant to provide for riverbank protection along the area of the Group Campground.

Today, if you visit Richardson Grove you can still see the slide that caused all the damage. Many of the trees on it still survive. The rising river surely did create **a flood of problems for us** - but they were not insurmountable. Oh yes, Margaret and Chris eventually made it home. They had to travel north to Redding, west to Arcata, and back down to the park. Highway 101 remained closed at Carl's Slide for months and when it finally did open it was to controlled traffic only for an extended period. Remnants of this slide still remain visible high above the river on the opposite bank

Yes, we experienced **a flood of problems** and they will happen again.

GONE TO POT

In the 1980's Humboldt, Mendocino, and Del Norte Counties were known in law enforcement circles as the "Emerald Triangle." Humboldt Redwoods SP was right at the center of that triangle. Within much of the park's relatively inaccessible interior there was a lot of space for growing marijuana. Along the park's western and southwestern boundaries lived many "alternative lifestyle" folks who weren't adverse to growing a little, or a lot, of pot on State Park property.

Without going into the social or legal issues of growing marijuana let me describe what would often happen when "weed' was grown in the park. Usually there was damage to the park resources. This could be in the form of removing vegetation, cutting trees and brush, tapping water sources and drying up springs that would normally be needed by native plants and animals, setting traps and poison bait to kill wildlife and contaminating soils with fertilizers. Beyond that there was also the matter of "booby traps" and armed guards to prevent any "intruders" from confiscating the plants. In truth it was a scary time for Park Rangers on patrol or the unwary hiker who might stumble upon a "pot garden".

It got so bad that we found it necessary to assign a Ranger as a liaison to CAMP (Campaign Against Marijuana Planting) i.e., a coalition of law enforcement agencies working to reduce illegal marijuana cultivation. It was our Ranger's job to take aircraft patrol flights with CAMP personnel and locate hidden gardens in the park. Some of these gardens were quite extensive and the plants in them worth millions and millions of dollars on the street. The conditions in HRSP must have been perfect for pot growing. Plants often reached 12' tall and 3" in diameter. The largest garden we ever removed was 1200 plants of this size. Chief Ranger Reinhardt made the NBC National News as he was shown burning 10 tons of Marijuana destroyed in the largest single crop harvest ever confiscated in the park. Some of the gardens were very elaborate and sophisticated. At one location, deep in the park interior, a hillside had been terraced and about 50 half drums of 55 gallon barrels used as planters. These were connected to a solar powered watering system. On another occasion we found a location within the park that was obviously being used as a central clearinghouse for distribution of bags of fertilizer and plastic hose. An 18-wheel tractor- trailer rig had dropped off the supplies. Fortunately, we got there first and hauled everything away for park use.

The smaller gardens, those of 100 plants or less, were usually destroyed at Park Headquarters by burning the plants in a steel BBQ grill. This practice had to be stopped after the smoke from the burning marijuana plants drifted into the park employee housing area and lifted the spirits of several spouses quite "High!" The "Stony" stares that greeted us told us enough was enough.

Eventually, things got so bad I had to call for help. I wanted to be able to import Park Rangers from other Districts to conduct periodic sweeps to remove the gardens. It could be dangerous work. We had a very competent staff who did an excellent job of locating the gardens, both from the air and on the ground, but it took more manpower than we had to remove the gardens and it interfered with normal park operations.

I made my proposal to Region Headquarters (Oh, yes did I mention that we had reorganized again) and got a tentative okay. Before proceeding, however, Assistant Regional Director Dale Buschke wanted to have a first-hand look on the ground at the situation. In preparation for Dale's visit I asked Ranger Ash to locate a typical pot garden we might show him. When Dale came from Santa Rosa all was ready. Dan had found a spot that he thought would be good to show Dale. It was in an area where there had been a garden the previous year.

We drove out in the park's rather small CJ-5 Jeep, through the Rockefeller Forest into the Bull Creek Area and on up to Panther Gap toward Honeydew. Turning off the highway we skirted the park's western boundary in and out of private property. At many locations there were people sitting on their front porches eyeing us warily. It was rather like a scene out of the movie "Deliverance."

We finally came to a locked park gate and passed through it into the park. Dan drove a distance and parked at a turnout where a faint trail led down into the manzanita-covered hillside. Quietly, he told Dale and me to wait while he went down the trail to check things out. We waited and <u>waited</u> and **waited**. No sign of Dan. I became concerned and told Dale to wait there while I went down the trail to check on Dan. I entered a thick stand of brush and heard two voices. I knew Dan had been alone. As I got closer, through the brush I could see that Dan had his weapon drawn. I immediately pulled my gun from its holster and proceeded cautiously ahead. When I came out of the brush into a clearing I saw another individual on his knees, with his hands clasped on his head. He was wearing camouflage clothing.

Dan raised his finger to his lips as a sign of quiet. He/we were not certain if this was the only person guarding this garden. From where we stood we could see other irrigation hoses leading out into the brush in several directions. Dan handed me the gun he had taken from the pot grower as he handcuffed the bad guy. About this time, Dale, who was getting antsy waiting at the top of the hill came down. Dale was not in uniform nor did he have a weapon. I handed him the gun that Dan had taken from our prisoner and in true western fashion said, "Keep us covered." Dan and I then proceeded to follow the other hose lines. We cut down about two dozen plants that were really thick and tall.

Now our problem was to take our prisoner and the plants out of this hellhole, drawing as little attention to ourselves as we could. We decided not to go back the way we had come. Instead, we would take a longer circuitous route on backcountry roads in order to avoid our "friends" sitting on their porches. We placed the prisoner in the front passenger's seat so I could watch him. Dan drove and Dale and I took the back seats crammed against the smelly, sticky, marijuana plants. It was awful!

Once on the road and at a location where we could re-establish radio contact, we radioed for Ranger backup to meet us at the Grasshopper Lookout Fire Road gate. It would take us over an hour to reach it. When we were almost to the gate we were in for a surprise. Unknown to us the California Division of Forestry crews had been in the process of replacing a small bridge near our destination. There were new abutments in place at each end of the bridge but no span as yet reached across the gap. On the other side were the Rangers we were to meet. The thought of going back around the way we had just come was unbearable. The heavy planks that were to be used to span the gap were lying on the ground awaiting installation. Dan, Dale and I eyed them. Could we place them across the span and go across? I asked Dale if he would do the accident report if it didn't work. He agreed. After placing the boards, Dale, the prisoner and I walked across on our makeshift bridge. Dan then carefully drove the Jeep across the makeshift bridge. Whew!

The Rangers who had come to meet us transported the prisoner to jail. It was dusk by now so Dan, Dale, and I went back to Headquarters. I'm not sure if Dale thought this was a set up (it wasn't) but we had no problem after that in getting the help we needed from Region.

"CHICKEN OUT"

Ever since I was a little boy I had this "thing" about chickens. I love them. Growing up in Linda Vista we had two pet chickens, "Blondi" and "Dagwood." Living in Fletcher Hills I had about a dozen chickens as pets also. We would gather eggs, of course, but I would never allow any of them to be butchered.

At Humboldt Redwoods things were different. Our house was semi-isolated from the campground and we had a large area where chickens could be raised without anyone "crying fowl." My family knew of my love of chickens and decided it would be okay to obtain some. One day while Abby was at school she learned that the feed store in Garberville had a supply of baby chicks for sale. She called Margaret on the telephone and told her about the chicks, which were supposed to be "sexed" to insure we had a proper rooster/hen ratio. Margaret agreed to pick Abby up after school and get the chickens as a surprise gift for me. When I came home from work that evening I was pleased to find my new brood chirping away in a box.

I built a temporary chicken coop that I placed on the back patio of the house. The floor of this coop was wire mesh. I was more protective of my chicks than a doting mother hen. The chicks prospered and grew. One night, when I was fast asleep, I was awakened by a commotion coming from the rear of the house. I got up, turned on the lights and dashed out to the patio. My little brood was in a panic as a small spotted skunk was attempting to make a late dinner snack of them. The skunk was under the cage and had grabbed a chick by the foot and was attempting to pull it through the wire floor. I picked up anything I could find and began shouting and throwing objects at the skunk but he wouldn't be dissuaded. I finally reached in the coop and pulled the young chick out. All the skunk got for his effort was a "Toe McNugget." Behind me I now became aware of uncontrollable laughter. Turning around I saw the family staring at me with their mouths agape. I guess I was a sight to behold standing there in the "altogether" consoling my toeless chicken!

The chicks thrived and grew in their coop. Eventually I built a larger chicken coop and a fenced enclosure some distance away from the house. As the chicks began growing their permanent feathers, an unsettling feeling came over all of us. A lot of them were beginning to look and **sound** like roosters. We were now the proud owners of a flock of eleven roosters and one hen! It didn't take long to sort that problem out and start over again with a new flock of the correct composition.

I did not like to keep the chickens cooped up during the day. To me it felt like they were in "jail". The chickens were productive members of the Chavez Family, going about their daily work of laying eggs. They deserved to be free. I'm afraid that Margaret did not agree with me. I tried to explain to her that the chickens were only rototilling and fertilizing her flower beds but she drew the line when they scratched out all of her cultivated flowers. We had a constant battle over this and I held my ground-for as long as I could before succumbing to her will and my own better judgment.

Sitting in my office at work one day I heard over the park's radio a Ranger reporting "chickens on the loose in the campground". I went out and got into my vehicle and drove over to the campground. Sure enough, there was a group of "redwood chickens" happily scratching about in the campsites. Not only that, but some campers were feeding them. These chickens looked very familiar, I doubted they could belong to anyone else but me. How embarrassing. Oh well, we did have rules and regulations about dogs on a leash but I couldn't recall any about chickens on a leash! I shepherded my wayward flock down the steep bank, across the creek, and up the other side to the safety of their home turf.

This incident wouldn't have been so bad if it weren't for the fact that it happened on several occasions.

The day finally came when everything came to a "head." As I drove through the Burlington campground I came upon my flock again. They were all gathered around a water spigot, drinking from a leaky faucet. Enough was enough. I did not have the heart to do in my chicken friends myself. I left the dirty work to my Chief Ranger, Ted, who had once worked on a chicken ranch. After his first day at work, I invited him over for an early Christmas dinner since his family was still back at Lake Tahoe and wouldn't move to HRSP for more several weeks. I told him I had a job for him to do before we ate dinner. He was good, swift and merciless as my chickens went off to the "Big Redwood Roost in the Sky". Poultry in Parks became a thing of the past!

"OTHER DUTIES AS REQUIRED"

The official job description for all Ranger positions in State service has at the end of it a sentence that reads in part: "...and other duties as required." This is a catchall phrase that covers a multitude of unexpected situations and work related requirements that could not be anticipated. However, in many instances the work that this phrase implies can be very interesting and sometimes enjoyable. That was the case for me often when dealing with the Save the Redwoods League (SRL) and it's Executive Secretary, John DeWitt. John and I had a very close working relationship. The SRL is a non-profit organization that over the years has been responsible for the acquisition of thousand of acres of redwood forest for inclusion into National, State, and local parks. Humboldt Redwoods was one of the primary beneficiaries of the League's efforts.

One means that SRL used to obtain matching funds to be used for land acquisition was through their Redwood Memorial Grove Program. Through this program a donor could select an area in the park to be designated in memory of a loved one. There are hundreds of such groves in HRSP ranging in size from 5,000 acres on up to much larger groves. When SRL had a perspective donor who was interested in choosing a grove, John would call me and arrange for a tour of the proposed grove. The cost of the grove to the donor was usually in the range of $20,000-$50,000.

Over the course of the eight years I was at HRSP I had the opportunity to meet and show many groves to some interesting (and wealthy) people. On one occasion, I had taken an elderly woman and her son out to view a grove that she was considering in memory of her recently deceased husband. It was a $50,000 grove. As I made my "sales pitch" I sensed some hesitation on the part of the women, but I could tell that the son wanted the grove for his father. I suggested that maybe the two of them would like to discuss the situation alone so I moved away from them and stood admiring the majesty of the cathedral-like redwoods towering above. I was thinking "they sure grow them tall here." It was quiet; so quiet I could not help but overhear part of Mother and Son's conversation. "But Mother, it's only $50,000 and that's less than a Mercedes. Dad would love it". They took the grove.

Once a grove was "purchased" by a donor, a Memorial Grove sign is put in place to commemorate the recipient and recognize the donor. It is very common for the donor, be it family, friends, or organization, to request a tour of the site. That is an important service we are obliged to provide.

Some of the groves have easy access. For instance the Memorial Groves that line the Avenue of the Giants can be reached directly from the highway. Others are more difficult to get to and required a walk or a hike to reach them. This is generally not a problem in the summer when there are temporary bridges in place to cross the South Fork of the Eel in order to reach groves on the other side. It is another matter if a person wants to reach the other side of the river in the spring before the bridges are in place.

One spring I received a call from John at SRL informing me that a Grove donor wished to see her grove and another one next to it that she had recently acquired in memory of her husband. Both of the groves were in the $50,000 category. Both groves were on the far side of the river and the summer bridges were not yet in place. The woman was the wife of a now deceased author of adventure books and she wanted to see the newest grove **now**, not in the summer. I explained the problem to John but he said we had to do it now because she was a very important contributor to SRL. He gave me the telephone number of the elderly woman's caregiver. I called her and again explained the problem. Again I was told that the donor was adamant about seeing the grove as soon as possible. "Okay," I said but this would require some special arrangements. I told her that we would have to cross the river by boat and climb a steep bank to reach a trail on the opposite side. I asked if the elderly woman was capable of doing this. When I was told she could, I then told the caregiver to make sure that Mrs. "D" was appropriately dressed and had proper walking/hiking shoes or boots.

At the time the donor had chosen to come for her visit, the river was too wide and deep to cross by wading, but too shallow, because of numerous sandbars, for the park's motorboat to negotiate. I decided to utilize my own personal "Sea Eagle" raft to which I had attached a small electric motor for the trip. I was confident that it could provide transportation for all three of us for the short distance we needed to go. My plan was to launch the raft from Gould Bar beach and float a short distance down river until we were opposite the grove and then climb the bank, and hike into the grove. The return trip would retrace our route (I thought) powered upriver by the electric motor.

I was in my "Spit & Polish" uniform for this important occasion when my guests arrived. "Oh my Gosh!" Before me stood an 80-year-old lady, in black dress with black 2″ heel pumps and an elegant black beaded handbag! Her caregiver was a little more appropriately dressed for the occasion, though she also wore a dress and in her arms she was carrying a large wicker picnic basket. I was beginning to feel that this was quickly turning into one of those "other duties as required" episodes. As delicately as I could I again explained the situation to the both of them. Unimpressed by my trepidation they said, "Press on."

We drove the short distance from Park Headquarters to Gould Bar to board and launch the raft. It was a beautiful spring day for the lazy drift down river to the area of the grove. The tall redwood trees, wisps of lingering fog and blue-green waters of the river added to the wonderful mood of the moment. When I judged we were at the right location I guided the raft towards shore and nudged into the **muddy** bank. After I had secured the raft I assisted the others out onto shore. Mrs. "D" was now wearing muddy brown pumps and her companion now had muddy brown tennis shoes. I didn't even bother to take note of my once polished Wellington boots. We now faced a major obstacle with the steep bank we had to climb. I found what looked to be the easiest route and managed to get the others up with the help of a rope. I would say this for the two ladies, they were determined! We arrived at the top of the bank and proceeded to walk deeper into the forest. The forest litter was thick and deep and travel was difficult. Walking would have been difficult for anyone in this thick duff, let alone for an 80-year-old woman in 2″ heels.

When I consulted the grove map that I had brought with me and announced that we were now in the appropriate location Mrs. "D" beamed and tears of joy came to her eyes. Then, she very formally, asked me to join her and her companion in a celebration in honor of her dear husband. We found a level clearing and the picnic basket that we had carried all this way was opened. A lace tablecloth was spread on the ground, and an elegant place setting of china and silverware was set for each of us. Next came the crystal champagne flutes and the champagne. "Would I join them in lunch and a toast to Mr. "D?" "Of course." Even though I was in uniform, wasn't this a perfect example of "other duties as required"?

After our lunch and celebration we made our way back to the raft. I hadn't noticed the wind blowing down river when we had started our trip. Now I could see it was going to be a problem going back up river against the wind. I wasn't so certain my little electric motor could propel us against the current and the increasing wind. No problem. I had brought a portable radio along for just such an emergency. My backup plan had been to float about two or three miles farther downstream to the Dyerville Bridge and be picked up by a park employee and transported back to our vehicle. That plan did not work any better than the portable radio I had brought with me. I could not contact anyone on it.

"Other duties as required". There was only one thing left to do. As I said before the water was fairly shallow but obviously too deep for my two passengers. I did not think it would be a problem for me though. Much to the surprise of my guests, I jumped into the river, uniform, boots and all and began pulling the raft upstream, back to Gould Bar. I was able to pick a route so that the water level never reached above my waist. It was a struggle, to be sure, against the wind and the current but after about 45 minutes I made it back to our starting point. My passengers thought this was one of the greatest adventures they had ever been on, so by that standard I guess the trip was a success.

Several weeks later I received a package in the mail. It was from Mrs. "D." In it was a silver bowl, supported on a pedestal made of Grizzly Bears. It is something I would have liked to have kept but, of course, I could not accept a personal gift of that value. Instead I had the bowl accepted as a Gift to the State of California and accessioned as an artifact. The last time I saw it, it was still on the Superintendent's desk at Humboldt Redwoods SP being used either as a candy dish or a receptacle for telephone messages.

IT'S A DOG'S LIFE

Chief Ranger Reinhardt and I had developed into a good working team and the best of friends on and off the job. Those who did not know us were a bit baffled by the irreverent banter that went back and forth between us. In fact, often when we attended meetings or training sessions together, many people thought that we did not get along with each other but nothing could be farther from the truth. Our families were close and we often did things together. Ted and I were double tennis partners and had won several tournaments in Southern Humboldt county and Eureka. Basically we knew what made each other tick. Today in retirement we live in the same community just around the corner from each other. It was Ted's job to transform many of my ideas into action. He did this well. Many years later, Ted was to tell me that he had to go back to talk to employees and assure them I had only been thinking out loud when I said I wanted "such and such' a thing done. He could have made an entire career out of cleaning up after me!

It got to the point where both of us would finish much of our daily work in the morning, leaving the afternoon free to "patrol". Frequently in the afternoon we would go "out in the field" to inspect progress on projects. Sometimes it was to Pepperwood to see how our reforestation work was going or to check on the lumber mill operation or see how Ranger Rick was doing over at Grizzly Creek. I think that in some management training circles this is called, "Management by Wandering". We just thought of it as goofing off.

On one beautiful, clear afternoon, we were driving south from Park Headquarters on the Avenue of the Giants toward the town of Miranda. As we often did we stopped to check various Memorial Grove parking lots and talk to the occasional tourist that might have a question for us. It was pleasant PR work.

As we approached Miranda we noticed a cloud of "smoke" billowing up out of the back of a camper shell on a pickup truck that was parked in one of the grove turnouts. On closer inspection we could see and **hear** two women, obviously in distress, screaming and waving their arms about with great agitation. We pulled off the roadway next to them and heard them shouting a name and words to the effect, "My baby, My baby". This called for immediate action, as it seemed a child was trapped in the back of this burning vehicle.

It was not until we got next to the truck that we realized that we were not seeing or smelling smoke, but **propane gas!** Now we could also hear a dog barking in the back of the camper shell. It was impossible to see the dog because the cloud of gas was so thick. One of the women was finally able to explain that they had been carrying a large propane cylinder in the back of the truck. It had not been secured and had rolled around and the gas release valve opened. Deadly, dangerous explosive fumes were still escaping from the tank. It was not to a child inside the truck the women had been shouting to but to a dog. Nevertheless, this was a very dangerous situation as any spark could ignite a devastating explosion. We immediately stopped all traffic on the Avenue as a precaution.

By now the dog's barking was becoming pitifully weaker and weaker until it ceased altogether. We again carefully approached the truck **(We later realized that this was a very stupid thing to do!)** but could not even see the propane tank in the truck because the cloud of gas was so thick. Ted finally reached over the tailgate of the truck and groped about feeling for the tank valve. His hand was freezing from the cold gas, which was still streaming out of the tank but he could not find the valve. He tried again, this time with success and turned the valve, shutting off the gas. Fortunately the 4' tall cylinder had been placed in the truck with the valve to the rear.

Meanwhile, I climbed into the cab of the truck **(how stupid is this?)** and opened a small sliding window at the back of the cab which gave limited access to the interior of the camper shell. I too reached my arm inside the back of the truck and felt around in search of the now silent dog. I felt some fur and grabbed hold. When I yanked, out came a small Welsh Corgi, just like the Queen of England's dog. As soon as I had the dog in hand I made a hasty retreat, a long distance away from the truck, and joined the others. The dog was not breathing and appeared lifeless.

Remembering the "other duties as required" clause of my job description, I began mouth to mouth (nose?) resuscitation on the dog. Some would call it CPR (Canine Pulmonary Resuscitation). It was successful! I placed the dog on the ground and for a moment it lay there. Then he got up on its front legs and tried to walk, dragging its hind legs. Finally, it stood shakily on all four legs. After a few moments it seemed fully recovered and proceeded to march over to a tall redwood tree, and lift his leg to do what all male dogs do. I tell you "it's a dog's life out there."

YOU NEVER KNOW WHEN

A year or two after my picnic adventure with Mrs. "D" I had another interesting encounter with a Save the Redwoods League member. Some time in the fall of 1986 I was working late in my office at Park Headquarters. There was no one else in the office as I was catching up on reading and other paperwork. It must have been around 6:00 pm when I looked out my window and notice an older couple get out of their car and walk up the walkway to the front door of the headquarters building. I knew that they had seen me in my office as the light was on and I was quite visible from the outside. It was past closing time for the office and the other employees were gone so of course the door was locked. The couple knocked on the door anyway.

There really was no way I could ignore the knocking since they knew I was in my office. I got up and went to the door and opened it and asked if there was an emergency I could help them with, tactfully informing them it was past business hours. "No", they said, they were just passing through the park and wanted to see the Visitor Center but it was closed. The couple, Mr. & Mrs. "S", identified themselves as members of the Save the Redwoods League. They were very friendly and personable. We had a pleasant conversation about SRL and the park. I hadn't remembered, but they reminded me, that they had a Memorial Grove in the park. I finally offered to take them down to the Visitor Center and open it up for them.

While they were delighted with this offer they at first declined because they were concerned about getting dinner someplace nearby before the few restaurants in the area closed. They were on their way to Eureka, about an hour's drive north on Highway 101. Taking the time to see the Visitor Center might upset their plans for dinner. Me and my big mouth. "No problem, why don't I show you the Visitor Center and then you can come over to our house for dinner? That way you can take a leisurely drive to Eureka without feeling rushed." Mrs. "S" asked, "Won't that be an imposition on your wife?" "Of course not, she would love to meet you and I'm sure if you're not fussy about food **we** can scratch something up."

I telephone Margaret and said, "I'm bring company over for dinner." Of course, since I had just met these people, there was not a chance in a million that she would know them. I explained the situation to her and she seemed to take it in stride as another of Carl's hairbrain spur of the moment schemes. I took my guests down to the Visitor Center and gave them a personal tour. The SRL had originally contributed $5000 towards development of the VC and this couple had heard about the VC through their association with SRL. They were very pleased with what they saw.

After touring the Visitor Center I had the couple follow me in their car to our house. I introduced them to Margaret and the kids and cheerfully asked Margaret, "What's for dinner?" I didn't quite get an icy stare, but I did notice a tightening of the jaw when she said we were having salmon. Luckily, Margaret's brother, Bill, who was a commercial fisherman, had stopped by the house earlier and dropped off a salmon that had a big hunk bitten off by a shark. It was still perfectly good to eat but not a salable fish for market. Our guests thought it was very exciting to eat a salmon that had been attacked by a shark. In any event, we enjoyed dinner and the company of our guests. They said their farewells and departed for Eureka. That is the last time I saw them.

Two years later, sometime in 1988, I was sitting in my office in Santa Rosa as Northern Regional Director of State Parks. My Secretary, Jan Thompson, informed me Mrs. "S" is waiting for me on the telephone. For the life of me I can't think who Mrs. "S" is. I asked Jan to transfer the call to me. Quickly I learned that this was the same Mrs. "S" that I had met at Humboldt Redwoods two year ago and invited to dinner with her husband. She informed me that her husband had passed away the year before and that the trip to HRSP and the redwoods parks north to Eureka had been the last really enjoyable trip she and her husband had taken while he was still in good health. She could still recall the details of the

Visitor Center tour and especially remembered the dinner at our house.

She then told me that her health was also beginning to fail and she was in the process of putting her estate in order. Part of her plan, she said, was to thank me for that last trip she took with her husband and she wanted to leave me $25,000 from the estate! "Gulp." I explained that I was very appreciative of her generosity but I could not accept a gift of that kind. I suggested that since she and her husband had enjoyed the Visitor Center so much, perhaps she would like to consider donating the $25,000 to the Humboldt Redwoods Interpretive Association instead. She readily agreed to this proposal. I gave her the telephone number and name of my replacement at Humboldt Redwoods, District Superintendent Don Hoyle. Mrs. "S" made that call and Don arranged for the funds to be placed in a HRIA bank account that would maintain the principal and utilize only the interest from the account for interpretive purposes by the Association. You never know when...!

NO SMALL POTATOES

At the north end of the park, along the Avenue of the Giants is the small community of Pepperwood, today made up of a few houses scattered here and there. Wonderful vegetables, especially corn, is grown in the area and sold by the local farmers from roadside produce stands. The December Flood of 1964 devastated the town, drowning several residents and essentially wiping it off the map. I remember as a student at HSC in the spring of 1965 driving to the area and being amazed to see most of the town's buildings crushed and piled up against the stands of redwood trees that surrounded the community.

After the flood, many of the remaining residents moved away. Since Humboldt Redwoods SP surrounded the community these properties were "in-holdings" that the park desired to acquire. The Save the Redwoods League began to purchase the property from willing sellers and to transfer titles to the State. This activity continues, as property becomes available.

Not all residents in Pepperwood were pleased at the prospect of the State acquiring Pepperwood property. Some were unwilling sellers and so the property remains in private ownership. In the mid 1980's most of the remaining parcels of land were relatively small, less than 5-10 acres. There was, however, one 40-acre parcel that was highly desirable. This property was situated between the Avenue of the Giants and Highway 101 directly in the middle of some prime old growth Memorial Groves. State Parks and SRL had coveted this property for many years and, but for a sick cow, would have acquired it after the 1964 Flood.

Negotiations for the property with the owner, Mrs. Madeline Holmes had gone on for many years before she agreed to sell. Finally a price was agreed upon. An entourage of State Park officials, including representatives from SRL and the Director of State Parks, drove to her house to seal the deal. The road leading to her house was a narrow track that wound its way, about one half a mile, through a beautiful redwood grove. The official party parked their vehicles in such a manner that the roadway to the property was blocked.

It so happened that Mrs. Holmes had a sick cow on her property so she had called a veterinarian from Fortuna to come out to care for it. The veterinarian came out but could not drive to the ranch because of the cars blocking the road. He returned home. The cow died and with it so did the land sale deal because Mrs. Holmes was so irate about the loss of her cow she refused to have any dealings with State Parks or the Save the Redwoods League. SRL Executive Secretary, John Dewitt told this part of the story to me.

I decided that I had to meet this independent woman I had heard so much about and introduce myself as her new neighbor and the new manager of the park. I had forewarning from park staff that Mrs. Holmes had no love lost for park employees and an even worse opinion of SRL.

We had both apple and pear trees growing in the orchards in front of our house. I had built a fruit dehydrator to dry the apples and pears and so decided to take a bag full of dried fruit with me when I went to see Mrs. Holmes. Carefully parking my vehicle so as not to block the roadway I walked through a gate. As I continued toward the house I could hear some banging and muttering.

Before me was a surprising sight. There was Mrs. Holmes, a tiny, perhaps 90 lb., 75-80 year old wisp of a woman, in blue jeans and flannel shirt, trying to hang a wooden gate on a corral **all by herself.** I quickly introduced myself and helped lift the gate so she could attach the hinges to the support posts. When we finished hanging the gate she said, "I won't sell".

I told her I hadn't come to purchase the property, only to meet her and bring her some dried fruit. Though still wary, she became a little more friendly and we talked a while, mostly about the past efforts and attempts of SRL to acquire her property. I returned several times to visit Madeline over the next couple of years. She was a very interesting lady. She was once a physical education teacher and had been a widow for many years. She lived alone on her ranch and had no surviving close relatives. On her property she had a few cattle and grew potatoes. There were also some fine redwood trees on the land, but for the most part it was a clearing in the forest. Mrs. Holmes had grown up and lived all her life in Humboldt County. On one of my visits she told me that her father had also been a rancher in the hills east of Grizzly Creek State Park near Bridgeville. As a little girl she recalled driving flocks of turkeys they raised on the ranch to market in Loleta, a trip that took several days walking. We continued to visit and became sort of the "Odd Couple". I gave her dried fruit and she gave me some of the huge potatoes she grew in her fields.

Once she burned her hand severely and when I came to visit her she was putting some greasy home remedy slave on her hand. I insisted on taking her to the doctor and she finally relented. We had built up a good friendship and trust at last over our potato and dried fruit exchanges.

One day I received a call from Madeline. She said, "Carl, I'm getting old. I want to sell the property to you (she meant the park) but I will have no dealings with that Save the Redwoods League." I told her I would be right over to talk to her in person. When I arrived we discussed her selling price, which was considerable. I told her that I would have to talk to my boss in Santa Rosa and explained that our Acquisition Section in Sacramento usually conducted negotiations for property. Again she insisted she would deal with no one but me. I told her I'd see what I could do.

Returning to my office, I immediately called Regional Director, Curt Mitchell, in Santa Rosa and explained what had happened. Curt was aware of the past history of attempting to acquire this property and was very encouraged and supportive of this window of opportunity. He promised to get right back to me after talking with the Acquisition Section in Sacramento and to the SRL. Curt was able to broker a deal that entailed the Department providing half of the funds and SRL providing the other half. The full check for payment, however, would be from DPR after SRL had transferred its share of the money to us. It was agreed I would do the negotiations with Mrs. Holmes with coaching from someone assigned from the Acquisition Section. There was to be no mention of SRL. A "Life Estate" was agreed upon so that Mrs. Holmes could live on the property until she passed away.

Everything worked out fine, but for some reason Mrs. Holmes insisted that she have two separate checks made out for payment of the transaction. That was no problem and the checks were made out and mailed to her. When Madeline received the checks she called me and asked if I would take her to the bank to deposit them. I agreed and drove to her house (I no longer needed to park outside her gate) to pick her up. We first drove to one of her banks in Loleta and deposited the smaller of the two checks. Next we drove to a Fortuna bank and attempted to deposit the second check. When we went into the bank it was very crowded with lines of people standing in front of every teller position. Madeline saw the lines and said she did not want to wait. I asked her to give me the check, which she did, and I walked over to a bank employee sitting at a desk. I told the woman that Mrs. Holmes had a check she wanted to deposit. The woman at the desk said we would have to get in line. I held the check in front of her to see the amount. Almost immediately the bank president was at her side and the check swiftly deposited. Money talks!

Several months later I again received a telephone call from Mrs. Holmes and was she ever mad. Apparently, her tax person, when preparing her tax returns, had come across the canceled checks for the property and there was a small notation on them with reference to the Save the Redwoods League! I hadn't noticed this nor had anyone else. The CPA inquired of Mrs. Holmes what the notation was about. She went "ballistic" and called me. She explained that as far as the deal was concerned she would honor the agreement but she insisted on being issued **new checks** that had no reference to SRL on them. Here was a woman of principle if I had ever met one! In a panic I called Curt in Santa Rosa still wondering if this would make the deal null and void. He became upset too, knowing how difficult it had been to acquire the property. He was mad at the Acquisition Section for this seemingly minor slip up on the check. Eventually, I retrieved the original checks and two new checks were written and mailed to me. I hand delivered them to Madeline and one of the strangest land acquisitions I had ever been involved with came to a happy ending. It had all started with dried apples, pears and no small potatoes.

DEPTHS OF DESPAIR

Things were operating relatively smoothly in the Eel River District in 1984. The Visitor Center and Interpretive Association were successes, the log salvage and lumber mill operation were going well, and we were even making some modest progress in our efforts to reduce illegal marijuana growing in the park.

The lumber mill operation was especial busy at this time. We still had a three-man crew but they now had a newer, heavy duty, portable mill know as a "Mighty Might" which utilized a Volkswagen engine as its power supply. The mill crew had been utilizing a much smaller "Alaskan Mill" when I arrived at the park in 1979. They were part of a federal funded "CETA" program (I can't even remember what that acronym stands for but it was something to do with job training) and were temporarily placed in a State job classification of "Laborer". After a couple of years in that classification our Sacramento Headquarters Personnel Department determined that that was not an appropriate classification any longer and a new one was needed. In order to correct the situation personnel didn't actually create a new classification, they found an older one that was still on the books but hadn't been in use since the 1930's. Apparently there still was a classification of "Lumber Mill Operator". In order to reclassify the positions a Statewide Open Examination would have to be given. Our three-person crew had been on the job since the inception of the park's lumber mill operation so that it was a forgone conclusion that they would continue to work after the examination. They need only pass the examination and be reachable on the list.

The State Personnel Department had delegated to our Personnel Department the authority to administer the examination. I was contacted by Sacramento Headquarters to come up with some examination questions, which of course, would have to remain confidential for the test. We had two equipment operators on staff, one of whom had put the lumber mill machinery together when it was first acquired. He was the most knowledgeable of its operation with the exception of the lumber mill crew itself. I asked him to write several questions for the examination, which he did. When I received the questions back from him, I read them briefly to check them for appropriateness and sent them on to Sacramento as requested.

Several months later the examination was given on a statewide basis. The day before the examination, the Park Maintenance Supervisor and the three lumber mill crew members came to my office. The Maintenance Supervisor asked if there was any advice that I could give the crew about tomorrow's examination. I got up and went out to the hallway and retrieved the Job Announcement from the bulletin board. I went over the key points for the position that were in the job description but I did not discuss the actual examination questions as was later alleged. After the examination list came out, only four names appeared on the list. The first three names were those of the current lumber mill crew and they were appointed to fill the new classification of Lumber Mill Operator.

Months later, most of the park staff was out at our Cuneo Creek Horse Camp for a staff potluck in the evening after work. The night patrol ranger stopped by to alert me to a problem. Tipped off by an anonymous caller, he had found water hoses connected from a park residence leading to several 55-gallon steel drums containing marijuana plants.

The next morning, Chief Ranger Reinhardt and I went to the residence and confirmed the report. We confronted the employee and he admitted guilt. Not only that, but he also expressed knowledge of the discovery of another 1200 plant garden in the Bull Creek drainage that he was considering taking plants from for sale. He had previous knowledge of that garden and had told no one on staff about it until now. The employee was a good worker and a friend so this turn of events was not only shocking, but also hurtful. Ted and I talked to the employee and his wife and told them that we would do all we could to help them, but also we would have to report this illegal activity. The employee was distraught and handed us his keys saying he was quitting. We refused the keys and told him do nothing until things were sorted out.

Unfortunately, things did not turn out too well for him. While he continued to work for us he and his wife became embittered when charges of illegal growing were brought against him. They apparently had assumed we would not press charges. As peace officers we had no choice. The day came when the employee's wife charged into the office and threw her husband's keys at me and said something to the effect that they would get even with me for cheating on the lumber mill examination. I had no idea what she was talking about as she stormed out of the office waving an envelope she said, "would do me in". After working out a deal between his attorney and the judge, the employee eventually resigned and went to work for another agency.

Again some time passed, when one evening I received a call from one of the lumber mill operators saying that he had received a telephone call from an investigator with the State Personnel Board (SPB). The SPB had received a letter alleging improprieties with the examination that had been given earlier (maybe a year previous) and was asking a lot of questions. Most of those questions dealt with my role and that of the maintenance supervisor in providing answers to the examination question. Now I knew what had been in the envelope that had been waved in my face!

The SPB investigation went on for some time. The Maintenance Supervisor and I were dragged in for questioning. While I had the full support of our Region Headquarters and my staff the situation was getting very serious. I could be fired for this. I simply could not believe that the SPB would not believe me and was taking the word of the employee and his wife over mine. I became very despondent and depressed over the matter.

The investigation seemed to go on and on. The Lumber Mill Operators were dismissed (they had done nothing wrong) and a gloom settled over the District. I must confess I had reached the depth of despair. I could not concentrate at work, could not sleep at home, and worried constantly. I was barely managing the park. Thank goodness for my Chief Ranger Ted and Supervising Ranger Jim Burke who stepped in to "cover for me". They were not only good employees, but also, the best of supportive friends. They recognized my depression and did everything to try and cheer me up. Even today they will tell you that they succeeded in getting me drunk to drown my sorrows (It didn't happen and I'm sticking to my story!). Ted became so concerned that he even called the Regional Office to complain about the investigation and the length of time it was taking. He told Assistant Regional Director Buschke that I thought I was going to be fired and had gone home depressed and upset. Ted was told to go over to my house and tell me in no uncertain terms that I was not going to be dismissed. That was the best news I had in several months.

The Region Office was doing battle with SPB to prevent my dismissal. I couldn't believe this was happening to me. Finally, a decision came down on my case. I was to be placed on a one-year probation and could not participate as a panel member on any State

Examination during that time. I had been a panel member on many statewide examinations and enjoyed this activity. It was an opportunity to interact with the new employees that would soon be coming into the Department and employees that would be promoting.

I had done no wrong. Should I appeal the decision or live with this stain on my otherwise unblemished record? My home life and my work had suffered. I decided to forego the appeal process and get on with life. Many times during the year I would receive requests to be on different examination boards. Since I had been barred from doing this I refused the requests without explanation, sometimes leaving the caller baffled as to why this sudden change in attitude. A new examination was given for the Lumber Mill Operator position. Of course the same three lumber mill operators came out number one, two, and three on the new hiring list and they were all reinstated to their former positions.

A year later I was to receive some satisfaction for the action taken against me by the SPB. In 1985 the Department of Parks and Recreation established a "Superintendent of the Year" award. I was the recipient of that very first award. Though the award was given to me by DPR, the State Personnel Board sanctioned it and the accompanying monetary reward that came with it. I do not know if it was a case of the right hand not knowing what the left hand was doing but the SPB, the very agency that had tried to fire me a year earlier, was now rewarding me for my management performance. It was the sweetest moment of my career.

CAREER DEVELOPMENT

When the Department reorganized in 1984 and established the new Northern Regional Office and Park Districts, the Northern Region was fortunate to have Curt Mitchell as our Regional Director. His office was in Santa Rosa.

Curt was very supportive of interpretive activities and visitor centers in our parks. In fact, so much so that when he became Regional Director he sent out a Directive that had as one of his goals the establishment of a visitor center or information station at each park within the Northern Region. The Eel River District had met that goal with a few exceptions, one of those exceptions being Grizzly Creek Redwoods State Park.

Ranger Rick Johnson was the Unit Ranger at Grizzly Creek. Originally, when I had arrived in the Dyerville Area, Rick had been assigned to Humboldt Redwoods. He was the first Executive Secretary of the Humboldt Redwoods Interpretive Association and the key person in obtaining its incorporation certification. Later he transferred to Grizzly Creek. There too, he established an interpretive association but, with only himself and one other maintenance person as full-time employees, it did not seem likely that he could build a visitor center as we had done at Humboldt Redwoods - but we could try!

I told Rick I thought we could do it. We had the lumber from the sawmill, we could get CCC help again, and I could divert some staff from HRSP to help also. Since I assumed the Directive from Region had given us tacit permission to proceed, I told Rick to go ahead and come up with some plans. He did, and together with Maintenance Worker Don Gray and help from the CCC the visitor center was built. Again, we did not tell Headquarters what we were doing. Why should we, they wanted it didn't they?

The VC that was built at Grizzly Creek was a two-story structure that was added onto the existing, standard park office building. It was a little larger than I had anticipated for a small park. I guess Rick just got carried away. It was built without any engineering plans or "in house" review of CEQA (California Environmental Quality Act). We went back and got that after the fact. It was strictly another "bootleg" job. In any event, when it was completed I called Curt up on the telephone and told him to come up and have a look.

Curt met me at the District Office in HRSP and we drove to Grizzly Creek. On the way over we struck up a conversation, which was sometimes hard to do with Curt because he tended to be a man of few words. At some point he asked, "Carl, what are your future career goals?" Without much thought or pause, and a bit flippantly, I blurted out, "I want your job!" I think Curt was a little taken aback by my response which was given half in jest. In truth, except for the SPB incident I was quite happy with my present assignment.

If Curt was surprised by my response to his question he was even more shocked when we drove into Grizzly Creek and he saw the visitor center. He had not expected to see a two-story visitor center of this magnitude in such a tiny park. He asked about permits and CEQA and I mumbled something like, "I thought we already had the approval through the Regional Directive." Anyway, after he inspected the visitor center and the displays inside he seemed satisfied and pleased with the results. I never heard anymore about that visitor center from my boss after that.

Later that year Curt was set to retire but because there was a vacancy in our Sacramento Headquarters he was asked to temporarily fill in as Chief of the Operations Division. This left the Northern Regional Director position vacant.

I had been in the Redwoods now for almost eight years. That was long enough for Abby to complete high school and Chris to reach his junior year. But Chris would be away in Denmark for his senior year as a Rotary Exchange Student. There would be no family conflict with a move this time if I should be lucky enough get the job. Also with the Region Office in Santa Rosa we would be close to Margaret's family home where she grew up in Sonoma County.

Several of us applied for the position and interviews were scheduled. When I arrived at the interview site in Sacramento I found that Curt and two others were on the interview panel. Of course, the inevitable interview question, "Why do you want this job?" was asked. I knew I could not answer, "Because I like people and the outdoors, etc.." It wouldn't work this time. Instead I pulled out a piece of paper from my jacket pocket.

In preparation for the interview I had made a list of shortcomings and needs for the Region that I had seen from my perspective as a District Superintendent. I had not expected my former boss to be on the panel. In effect, my list was a mildly critical analysis of his operation (it really wasn't that bad). Well, I figured Humboldt Redwoods wasn't such a bad place to live so I went ahead and discussed the list with the panel, outlining what I would do differently. Curt, professional that he is didn't even bat an eye. I went away from the interview not knowing how I had done or what to expect.

A few days later I was in Eureka, where I had taken my first State Park Ranger examination 20 years earlier (almost to the day). I was attending a "Career Development" class that was being presented by our Sacramento Headquarters Training Section. About midway through the session I was handed a note to telephone the Director of State Parks immediately. I got up and left the meeting to make the call. The Director told me that I had been selected for the new Northern Regional Director position. My response was, "You've got to be kidding." It was the Director's last day on the job and it appeared that I was one of those "Midnight Appointments" one hears about in government. I was to serve at the pleasure of the next Director to take office. I think I was more stunned than happy.

My time in the Redwoods was over. May 1,1979 to March 31,1987 had been good years.

REDWOOD SKETCHES

Carl S. Chavez

AN UNEXPLORED REGION

The eight years we had lived in the redwoods had been the longest that Margaret and I had stayed in one place since we were married and I had begun my career with the California State Park System. In three of the five previous moves we had lived in State Park housing. Now the kids were starting to leave the nest. Chris was off to Denmark for his high school senior year and Abby was away at college. It was now or never to make the biggest career decision of my life. At least now we would have the opportunity to purchase our own home for the first time. It was an idea we could embrace with pleasure.

So it was on April 1, 1987, that I was appointed Northern Regional Director (RD). I wondered if there was hidden meaning in the fact that I was starting on April Fool's Day. The worst part about my appointment was the fact that I would have to live out of suitcase in a motel for several months until Margaret and I were able to find a permanent place to live. Also until I was able to appoint my replacement in the Eel River District, I would be going back and forth between Humboldt Redwoods and Santa Rosa every week. The 5-hour drive is a pleasant one in daylight but I never did like the night drive on Friday evenings.

Speaking of drives and vehicles, I did have a strange incident occur while staying at a motel near the Region Office. For some inexplicable reason, the regional directors were assigned big white Ford LTD sedans with "undercover" license plates and gasoline credit cards with fictitious business company names on them. The problem with the "undercover" cars was that they stuck out like sore thumbs with their blackwall tires (low bid) and almost anyone who cared could recognize them for what they were. I couldn't have had better proof of this when one night there was a knocking at my motel door and a young women asked if I was police officer. She said she had seen my car and assumed it was an "undercover" car because "it was like all the other ones." She wanted to report a drug operation in a room next to hers. I explained that I was a Peace Officer, but perhaps in this instance we should call the local Santa Rosa Police Department to respond to her concerns. She explained that she would have done that but upon recognizing my car as an "undercover" vehicle she thought I might have been part of a police sting operation. We called the police.

The initials "RD" could stand for a lot of things. In my case they stood for Regional Director. Others might say they stood for "Real Dumb". I had left the safety and security of a wonderful job "in the field" to enter into the world of management, far removed from the lifestyle I had grown to love. With my appointment I became one of the youngest Regional Directors in the Department's history and would be following in the footsteps of icons of the California State Park System. It was a very humbling thought.

The Northern Region, with its headquarters in Santa Rosa, was comprised of eleven Districts and some 80 units stretching from Angel Island in the south to Pelican Beach at the Oregon border and from Mendocino Headlands in the west to Ahjumawi Lava Springs in the east. Geographically it was the largest of the five Regions in the State. The most immediate effect my appointment to Regional Director had upon me was a dramatic change in mind set. Where once I was dealing only occasionally with my fellow superintendents as peers, I was now suddenly thrust into a leadership role as their immediate supervisor.

If anything was certain upon starting this new phase of my career it was the sure knowledge that I had the support of the "Troops in the Field". Calls from well wishers were frequent and a boost that helped calm the butterflies in my stomach.

Without question the move into the Regional Office in Santa Rosa could have been much more difficult for me had it not been for those around me in supporting roles. First and foremost were the Superintendents of the eleven Districts in the Northern Region. One moment we were peers and the next I was without peers. The ability of the superintendents to make this shift seemed easier for them then it was for me. I think this stems from the fact that I was always task and goal oriented and could initiate something and see that it was concluded in a timely fashion. Now I felt that I was in a supporting and advisory role and the superintendents really had the more enjoyable job and could see the direct results of their programs.

As Superintendent of the Eel River District, I was always in a friendly, even playful competition, for resources with the other Districts. Every superintendent wanted the same thing: the best programs, the most funding, the best personnel, and the fastest filling of vacant positions. Still, as I said before, in times of crisis all bets were off and we helped each other without question. Now that I was Regional Director I immediately had to switch my thinking totally away from competition and into a mind set of cooperation. As Regional Director, I could play no favorites among the districts. Even my old Eel River District must now compete on fair terms with the other ten Districts.

Within three months of my appointment there were several retirements and promotions in some of the districts that allowed me to select the replacement superintendents. At least I hoped all of the vacancies weren't a result of my appointment. I preferred not to see a cause/effect relationship! In any event the Mendocino, Cascade, Klamath Districts, and of course my old Eel River District, all had new superintendents. I was grateful that I had been able to put together a team that meshed well with the other incumbent superintendents of the Northern Region.

It was my management style to adapt my methods of operation to the style and idiosyncrasies of the individual superintendent in a particular District rather than requiring them to meet my style. I figured it was easier for one person to adapt than eleven. Thus, when Dave Bartlett of Mendocino would telephone, I knew immediately when he said, "Chief" (He **always** called me Chief), that we would first have five or ten minutes of friendly joking and bantering before we got down to business. If Bill Beat called, which he often did, sometimes several times a day, it was not to ask for advice or funding, but rather to keep me informed of the many on-going projects he was so proud of. Others, like Marin District Superintendent Ron Brean, rarely called and that was not of much concern to me as I was well aware of his programs and competence. There were a few I checked on regularly to ensure we were on the same page. Each and every one of them was great to work with, and they and their staffs made great contributions in carrying out the Department's Mission which is: "To provide for the health, inspiration, and education of the people of California by helping preserve the state's extraordinary biological diversity, protecting its most valued natural and cultural resources and creating opportunities for high-quality outdoor recreation."

Park Superintendents, as a whole are very resourceful and creative people. If in the 1970's we had developed into "Renaissance Ranger's," in the mid-1980's we were developing some very bright "Sophisticated Superintendents" who were now becoming public relations specialists and quickly learning the ins and outs of politics and special interest groups. We were no longer in the era of the "Good 'Ol Days" but rather in a period of much greater responsibility and accountability.

Assistant Regional Director Dale Buschke, who gently eased me in and guided me in my first couple of months on the job before he too retired, helped my transition into the role of Regional Director. It was several months after Dale's retirement before I was able to fill his vacant position, so I had plenty of opportunity for my own extended period of self-taught, on-job-training. When I was finally able to select Ted Crane as my assistant, all was in place for a productive seven years in Region.

It is said that behind every successful man there is a woman. That was certainly true in my case and Margaret was my loving proof of this relationship. I found it also true that behind every successful manager there is a dedicated and efficient secretary. Jan Thompson filled that role for me. She was fast, efficient and energetic on the job, but I must admit that I was most impressed by her ability to shop and accomplish so many personal errands on a one-hour lunch break that would take most people a week to do. How she did it, speeding across town without ever getting a ticket, is beyond me. Ted, the Assistant Regional Director, possessor of photographic memory, was the best "completed staff work" person I ever had the pleasure to work with. As long as he had his October hunting trip to the Rocky Mountains, he was happy. Without Ted things would have been tough as he filled the void when the parade of Administrative Officers changed from Larry Hill to Kathy Ryan to Tom Ward. Ted should have been called Peter, for he was The Rock (well, with his physical stature maybe only a pebble). Don Ito was our quiet, unassuming Visitor Services Manager with an easy disposition. It was a joy to be around Don and to take afternoon walks around the block to get the kinks out. For excitement there was always Technical Services Manager Jim Hart, a legend unto himself, who we will hear more about later. Rick Royer was our Interpretive Specialist who was the epitome of persistence. Once a fine field ranger, he and his family had been involved in a serious automobile accident that had injured Rick to the extent that he could no longer perform peace officer duties. With strength, and a will of self-determination, he recovered from his injuries and we were able to accommodate him in the Region Office as the interpretive specialist. Vic Maris, on the other hand, made the conversion in the other direction, moving from Interpretive Specialist to Safety and Enforcement Specialist where he was very effective in revitalizing that section.

Our Resource staff of historian, ecologists and archeologist were, for me, the most interesting to work with. More than any other staff members they were, for the most part, single focused individuals and advocates of their discipline. The exception was Breck Parkman, the archeologist, who is such a thoughtful and dedicated person and thinker that he had the ability to see all sides of an issue. I much valued his input and advice on matters even outside of his area of expertise. In any event, I saw it as my job to help staff see the big picture on issues that increasingly seemed to require "losing the battle to win the war" when politics and special interest group pressure was added to the mix. Even in disagreement, however, I never questioned their motives. They **always** held the interest of the resource at heart and caused me to pause on any decision that directly affected and/or impacted the cultural or natural resources of our units.

Overall it was a great staff to work with in Northern Region Headquarters but it would be naive to think that some problems didn't exist. After all, it seems to be human nature to have some "office politics" in every profession with the resultant cliques that seem to form from time to time. These little "bumps in the road" were usually of short duration and a distraction that occasionally turned out to be quite humorous. For example, one time an employee was having a problem with another employee and her supervisor in the administrative section. The physical layout of the office was such that there were several desks in a row, one behind the other, maybe five feet between them. The upset individual instead of turning around to talk to the person behind her about the problem actually telephoned requesting an appointment for a meeting. It was hard to take that kind of situation seriously.

But overall it was an excellent staff and I enjoyed working with all of them. I could tolerate the idiosyncrasies of individuals if they could tolerate me. Without peers close by I had no other choice. There were bigger problems ahead than a five foot telephone call!

HOME IS WHERE THE HEART IS

The move from Humboldt Redwoods State Park to Northern Region Headquarters in Santa Rosa gave me pause to reflect on the wonderful places our family had resided in State Parks. True we now had a home in Windsor that we could at last call our own but it lacked the unmatched real estate of park lands. Here are some of my thoughts on the subject.

When a park employee tells a visitor, acquaintance, friend or relative that he or she lives in "State" housing, the usual reaction is one of envy. The thought of residing in an area of idyllic natural surroundings sounds too good to be true. That can be, and is often true, but it can also come with a price.

Living in a park is a subject of much debate within the ranks of park employees who will argue the "pros and cons" of such habitation endlessly. To be sure there are some benefits such as relatively cheap rent and utilities, prime real estate locations and an opportunity for that idyllic lifestyle we all dream about. On the other hand there is the downside of things such as "living in a fish bowl", never off duty, no equity in a place of your own and sometimes substandard living conditions.

I have lived in park housing in five of the nine locations I was assigned. Those five were at Bodie SHP, Morro Bay SP, Cuyamaca Rancho SP, Plumas-Eureka SP, and Humboldt Redwoods SP. Each of these locations offered some of the pros and some of the cons I referred to above. Let me take you into our homes to give you some examples of the expected and unexpected consequences of living with the job.

BODIE SHP, RESIDENCE #1

You have read of my experience and the difficulty Margaret and I had moving into our home in Bodie. Originally built on the corner of Park & Green Streets for the town banker, James Stuart Cain, in the 1890's, it had undergone some modification over the years in order to make it more habitable for more recent residents like me. Among other things, we now had propane heat and a propane-cooking stove with a wood burner on the side. One of the unique features of the J.S. Cain House is the front porch that has been glassed in to give a sunny atrium effect to the structure. When we lived in Bodie the shelves on the porch were stocked with purple glass bottles that had been found in the area. The sunlight shinning through the greenhouse-like panes gave a sparkle and color to the otherwise drab exterior of the structure. I cataloged and accessioned all of the bottles, including those I found and added to the collection but they are no longer on display and I do not know what happened to them. Perhaps most missed from the collection is a beautifully shaped translucent, purple urinal that always attracted the most interest from visitors.

Additionally, one of the rooms had been converted in to a park office so that commuting to work only required walking from one room into another. There was a fireplace in the parlor but it was not safe to use. The two-story house could not be adequately heated in winter because of the many large rooms with high ceilings. We normally "lived" in the kitchen because it was the warmest room with wood burning constantly in the trash burner attached to the stove. There was no insulation in the walls, only "Celotex" fiberboard added to the walls in some rooms and sheets of plastic storm window material covering the windows in the winter. Despite this, if a blizzard were blowing, the snow would accumulate on the inside of the window sills. Additionally, the snow would accumulate, drift and slide off the roof to such a depth on the outside that it would completely cover the dining room window and one of the kitchen windows making the house eerily dark in the day time. We had no telephone or television and only limited radio reception from one station during the day and a second one at night. We got all of this for $22/month including utilities but for sure there were times when we thought even this was too much!

When we first moved in to Bodie we did not have much in the way of worldly possessions. We had neither refrigerator nor freezer. During the coldest winter months any frozen items we had we placed in a screened cupboard in an outside anteroom that was attached to the kitchen. The cold temperatures were sometimes as low as -30°F and frequently did not rise above freezing during the day so that nature's freezer served us well in keeping food frozen.

As for preserving other perishable foods we used an old traditional method. There was a trap door in the floor of the kitchen with steps leading down to a root cellar. Temperatures stayed at a relatively constant temperature of about 40°F year round. Our solution was to place food in plastic containers that would keep the mice and pack rats out of the food and then place the containers on the steps leading down to the cellar. This probably wouldn't have met public health standards but it worked out fine for us until the spring thaw arrived.

When we moved into the house in late October we had noticed some unusual plumbing and electrical wiring in the root cellar. Since nobody at Bodie at the time, other than the previous occupant knew anything about the house or it's systems we were not aware that there was a sump pump buried in the floor of the root cellar. Later we were to learn that the sump pump was supposed to operate automatically when water reached a certain level. We were also unaware that the pump was out of order.

The root cellar was about 8' x 8' x 8'. Imagine our surprise one morning in the spring as the snow was melting when we opened the trap door to find we had an indoor swimming pool! All the containers were floating about and water was within 4" of the kitchen floor. Now I understood what that recently uncovered hose that had been buried all winter protruding from the exterior kitchen wall was for. It took my first trip to Plumas-Eureka SP that spring to borrow a sump pump before the problem was rectified.

Bodie was also the first place we lived where we had that all-to-frequent job hazard of people walking right into the house as we sat down for dinner. Because of the outward condition of the J.S. Cain House, visitors could not always tell which houses were occupied and which were "ghost" abodes. Park visitors were forever peering in through the windows to catch a glimpse of the past. On one occasion a young man peeking into our kitchen called out to his mother, "Hey look, this in these times". We took delight on occasion in sneaking up to the window and scaring the daylights out of the peaking intruders.

The carpets in the J.S. Cain House were threadbare but most of the house was furnished with original furniture that even by standards of 1966-67 would be classified as valuable antiques. I spent much of the winter cataloging and accessioning all of the furnishings in each room. The shame of it is that some of it was missing when we made a return visit in the late 1970's. Though I'm sure a park employee stole some items we were unsuccessful in proving that point. Somewhere, perhaps in a home down near Mono Lake, sits a cherry wood rocking chair that we spent many pleasant hours in while enjoying the Bodie experience.

"Our" Bodie house is perhaps the only home we have lived in that may have been haunted. Many stories of ghosts abound. Most centered on tales of candles glowing in an upstairs window when no one was home. The only "proof" of this that I ever noted was the shoe print embedded in the glass of one windowpane where perhaps a ghost had left its mark! It gives different meaning to that park saying, "take only pictures, leave only footprints"

MORRO BAY SP, RESIDENCE #2

After a hiatus of 4 years we were back in State Housing. This time we were living in a "standard" state park house. These homes were built to a set plan and were and still are seen in many units of the State Park System.

Originally built as two bedroom homes, many of them were modified for expanding families by converting a laundry room into a third "bedroom".

Our house at Morro Bay was of the original two bedroom variety. It was situated in a nice location, with a fenced yard, the back of which abutted the park maintenance yard fence. It was also located further, and somewhat concealed, from the campground check station and thus not subject to the intrusion of the park visitors when I was off duty. We were able to have a garden and enjoy the benefits of living in a park with easy walks with our children to the tidal flats or the adjacent golf course after it closed in the evening. We could also stroll or ride our bicycles "incognito" through the campground to enjoy the sights and smells of campfires, camp food, and people having a good time.

Living in the park at Morro Bay was my first real experience having a lot of park employees as neighbors. My next door neighbor was John Myers who I now supervised. He is the Ranger I replaced at Bodie when I first was hired. Later, after John retired, Ken Leigh was my neighbor. Ken was to work for me later at Plumas-Eureka and again when he was Superintendent of the Marin District parks. A memory of our time together there was taking care of his eldest daughter Stacy on the night that his youngest daughter Kassie was born.

There really were few negatives living at Morro Bay. "Call-outs" from the local police department for the many false burglar alarms at the museum were more a nuisance than a hazard, the occasional rescue on Morro Rock only added excitement to the job, and taking care of fledgling birds was our little part in helping nature's critters. All in all, I could live there again.

CUYAMACA PEAK GATE HOUSE, RESIDENCE #7

It is an odd experience to move several hundred miles from one house to another and find yourself looking at a home that is almost the exact mirror image of the place you just left. That was the case when we moved from Morro Bay to Cuyamaca Rancho SP, in the mountains east of San Diego. It was the same house except the laundry room had been modified into another tiny bedroom. Otherwise, it was essentially the same floor plan reversed. We told the moving company employees to remember where everything was when they loaded the truck in Morro Bay and put things in the same place in our new home. It was a very easy move for us.

Again we were fortunate to have this house. It was located back off the highway, not too far from the maintenance shop. A paved fire road, behind a locked gate, was located behind the house. This road led up to the fire lookout on Cuyamaca Peak. Though campers and hikers often took the road up to the lookout it was far enough away to be of little distraction. Our house was certainly in a better location then the dreaded "gate house" at the entrance to the Paso Picahco Campground where its occupant was sure to be in constant demand on or off the job.

Wildlife viewing was a plus at this location. We often would see many birds, deer, bobcat and coyotes in the yard. Of course the raccoons would come right up on the porch and beg for food while peering in the front window. They were most upsetting to our cat "Lumper" who disliked this impingement upon his territory. Lumper was the off spring of our wayward Morro Bay cat. If Lumper had gotten outside the raccoons would have made short work of him.

Winter at Cuyamaca sometimes did pose some problems for us. For one thing, when it snowed it seemed like all of Southern California would decide to come to the park. Highway 79, which bisects the park, winds it way over the summit at Paso Pichaco, just below our house. There were many accidents there that we had to respond to. The winter of 1974 we had several feet of snow during one storm that pretty much paralyzed park operations for a day or two. Apparently it paralyzed the brains of some of our visitors too as they went about their snow play. Coming home one evening I found a lady who had an urgent "call from nature" squatting in my parking space next to our house relieving herself. That sort of thing takes the idyllic out of the home equation.

One of the most memorable incidents I recall at Residence #7 involved a day off. I was relaxing at home in my easy chair when the telephone rang. It was the Area Manager on the telephone telling me to rush over to the adjacent maintenance shop to help an injured employee. The employee had called down to the Area Office, which was located several miles down the road, and requested assistance stating that he had hurt himself working on a chain saw. You can imagine what went through everyone's mind on hearing this. The Area manager could give me no other details, as the employee had sounded somewhat confused.

I immediately bounded out of the chair and ran over to the shop. On entering the room where the employee had been working I observed a chain saw resting on a workbench and the employee standing there with blood running all over his hand and down his arm. I made the same assumption that everyone else had made and so I immediately leaped into action and grabbed an oily rag that was laying on the work bench, wrapped it around the employee's hand, and applied pressure to staunch the flow of blood.

Next I hustled the employee, who did not appear to be in shock, into a vehicle and started down the road to the nearest medical services about 30 miles away. As I raced down the road I radioed the Area Office to tell them that we were enroute to the hospital for treatment of a severe hand wound. It was only at this point that all of us learned that the accident was not a direct result of a chain saw cut. Though indeed the wound was deep and dangerous, it was caused by a knife and not the action of the saw. It seems the employee was slicing down the length of a garden hose in order to make a safety cover for the chain saw when the knife slipped and cut his hand. It turned out that this was the "Chain Saw Massacre That Wasn't" and in the end the employee survived despite my first aid.

The house at Cuyamaca was also a reminder to me of those who had lived there previously. Each house is filled with the memories of park employees who may have proceeded the present occupant(s). One day while I was cleaning the detached garage of Residence #7 I chanced to look high up on the wall between two studs and noticed an area that had obviously been sealed off for some unknown purpose. I got a ladder and climbed to check it out. I was able to pry off a board and peer into the cubbyhole between the studs. Inside was a treasure trove of "stuff". A couple of old "Beaches & Parks" half moon patches, a soapstone carving of a bear, some papers, one of which had the name "Vaught" on it and a few other miscellaneous trinkets. My guess, though I have never verified it, is that the children of long retired Ranger Lew Vaught, had secreted these items many years before we moved into the home. After examining the items I resealed the chamber. I wonder if they are still there to be discovered by another generation of rangers?

JOHNSVILLE, RESIDENCE #2

You will note that I indicated this home is located in Johnsville, not Plumas-Eureka SP. That is because the old gold mining town of Johnsville is actually a private in-holding, surrounded by the park. The house was purchased by the State from Ora White, a grand old lady, who was still the rural mail delivery person when I arrived on assignment. For our family, living in Johnsville was the "Shangri-La" of our park experience. I have previously written of family life in Johnsville. It was everything and more we could have asked for in a place to live.

Residence #2 is a large two, no actually three, story house. The ground floor is a two-stall garage with the living room, kitchen, bath and two bedrooms on the second floor and another bedroom, great room and bathroom on the upper level. A large porch surrounds two sides of the house. The best thing about the house was the living room window that extended across the entire front room and faced the rising sun. This was especially appreciated in the winter when sunlight was at a premium and to be cherished. One year we marked the windows each week so we could track the progress of the sun as it rose on its annual solar journey across the heavens. The worst thing about the house was that the roof slope of the house dumped all the snowfall off the roof directly in front of the garage doors. The snow would accumulate so fast that you could walk from the street level up the roof created snowdrift and look into the second story windows. It sometimes took a lot of shoveling or tractor work to get our cars out of the garage.

The next best thing about the house was the kitchen (if you disregarded its bright pink color). It was large and roomy and as in the Bodie house we tended to congregate and spend a lot of time in that kitchen. What was bad about the kitchen was the ant problem. Millions of ants hid behind the sink cabinets, stove and refrigerator; we could never entirely get rid of them. They didn't get into the food, but they wandered around and over whatever was on the counters. When one was stepped on or died by other means, within minutes there would be a dozen or more other ants on hand to carry off the body. These were big black carpenter ants, so it is surprising to me that the house is still standing and in use.

The very best thing the Johnsville house had going for it as far as I was concerned was its location. We were in God's Country, with fishing at our doorstep, a short walk to work and a town that came to life each summer and was "returned" to us each winter. It is that experience that prompted us to return to this area in retirement

If I recall correctly, we paid rent of less than $100.month including utilities. That was a bargain. On the other hand, unless one was frugal, it was easy to waste those savings on less needed items and fail to plan ahead for the future. In our case we used our savings to purchase some land in Plumas County and made payments just as if we were living in the real world with real house payments.

Later in my career I was to see employees retire who had lived their entire career in State housing with nowhere or no home to retire to because their housing windfall had taken advantage of them instead of vice/versa. This squandering of finances in the end would lead to some sad endings to otherwise wonderful careers.

HUMBOLDT REDWOODS , RESIDENCE #1

For shear beauty of location you could not beat Residence #1 at Humboldt Redwoods SP. Known as the Chapman House, for the original private owner of the home, it had been purchased by the State as an employee residence. It is located next to the Burlington Campground, separated from it by Robinson Creek, whose Dogwood lined banks provide a beautiful screen from the sounds and sights of a busy campground. It was a short walk across a small footbridge to the park headquarters where I had my office.

The entrance to our "estates and garden" was spectacular to say the least. A turn off of the Avenue of the Giants brought you up a long driveway lined with towering redwood trees, many of which were more than 12 feet in diameter and over 300 feet tall. The house itself was surrounded on three sides by redwood trees but the front was open to a clearing with a circle driveway. There was a large orchard with apple, pear and cherry trees that were beautiful when in bloom and tasty in maturity. It was a 3-bedroom home with wonderful, though dark redwood paneling on the interior. It was that darkness that we would come to dislike in winter when the sun was low in the sky and we were starved for the little sunlight the tall redwoods blocked from our sight. One of the most interesting things about the house was its wonderful stone fireplace.   Apparently Mr. Chapman was a gem/stone collector and, in fact, for years had, or may still has, a rock shop along Highway 101 near the town of Fortuna.   The fireplace was a masterpiece of stonework.   It had matched stones on both sides of the hearth comprised of semi-precious rocks such as jade, turquoise, and quartz as well as more common river worn stones of chert.   Also embedded and worked into the design were two Native American pestles.   The large, wide mantle was made of fine slate and served as the warm roost for newly acquired cat "Cricket".

Adjacent to the main house was another smaller building that had apparently served as a workroom at some point.   It had a bathroom and we were able to convert the building into a guest house and seasonal quarters complete with kitchen.   Because of the large clearing the house was situated in, there was plenty of room for other activities.   I was able to have a fenced garden and chicken coop area.   Later we used much of the area as a storage yard for the lumber produced from the park's own saw mill operation.

The downside of living here was the dark, damp dreariness of the rainy winter, which tended to make for a dreary disposition.   That, coupled with the striped skunks that took up residence under the house, could make living conditions that were less then ideal.

Most of the time the location was such that noise wasn't a problem, either from the campground, the Avenue of the Giants, or US 101 that was high up on a bank behind the house.   However there was one memorable night I will never forget when the night stillness of the redwoods was shattered by the sound of gunshots seemingly directed at us.

We were sound asleep when a series of gunshots sounded.   The shots were near enough that even in the house we flinched.   The sound woke all of us up and I immediately told everyone to keep their lights off while I quickly dressed and put on my enforcement gear.   It was around 3:00 am when I went out the door. I ducked as more shots were fired, but it was impossible to determine exactly where they were coming from, though they seemed to be going over the house. I got into my park vehicle but did not turn on the headlights as I drove toward the campground. I wasn't at all surprised to find Rangers Reinhardt, Hardcastle and Ash already gathered together discussing what to do next. No one had called each other out; we had all just naturally met in the same place. They also thought that the shots had been aimed in their direction. We concluded that the shots, that were continuing, were coming from somewhere up on the freeway.

We decided to split into two teams with one team driving south to Myers Flat and getting on the freeway there to head north. The other two drove north to Weott and got on the freeway to drive south. We met on the freeway at a location roughly above where I lived and we saw a car on the shoulder of the freeway with a person leaning across the hood of the car with a rifle.

Approaching cautiously we quickly realized that the shooter was not sober. Fortunately for us, he was a "friendly drunk". We confiscated his rifle and arrested him. When questioned he told us that he was firing the rifle because "he loved to hear the sound of the echo reverberating across the mountains". I pointed out to him that it was also reverberating off my bedroom walls in the house down the bank below where his car was parked. Perhaps he sobered up a bit on the ride to jail. Such is the life of a Ranger in park housing!

It was over 21 years since we had first moved into State Housing at Bodie. We did not purchase a home of our own until after we left Humboldt Redwoods in 1987 and moved to the Santa Rosa area. Don and Nancy Hoyle followed us to Humboldt Redwoods and were the last occupants of the Chapman house. They kept up the house, grounds and orchards until they left with the Department's reorganization in 1993. With their departure, reduced budgets, and a general movement of staff out of park housing due to rising rents and utility costs and a desire to own their own homes, the residence was converted into an office facility for trail maintenance crews. Residence #1 has since fallen into a state of disrepair, and the grounds have taken on the appearance of a slum that belies what once was. It is a disservice to all who have lived there.

PERSONAL OR PERSONNEL ?

Sometimes when you are dealing with personnel issues, things can get personal. In my job as Regional Director I found myself in the inevitable position of often having to conduct "Skelly Hearings". This is an appeal hearing for an employee who has had some adverse action taken against him or her. It is the employee's opportunity to present his/her case before the action goes on to the State Personnel Board. As Hearing Officer I would have the opportunity to take no action or modify the action by either increasing or decreasing the severity of the punishment.

Because of my own personal experience when charges were made against me, I was very sensitive to the feelings of employees, who often felt they had done no wrong. Because of this I was careful not to become involved in the direct investigation of allegations until I conducted the Skelly Hearing. Other Region or District employees would conduct the initial investigation, usually under the direction of Assistant Regional Director, Ted Crane or his predecessor Dale Buschke.

What I found interesting about this process was that it always seemed easier to reach a decision on the more serious transgressions. If an employee was to be dismissed or receive a demotion, the investigations often seemed so clear cut that I could quickly make my decision. On the other hand, I agonized over the comparatively trivial personnel actions that might result in only a Letter of Reprimand that would later be removed from the individual's personnel file. Of course, to the individual named in the action, none of this was trivial.

The hearings that I conducted while I was in the Region Office covered the entire gamut of human follies, with the exception of murder (Thank Goodness!). I talked with employees, and often their union representatives and/or attorneys who tried bluff, brashness, sympathy, humor, remorse, and yes, even honesty. At one hearing I was even served lemonade and cookies! I also conducted hearings where I was concerned for my safety. On two occasions I placed my service revolver in my desk drawer and told another employee to stand by in the next office just in case. As in every line of employment, not all employees are emotionally stable. Take for instance the employee who made it a practice to telephone either Ted Crane or me at home or at the office on the anniversary date of his dismissal and say some not very nice things about our ancestry. I guess that person finally got over his anger since I haven't had a call from him since I retired (I hope he's not reading this book.).

Then there was an employee who was facing dismissal and decided to call me at home late at night. I'm sure you know the feeling: the telephone rings at 2:00 am and awakens you from a sound sleep. That's bad enough, but then all I hear on the other end of the line is a very heavy, menacing breathing, and finally silence when the individual hangs up. Of course my adrenaline is flowing and my heart is pounding. I can't go back to sleep. "It's okay, dear. Go back to sleep," I tell Margaret. Minutes, hours (?), go by and the telephone rings again. The same thing happens. Finally the telephone rings a third time and I am really mad. In my pounding heart I know who this is. I shout into the telephone, "Okay, ******, I know what you're up to, cut it out" (or not so nice words to that effect). This time a voice, "Dad?" It is my son Chris calling from London where he is attending college. It's about noon in London and he forgot the time difference. At least this was a call we gladly accepted. I slept better after that.

The very first Skelly Hearing I conducted, only a few days after I arrived at Region was interesting too because what seemed like an open and shut case on the surface, raised some interesting questions for me about one District operation. It seems that an employee had been AWOL from the job for over two weeks. The staff at this District conducted an investigation and filed the appropriate action against the employee. What did not come out until the hearing was that the District staff where the employee worked didn't even know the employee was missing until after he returned to work! At least at Plumas-Eureka SP when no one noticed my absence, I had been away on approved vacation. I wasn't sure if I should sustain this action or initiate new action against his supervisor. Was he so over staffed that he couldn't keep track of his employees? I think I ended up disciplining both employee and supervisor.

I had a rather embarrassing hearing on another occasion involving poor driving. An employee had had a series of vehicle accidents over the coarse of a few years. Many of them were not serious, but all had caused damage either to the State vehicle or a private vehicle or property. There were about one dozen documented accidents. As a matter of convenience for the employee and his/her representative I agreed to meet them at another park midway between the Region and the employee's unit. I left the day before the scheduled hearing and stayed overnight in a nearby town. In the morning I decided to drive into one of the nearby parks for an inspection tour since I had plenty of time before the hearing. Upon leaving the park I collided with another vehicle. It happened so fast that to this day I can't tell you how it happened, but it did. The other vehicle rolled over but the occupant wasn't severely injured. I was unharmed and my vehicle was still drivable.

I called the nearest park on the car radio and requested Highway Patrol assistance. They responded and conducted the investigation. Soon I was on my way to the hearing and a little chagrined at the appearance and impression my vehicle would make in the parking lot next to the union representative's undamaged vehicle. I decided that discretion was called for, so I drove into the park maintenance yard and parked the car out of sight behind a building. I'm afraid in this instance I had to tell the employee to do as I say, not as I do.

It is rare, but it happens, that an employee will actually thank you for your decision even when an adverse action is sustained. One time an employee who had an otherwise spotless record was involved in an automobile accident caused by a serious oversight in vehicle operation policy. Fortunately no one was hurt, but there was property damage involved to a private vehicle. The employee, who was within a year of retirement, was very distraught over the incident. Her main concern was that when she retired she did not want to have a reprimand in her file. It did not matter that in all probability no one would ever look at the file again after she retired. It was the principle that was at issue. When I told her that the Letter of Reprimand would be sustained against her **but would be removed** from her file one day prior to her retirement she was overjoyed and couldn't thank me enough. A rare occasion indeed under those circumstances.

Now imagine a bizarre, hypothetical case involving a longtime employee in a position of leadership and trust. Assume the employee has been with Department for almost 25 years. Suddenly, other employees notice behavior and absences that do not seem appropriate. Imagine that this employee's supervisor also begins to notice strange happenings and stories that don't compute with reality. Meetings are missed and excuses are given. The missed meetings and absences are explained away with tales of having to make an emergency landing in his/her private airplane or take on a secret assignment with Special Forces in Operation Desert Storm. After a while you began to wonder.

Suppose at this point the supervisor decides that an investigation is warranted and he assigns staff to undertake that investigation. A tangled web of deceptions begins to unravel with the investigation. Major discrepancies are found. Things like the airplane exist but hasn't been flown in years. The person is no longer in the military and never attained the high rank indicated. This person never attended medical school as he/she said, and in fact never graduated from college at all as stated on the employment application. Much of the employee's life has been a fabrication of the mind; so much so, that not only has the Department been fooled for almost 25 years, but the employee's family has also been deceived all this time.

Now this hypothetical employee is in his supervisor's office for a confrontation of the alleged facts. As a precaution to the events that might unfold at this meeting, the supervisor has another witness present. Confronted with the facts, the employee declines to answer questions based upon the Fifth Amendment and issues of national security! The supervisor and his assistant decide to let the individual sit and stew a few minutes and think about it while they leave the room.

Upon returning, the supervisor informs the employee that he is placing him/her on administrative leave and relieves him/her of his peace officer powers and weapon. At this point the employee's demeanor suddenly changes and the confidence is gone. Hypothetically, mind you, the employee then takes out a three-page letter that had been previously prepared, again detailing the Secrecy and national security reason why he/she can't answer the questions. Hypothetically, the supervisor fires him.

AN IN-BASKET FULL OF PROBLEMS

Each and every one of the eleven Districts that comprised the Northern Region had its own, often unique problems beyond those of personnel issues. A listing of each District with just two of the issues that we were

251

dealing with while I was at Region will give the reader a better perspective of the wide range of problems that reached my "In-Basket":

Klamath District
1) US Highway 101 Bypass, Jedediah Smith Redwoods.
2) Vehicle fishing access at Gold Bluff Beach, Prairie Creek.

Eel River District
1) Sinkyone Wilderness trail development.
2) Benbow dam installation/repairs and fishery.

Mendocino District
1) Navarro River homeless camping.
2) Jughandle State Reserve gorse (exotic plant) removal.

Russian River District
1) Salt Point commercial/recreational mushroom gathering.
2) Sonoma Coast and Ft. Ross grazing leases.

Marin District
1) Mt. Tamalpias Run to the Sea Race.
2) Angel Island concession contracts.

Sonoma District
1) Annadel SP housing encroachments and trespass.
2) Sugarloaf SP star thistle (exotic plant) removal.

Napa District
1) Ritchey Creek dam obstruction, Bothe-Napa SP.
2) Bale Grist Mill waterwheel operation.

Clear Lake District
1) Anderson Marsh SP highway realignment.
2) Clear Lake domestic water supply problems.

Cascade District
1) McArthur-Burney SP power company agreement.
2) Weaverville Joss House SHP closure.

Upper Valley District
1) Bidwell Mansion SHP kitchen annex demolition.
2) Bidwell Mansion/Chico State University parking.

Lake Oroville District
1) Bass fishing tournament fees and policy.
2) Lime Saddle Marina concession contract/development.

What wasn't unique about all of the above problems, and many others like them, was that each of them inevitably took from one to two years to resolve (if ever). Most often these issues resulted in the personal involvement of a State Assemblyman or State Senator or aides from his or her local office which creating an immense workload in answering all of the Controlled Correspondence generated by constituents who wrote to their legislator or the Director of Parks.

I have chosen three major issues, not previously listed, in order to illustrate some of the problems we faced in resolving major problems. The first deals with wine, the second with exotic plants and the third with fees. They are tales of troubled times that follow.

WINE WARS,"THE WRATH OF GRAPES"

Most people associate the Napa and Sonoma Valleys with the fine grapes and wine produced in the region. The area has a rich historical heritage with the Sonoma Mission and Barracks and the General Vallejo Home that are all part of Sonoma State Historic Park operated by the Sonoma District. It is the site of the California "Bear Flag Revolt" of 1846. One hundred forty-six years later battles of another sort took place.

Often when a State Park facility is located adjacent to or in the center of a town as is Sonoma SHP, a love/hate relationship can result over clashes of policy, operations, crowds, noise, financial impacts (either positive or negative) and appropriate use of facilities. Extreme pressure is often placed upon park managers to consider what may not be in the best interest of the natural or cultural resources we are sworn to protect. Sometimes the almighty dollar, coupled with political pressure, is used to circumvent the best judgment of the park professionals in the field. It takes a pretty dedicated and thick-skinned manager to face this pressure and the sometimes personal attacks on their integrity when taking a stand defending the State Park System. Fortunately, time and again our mangers have stood up for what is right in making decisions that have a long lasting impact rather then taking the easy way out for a short sighted gain. Larry Ferri, Sonoma District Superintendent was such a manager.

General Mariano Guadalupe Vallejo is a name associated with early California history during the mission period. From about 1823 until 1855 many structures that are now a part of Sonoma SHP were built under General Vallejo's direction. One of these was the Vallejo Home, *Lachryma Montis (Tear of the Mountain),* which is operated as a house museum. Adjacent to the house is the carriage house that today serves as a visitor center/museum.

In 1988 some influential businessmen used their influence to get board members of the Sonoma State Historic Park Association to agree to the sale of wine and bottled water (there is a public drinking fountain right outside the door) in the State Park under the label of M.G.Vallejo Winery and under the guise of the Cooperative Association's ability to sell interpretive items. It was deemed good marketing strategy to have the carriage house at the Vallejo Home as a point of sales and wine tasting. In order to implement this plan half of the carriage house museum would have to be utilized. Since General Vallejo once grew wine grapes on the property it was rationalized that this was an appropriate interpretive activity.

Never mind that busloads of school children visited the Vallejo Home by the thousands as part of their 4th grade California history studies. Never mind that half the historic interpretive displays would have to be removed. Never mind that the sale of alcoholic beverages in State Parks is strictly regulated and must be approached by the State Park Commission. The battle lines were drawn as our Region and District staff answered the challenge with a resounding "Never!" and began an almost two year effort to remove this intrusion upon the historic scene.

Initially the winery advocates were successful in circumventing park staff in order to get the Director of Parks to take the issue to the State Park Commission (SPC) for approval of alcoholic beverage sales. The SPC authorized a one year trial period for sales with the stipulation that park staff would monitor and record complaints and any disruptions to the school children's field trips. Soon it seemed that Larry, Deputy Director Jack Harrison and I were having endless meetings with legislators, media reporters and both opponents and advocates of the Vallejo Home wine sales. Over the year Larry and I had to respond to literally hundreds of "controlled correspondence" letters. A controlled correspondence is usually a complaint letter written to the Director of Parks by a citizen or often from a state legislator. The response to these letters was not written by the Director, but rather by Larry or me, for his signature. This can be a delicate thing as one tries to read the mind of another person and manage an outcome that is in the best interest of the Department and the citizens of California. Many of the letters we received were from school children and their teachers. The park staff's tracking of complaints reaffirmed our belief that the trial wine sales program had to go. Still it was difficult since advocates made direct contact with the Director, various State Park Commissioners, and even legislators in order to offer samples of the products.

The advocates had done a good job of getting the Association board of directors to acquiesce to the wine sales, but after over a year of dissension in the general membership of the Association, the issue came to a head. An overflow crowd gathering at the Sonoma Barracks for a final vote. There had been a lot of behind the scene maneuvering on the part of both sides. Finally, it took a roll call vote of the general membership to override the Association Board of Directors and bring a merciful end to this ugly assault upon the primary mission of the State Park System.

Often when such a high profile issue is played out in the media, as in this instance, there are no winners or losers. However, this time the wrath that the grapes generated, served to stop this intrusion into the historical integrity of the Vallejo Home, and the clear winners were the many 4th grade school children and other visitors who can now gain a better understanding of their cultural heritage. Oh yes, many varieties and labels of wines are still available from the 57 nearby wineries in the Sonoma Valley. I think that very few wine aficionados mourn the loss of this one sales area. Certainly, General Vallejo can once again rest in peace now that this revolting development has ended.

P.O.E.T.S & POLITICS

Angel Island, discovered in 1775 by the Spanish explorer Juan Manual de Ayala, and by the Native Americans before him, is situated in San Francisco Bay at the juncture of Marin and San Francisco Counties. It commands magnificent vistas of The City, the Golden Gate Bridge, Tiburon, Mount Tamalpias, Alcatraz Island and the East Bay Oakland Hills. In turn, it is highly visible from these points by the millions of people who live and commute to work in the area.

The history of Angel Island before it became a State Park belies the serenity and peaceful nature that one would normally associate with its name. The strategic importance of Angel Island at the entrance of San Francisco Bay resulted in development of a number of military installations that remain to be seen and explored. Ayala Cove, the site of Ayala's first anchorage and landing was known as Hospital Cove in 1893 for the quarantine station that was located there. Military officer's residences that remain today serve as the park headquarters/visitor center and employee housing area. There is a dock at this location that is utilized by the ferry companies that transport visitors to the park. Continuing from Ayala Cove counter-clockwise around the island one comes to the Civil War era Camp Reynolds with its parade grounds, barracks and officers houses still intact. At East Garrison's, Fort McDowell, are the remains of the facilities that were used for training and housing of the thousands of troops that were shipped off to the Spanish-American War, World War I and to the Pacific Theater during World War II. Finally, continuing around the island you come to the remains of the Immigration Station that was once known as the "Ellis Island of the West." It became an immigration station in 1910, or more accurately by some accounts, a detention center for Chinese immigrants. Stories, dreams of hope, heartbreak and woe can be read in the poetry written on the walls of the historic barracks building which remain today. Scattered around the island are numerous gun batteries dating from the Civil War, World War I and World War II as well as Nike Missile sites remaining from the more modern Cold War era.

Most people who come to visit Angel Island arrive by ferryboat service intent on a day trip or picnic. There is anchorage in Ayala Cove for private boats and there are a limited number of "Environmental Campsites" on the island for overnight stays. Angel Island, with its rich cultural history also supports a natural history that was once unspoiled but has changed much in the 227 years since Captain Ayala anchored in the cove bearing his name.

The work and influence of man has changed the landscape, as can be seen when looking at the many exotic non-native species of flora (and to a much lesser extend fauna) that has invaded the island. Most conspicuous of the plants that dominated the recent scene are the eucalyptus trees. Originally brought to California from Australia for firewood, railroad ties, and furniture, they have been spread intentionally by man as well as by natural processes throughout the West. On Angel Island, rows of trees, some of which are now considered historic, were planted in conjunction with the military housing areas. Quick to grow and gain a foothold on Angel Island, the eucalyptus spread, replacing native plants which were either crowded out by the fast growing eucalyptus or smothered under the oily and highly flammable duff of the trees. That is not to say that there are/were not visitors to Angel Island who tolerated the eucalyptus tree and its pungent odor. In fact there were individuals and groups that loved these trees. On the other hand, there were those of us who felt that we should be true to the State Park's Mission Statement and comply with the policies of the State Park System to preserve natural ecosystems.

Specifically, in the case of Angel Island SP it was our desire to return the vegetation to a state that more closely replicates the conditions of Pre-European contact. This meant removing most of the eucalyptus trees on the island. Dave Boyd, our Regional Resource Ecologist was the prime advocate of this program. In 1985, he had initiated a program that had some success in removing eucalyptus trees, after much trial and error, at Annadel State Park near Santa Rosa. Because the eucalyptus trees produce such prolific stump sprouts after they are cut down it is no easy matter to get rid of them. Also disposal of the logs and slash materials from the necessary logging operation poses many problems.

Any problems that had been encountered at Annadel SP would be compounded many times over by the geographic setting of Angel Island. Everything would have to be shipped to the island and **off** the island, including the logs themselves. The problems of log disposal at Annadel had been solved by having the tree removal done, at no cost to the State, by a logging company that was able to sell the logs as pulp material at a time when the pulp market was high. We were not so fortunate in the case of Angel Island because the pulp market crashed shortly after the eucalyptus tree removal program began.

To be sure, there was no unanimous agreement even among park staff that the program should go ahead. Some felt that the trees were now a part of the "natural" evolution of the Angel Island and the disruptions that the logging operation would cause would have too much of an impact on the visitors' experience. I viewed this as a short-term outlook and decided we should look toward the long-range benefits. We would proceed with the project. We knew we would have some strong opposition from the public, as was evident by the fact that staff at the Golden Gate National Recreation had decided to abandon their efforts to remove eucalyptus trees on Marin Headlands after receiving pressure and resistance to their program from the public

Resource Ecologist Dave Boyd, to his credit and thick skin, stuck to his principles despite being labeled "an out of control" ecologist in the media. He was able to find a logging contractor who agreed to take on the project. The island situation dictated that this time there would be costs involved much greater than those at Annadel. What was not anticipated was that the barge that would be used to haul the logs to the Port of Sacramento for transportation to Japan would have a hole knocked in it's hull near the shore of Angel Island when it first arrived. That was an immediate cause for increased cost and delay

Any logging operation, no matter how carefully and "delicately" performed, looks like a disaster area while in progress and immediately after completion. That, coupled with the fact that the burning of slash materials on Angel Island produced smoke that was visible in all the surrounding communities, made a project of this magnitude subject to much scrutiny and criticism. It even brought out the poets among us.

POET, better known as **Protectors of Eucalyptus Trees,** arose from media blitz that began as soon as the logging started. It did not help that the front page of the San Francisco Chronicle showed a photograph of one of the Environmental Campsites, with The City in the background, sitting in the middle of a logged off area that appeared to have been in a tornado or recent bombing. Debate over the project raged on, and on. It was the subject of Public Radio talk shows, television reports and letters to editor. Wars seemed to never end. Finally in 1989, P.O.E.T. was successful in obtaining a court injunction that stopped the project. This coupled with the depressed pulp market placed the logging company on the verge of bankruptcy and threatened to permanently stop the project.

While Dave worked to overcome the court injunction by producing a focus environmental study that would meet the intent of the injunction requirements, Rick Rayburn, Chief of the Department's Resource Management Division and I worked behind the scenes to save the contractor and secure additional funding. At one meeting the contractor, who had mortgaged his home and business, was in tears as we struggled to save the project. Fortunately for him and for us we did find the funding. But nothing was easy about the project. Even after the logs were being shipped to the Port of Sacramento, labor union issues arose with longshoremen that required off loading of the logs in the ship canal rather than the port. In the end we were required to hold a public meeting in Mill Valley where the findings of the focused study were presented and the results accepted, if not by all, at least to the degree that allowed the project to resume.

Major restoration of the logged areas has occurred with the re-introduction and planting of over 20,000 native plants and shrubs. The dire consequences that opponents to the project predicted did not occur and Dave's belief in the project proved to be his vindication. Additionally, after the devastating Oakland Hills fire of 1991, many of the opponents to the removal of the fire prone eucalyptus trees were writing a new verse to the poems of POET.

Today, the invasion and intrusion of exotic non-native species into the environment remain, along with biological diversity, the two greatest threats to the California State Park System. Extensive restoration programs are now taking place in many state parks in order to deal with the former, and many new acquisitions have occurred to provide for linking corridors to address the latter.

FEES. FIE & FOES

In all the time that I was in Northern Division Headquarters nothing approached the animosity, disgust, and opposition that was generated by proposed fee increases along the Sonoma Coast. Events that occurred then were a public relations nightmare that had direct physical effect on my health and well being. It is a tale worth repeating because what happened is yet another example of seeking short-term gains at the expense of a well thought out program.

A little background is necessary to set the stage for the drama, which was played out over a two-year period within the Russian River District from 1990 to 1992. Until the early 1960's, funding for the State Parks System was about 80% by taxes, the majority of which came from offshore oil revenues and the other 20% generated from user fees. Over time, budgets became more restrictive while mandated programs continued to increase. There was a gradual erosion of tax supported funding for parks and an ever increasing **requirement** placed upon the Department by the State Legislature to become more and more self sufficient. It reached the point in the 1990's that the 80% to 20% ratio was reversed to the point that some "bean counters" eventually decided that the State Parks System could entirely pay its own way. The only way to do this was by increasing fees, cutting back on service, instituting new fees, and not approving any new programs or services unless they generated enough revenue to pay for themselves. The one exception to this last item was if it could be proved that a very real and present health and safety issue was in question.

Forced into a corner by budget cutbacks, staffing vacancies and "salary savings" requirements, all districts scrambled to meet the mandate. Salary savings requirements were one of our greatest nemeses. Apparently, at some point in the depths of a dungeon in the Department of Finance offices, some bright, cheery accountant figured out that every time an employee vacancy occurred it would take some time to re-fill the position. That period of time between when the vacancy occurred and when the position was refilled resulted in salary savings since the position was budgeted for the entire year. Thus, if it took three months to fill a position, three months salary was saved. Eventually, that logical program was expanded so that Departments were **required** to hold the positions longer than the normal time it would take to fill the position, resulting in even more savings. Soon a position that was desperately needed in the field was being held vacant up to a year or more. It was/is a maddening and perverted system.

In any event, the Russian River District came up with a two-prong program in an attempt to plug the holes in the budget/financial dam. It was decided that fees would be collected at a number of beaches previously designated as free along the Sonoma Coast between Bodega Head and the mouth of the Russian River. All of the locations that were chosen had developed facilities such as paved parking lots and restrooms. Those areas that did not have improvement would remain free. Initially it was proposed that a $5.00 per car day use fee (less than the cost of a movie) would be charged. This was less than the fees that were charged along the beaches of Central and Southern California that had similar facilities.

In addition to the fees it was proposed that lifeguard service be introduced to the Sonoma Coast. There was real evidence that it was needed. A study quickly showed that Sonoma Coast was the deadliest unit in the State Park System when it came to visitor accidents (drowning). What appeared to be a gently sloping beach could turn fatal when unexpected "sleeper" waves caught the unsuspecting beach stroller or swept the unwary fisherman from the rocks. A lifeguard program was definitely needed and there was sufficient justification for its implementation. Unfortunately, the local citizens did not take kindly to the new lifeguard program. It was too closely linked to the initiation of the new fees. Reaction from the public, local county representatives and state legislators was immediate and swift.

A citizens group, **SOB** (Save Our Beaches) formed immediately and took us to task. Protests were held both at the Region Office and at the check stations where portable kiosks (on wheels so they could be moved at night and not destroyed) were in place and SOB made sure that the media was there. I saw some very interesting protest signs, some of which were personally directed at me, and heard some clever chants about my ancestry. The letter writing campaign and volume of controlled correspondence exceeded that of any other issue we had dealt with, including Angel Island.

I found the politics of the situation very interesting, but I was not surprised when some of the very politicians that had been urging the Department to become more financially independent were now chastising the Department for doing some of the very things they had directed us to do. As they say in cards, "There's a time to hold them, and a time to fold them." We folded, at least on the fee issue at Sonoma Coast.

The lifeguard program was another matter. In that instance we were dealing with peoples lives. Over 23 people had drowned in the 5 years previous to the initiation of lifeguards on Sonoma Coast. The lifeguard program, however, got off to a shaky start due to some, rather poor public relations and criticism. Some of it may have been justified. I know one thing; it never pays to arrest Santa Claus. The lifeguards, like park rangers, are fully sworn peace officers and like rangers carry a full compliment of peace officer equipment including a pistol. The lifeguards on Sonoma Coast do not have lifeguard towers that they operate out of. Instead they patrol the coastal cliffs and beaches from their patrol vehicles. Their main job is to warn people of potential danger, which is easier to do than actually go in the water for a rescue or body recovery. The first lifeguards to be assigned to the Sonoma Coast were readily recognizable both on and off the job. Locals did not treat them with respect at any time, as feelings were still very raw from the period of protest and confrontation. Things came to a peak over the Christmas holiday when one of the lifeguards arrested a gentleman dressed as Santa Claus who was standing up in the back of a pickup truck during a Bodega Bay Christmas Parade. It was reported that the truck was going at an unsafe speed and Santa Claus was in danger of becoming a casualty. I don't know. I wasn't there - **I only read about it in the local newspaper!**

It only took a few dramatic rescues and a new District Superintendent (thank you Bob La Belle) who was much more personable and media savvy to turn things around and show the citizens of the Sonoma Coast what a valuable asset to the community the lifeguard program was. The number of fatalities along the coast has dropped dramatically and the well-deserved recognition of the lifeguards has at last been realized. It was another instance where the Almighty $ lost, but the public won.

OP, FM. MBO, TQM. ETC. ETC.

I am sure that in almost every District or Unit Office, perhaps on a dusty shelf or boxed in storage somewhere in a closet, there are several large green binders with a label on the spine that reads, "Area Operations Plan". Those documents represent countless man-hours of work and effort that the Department expended in an attempt to measure and "quantify" what we do.

This undertaking was a Sacramento Headquarters "bean counters" dream. Now "they" would be able to look in a book and tell us exactly what, when, where and how much o a particular task, item or repair should cost. But for my generation of park rangers it marked the end of "The Good 'Ol Days". It was sometime between 1969 – 1970 that the major changes occurred that divided the park field staff into Maintenance Services and Visitor Services. It is also the period of time when a new facilities maintenance program was introduced statewide and we undertook the monumental task of developing Area Operations Plans.

For years, in order to keep track of payroll, we had utilized a simple form to track hours worked. With the concept of the Area Operations Plan a new form, DPR 202, was initiated that required us to break down all tasks in 15 minute increments of very specific jobs within a series of broader categories. For example, under a category such as Patrol, there might be subheading such as "Vehicle Patrol" or "Campground Patrol", but this would not include such things as Resource Patrol, Aquatic Safety or Camp Check and Fee Collections. Confused yet? We were. What did we do if we were on "patrol" but also collecting fees, providing visitor information, rescuing someone from drowning, apprehending deer poachers, all on the same work shift. I can assure you we weren't looking at our watches and tracking how many minutes each of these activities was taking. Most of us made up and took educated "guesstimates" of how much time we allotted to each activity and entered our guesses at the end of a shift or, in some cases, at the end of the week. The figures were suspect from the beginning and as the modern computer gurus of today say, "Garbage in, garbage out".

In any event, The operations plans did serve at least two useful purposes. The primary content of the operations plan was comprised of an "Area Description and Workload Description." To an employee new to an Area these sections provided a quick, easy reference and orientation to the park's resources and workload priorities that could be helpful. Perhaps more importantly to the park manager, was the ability to use the Operations Plan data, however flawed in might be, as budget justification for additional manpower, equipment, and facilities and programs. The Maintenance Facility portion of the plans probably had the longest lasting positive effect on the public. It was the basis for the program that is still used today and which resulted in better services to the public.

Whether I wanted to or not, I was to become very familiar with Operations Plans since I was the primary author of the first Point Mugu Area Operations Plan and Facility Maintenance Program documents. Bob Freeman, the first Maintenance Supervisor for the Point Mugu Area, had to make very few changes or additions to the program he inherited when he joined the staff. As for me, a State Park Ranger I at the time, being involved with the writing of the Operations Plan to the degree I was provided me with the opportunity to gain insight and responsibilities far greater than many of my peers.

When I transferred to Pismo Beach in 1971 I arrived in the midst of the formation of the San Luis Obispo Coast Area. There too, development of an Area Operations Plan was underway so that one of my first tasks was to assist the Pismo Beach crew with the completion of their South Sector portion of the plan. Because of my experience at Leo Carrillo preparing the final plan that combined the work that had been done with the plan at Pt. Mugu, the San Luis Obispo Coast Area Manager "selected" (read, ordered) me to help do the same with the North and South Sectors of SLOCA. This meant that almost every day, for several weeks, I had to drive from Pismo Beach to Morro Bay to work with the area manager compiling and editing the data and narratives of others into a cohesive document.

The two of us worked in a small trailer that served as an office. The most remarkable thing I remember about this experience was the amount of adding machine tape, with literally hundreds of work, hour and dollar figures on them, laying all about the office. It was even worse than the Report of Collections problems we had at Point Mugu. I usually took my lunch with me and while the area manager walked to his house at noon for lunch I would seek out a quiet place in the park to eat mine, and, more importantly, to clear my head of numbers, figures, and words. One day I decided to have some fun when the manager went to lunch. I stayed in the trailer and begin to drape all of the adding machine tapes that were laying about and hang them from the walls, curtains, lamps or anywhere else I could attach them. When I had finished the interior of the place looked like a house that had been "toilet papered". When the manager returned he walked into a jungle of paper "vines". Unfortunately, I was the only one laughing at what I deemed the best work to date that I had done on that Operation Plan. We eventually finished our work and I was finally able to return to my real job as a park ranger, which was ever more satisfying.

Like a rain cloud over my head that followed me everywhere I went, I was not quite done with my involvement with Area Operations Plans. On my promotion to Chief Ranger of the Montane Area in 1973, I arrived while the staff there was just finishing up its OPS Plan. Sam Bitting, the Maintenance Supervisor, was swamped and saddled with the responsibility of completing the document since the Area Manager was away on vacation and training. I took pity upon poor Sam and spent considerable time in helping him finish the task of combining the Palomar and Cuyamaca plans. He still owes me for that.

When I left the Montane Area for Plumas-Eureka in 1975, I was so glad to see a relatively simple plan that was completed and in need of few revisions (with the exception of adjusting maintenance cost figures that would reflect the real world of inflation). The surgery had been completed with this operation!

Of course, the California State Park System is a bureaucracy, and as such you know that there are probably more "bean counters" than Operations Plans. Unfortunately, the "bean counters" can come up with more "new" ideas then the Operations Plans provide solutions to.

That was the case in 1977 when the Department jumped aboard the latest trend and charged ahead with the development of "Management by Objective (MBO)" plans. For the benefit of reader's sanity I won't go there in detail. I would only say that it was more of the same. In researching this section of the book, I returned to Plumas-Eureka to seek out and find the Operations Plan for that unit. Indeed, it and the MBO Plan were there gathering dust on a shelf. I noted with some satisfaction that the cover sheet for the MBO plan that I authored in May, 1977, was still intact with the title that I had purposely changed to see if it would be noticed (it wasn't) in Sacramento Headquarters. It read "Management by **Objections**". After we had given MBO its opportunity to gather sufficient dust upon the shelves of bureaucracy, it was in the 1990's before we again had to update to the next trend in management styles. Total Quality Management (TQM) was now in vogue and on the operating table waiting its turn to be "doctored up." This, of course, required the creation of a whole new section and staff in Sacramento Headquarters to implement it, a natural course of events for a bureaucracy to initiate a new program. Since I retired I have often wondered if the "patient" survived or the time has come to bury TQM too and move on to another "new" management effort.

I do not want to give the impression that all we dealt with in Region was problems. There were many outstanding projects in the field that presented challenges on the road to completion, and the results were well worth the effort. For example, Bill Beat, Superintendent of the Klamath District, was able to complete the Native American Village at Patrick's Point SP that had been initiated by his predecessor, Herman Schlerf. I was able to participate in the dedication ceremonies for the Visitor Center at Clear Lake SP that Superintendent Steve Hill was responsible for, I also was Master of Ceremonies for the dedication of the Bale Grist Mill water wheel dedication. In addition, through the efforts of both Region and District staffs, we were able to complete many important acquisitions of property to the State Park System which are perhaps a more lasting legacy.

A STRONG FOUNDATION

A few weeks after I was hired in 1966 as a Park Ranger, Ronald Reagan was elected Governor of California. From my viewpoint he immediately did two things that had an effect on the State Park System, and thus my career. First, which I perceived as negative, he instituted a hiring freeze that kept us woefully understaffed for several years and basically stopped all promotions. No Ranger II promotional examination (the next step up the career ladder) was even given for almost four years. Second, which I felt was more positive, he appointed William Penn Mott, Jr. as Director of the California Department of Parks and Recreation. Mr. Mott was a very energetic and dynamic idea person who had a distinguished career in parks. He was later to become the Director of the National Park Service.

Isolated as I was in Bodie, I did not have the opportunity to actually meet the Director until about 1968 when I worked in the Point Mugu Area. I remember my first meeting with him quite well. The Department was in the process of opening a "special" Assistant to the Director office in the Los Angeles area. The location of the office was in Olvera Street, the birthplace of the City of Los Angeles, in a building that once had been a Chinese Laundry. The building had been restored to an "adaptive use" for the recently appointed Deputy Director and to provide an information center for drop-in visitors. The new Deputy Director was no other than my good friend and mentor Carl "Andy" Anderson. Andy had requested my services for two weeks to assist with the grand opening ceremonies and to staff a special exhibit trailer that was moved into the Plaza. So for two weeks I commuted from my home in Oxnard to Olvera Street.

There had been a rush to complete preparations of the office. The idea was to have the office look like the laundry it had been in the 1800's. To enhance this effect we had to tie bundles of brown paper and stack them on the shelves to simulate laundry ready for pick up. When I arrived the morning of the opening ceremonies I found a white haired gentleman in the office frantically tying these bundles together. I recognized him from photographs I had seen, as none other than our Director, Bill Mott! Quickly introducing myself, I too began tying up the bundles until we had all the shelves well stocked with "laundry." I thought that this was a real "hands on" director that I could like and respect. He would do whatever it took to get a job done even if it meant tying bundles of laundry together himself. Here was a political appointee who was doing something other than laundering money – I was impressed.

In 1969 Mr. Mott established the California State Park Foundation (CSPF) and later became its Executive Secretary after he left DPR. The CSPF is a non-profit organization that thrives today thanks to Mr. Mott's vision. It has taken on many projects involving restoration of facilities and acquisition of properties. I saw first hand evidence of one of the Foundation's first major projects at the Fort Ross Russian Orthodox Chapel in Sonoma County. In October 1970, while visiting Margaret's parents, we decided to take a drive up the Sonoma Coast to Fort Ross State Historic Park. As we approached the Fort from the south on Highway 1 we could see a column of smoke rising from a jumble of burning timbers that were the remains of the chapel. It had burned completely to the ground during the early morning hours. It was the CSPF that raised the funds for the reconstruction of the chapel that can be seen today.

My main involvement with the CSPF began when I was in the Santa Rosa Region office. The CSPF was involved in another major project known as the Marconi Conference Center (MCC). Guglielmo Marconi, of radio invention fame, had established a series of broadcasting and receiving stations around the world in 1914. There was one in Nova Scotia, one in Hawaii, and one in the small village of Marshall on the bluffs overlooking Tomales Bay in Marin County near Point Reyes National Seashore.

In 1984 when the 62-acre parcel was acquired by the CSPF, it still had a number of the original buildings, including a powerhouse, administrative building, and several houses for managers and a massive three-story hotel for station workers. On the rolling hills behind the facility were the foundation remains of the receiver towers. The Radio Corporation of America (RCA) purchased the facility in 1920 and operated it until 1939, though they held title to the property until 1947. After that it changed ownership several times until Synanon, a drug rehabilitation organization, that utilized it as their world headquarters from 1965-1980, finally acquired it. Synanon had some very unique "alternative lifestyle" housing units, color schemes, and hot tubs. They also had a very sophisticated (for the time) computer facility and a huge metal building of some 10,000-sq.ft. for a recreational and classroom facility.

When the Synanon project folded in 1980, the Buck Trust, a local non-profit organization in Marin County, took over and in 1984 sold it to the CSPF for the fair price of $1.00. The sale agreement stipulated that the property would be developed as a conference center and that it was to be opened by July 1, 1989.

When I entered the picture in 1988, the buildings and infrastructure of the facilities were being renovated by the CSPF. They had hired very capable manager, Wayne Zion, to oversee the project. He had made remarkable progress with limited funding and staffing. The plan all along, had been for the CSPF to develop the property and then turn it over to State Parks to be run as a non-profit corporation similar to the Asilomar Conference Center on the Monterey Peninsula.

My first job after the property was turned over to the state was to participate in the selection of a seven member Board of Directors to oversee the operations. I did this in conjunction with Les McCargo, Deputy Director in charge of Development and Acquisition. Next, we attempted to integrate the MCC with our Marin District operations so that we could utilize personnel, equipment and materials to assist in development in order to meet the fast approaching opening deadline. I offered the services of my secretary, Jan Thompson, as the recording secretary for the Board until there was sufficient funding available for the MCC to hire their own personnel to perform that function.

Attempting to meet the opening deadline was not without difficulty. There was a major lawsuit to deal with, insufficient funding, local community protest over removal of non-native vegetation, the use of herbicides and the use of the facilities (at no cost) for locals. Wayne was successful in meeting the opening deadline-just barely. The MCC was open for one day on July 1st, 1989 in order to meet the "letter of the law" if not the "intent". It was later opened for full operations despite a few problems that sometimes proved funny, For example, Mr. Zion received one positive response from a conference attendee who thanked him for the warm water in the toilets which made sitting on the toilet seats very comfortable in the cool of the morning. When he investigated this he found that the plumbers had mistakenly hooked up a hot water line to the toilet!

I was fortunate to attend the official grand opening ceremony for the Marconi Conference Center. In attendance was Guglielmo Marconi's daughter who had flown out from Italy to attend the ceremonies. At the dinner we attended after the event I was able to talk with her as she recalled her famous father's radio invention and business.

Today the MCC is doing very well and has expanded its services. It is an excellent facility and conference center for groups that seek peace and serenity of a natural setting away from the hustle and bustle of a more traditional conference center. It all started with a strong foundation and the vision provided by William Penn Mott, Jr.

A BROKEN HEART

One of my life goals has always been to see a total solar eclipse. The thought and mystical power of daylight turning to night in the blink of an eye has intrigued me as long as I can remember. Oh sure, I had seen partial eclipses before but never the real thing. When we were living in Johnsville at Plumas-Eureka SP the family was all packed to drive north to Oregon to observe the eclipse that occurred in February 1979. Unfortunately a big snowstorm arrived and dashed our hopes for the trip.

Now, in 1991, a year that had seen much stress and turmoil with the myriad of problems I was dealing with in Region, I definitely needed and was looking forward to a vacation. The previous year I had learned that there would be a total eclipse of the sun in Mexico that would be visible south of Acapulco. I contacted our friends Ted & Jeanne Reinhardt who agreed to join us on the adventure. In preparation for the trip, Margaret and I attended classes at Santa Rosa Junior College that were conducted by the astronomy instructor who would lead the trip.

As July approached I was working in a frenzy to complete several projects before we left on the trip. One of assignments had nothing to do with work. I was a member of the Windsor Rotary Club and was in charge of putting up signs for the upcoming Sonoma County Hot Air Balloon Festival. Last minute preparations and meetings were taking place that I had to squeeze in between work at the office.

At work I was also in the middle of interviews to select a new District Superintendent for the Russian River District a task I wanted to complete before I departed on vacation.

A lot was happening. Unfortunately, some of the happenings were occurring within my body. On June 25th, after conducting about half a dozen interviews, the other panel members and I adjourned for lunch at a local restaurant. During lunch a wave of nausea swept over me and I broke out in a cold sweat. I knew this wasn't normal and from my first aid training I was aware that these could be symptoms of a heart attack. I said nothing to the others seated with me. I decided to wait and see if I felt any pain in the arm or chest. I didn't, and the moment passed. I didn't know it at the time, but I had in fact experienced a mild heart attack and was in a classic state of denial.

There was no way I could be having a heart attack. First, I was too young (47): secondly, I lived a healthy lifestyle. I didn't smoke, drink to excess, and Margaret fed me all the right foods. Finally, there was no family history of heart disease in the family. This could not be happening!

We returned to the Region Office and completed the interviews. We made our choice and Robert LaBelle was selected. I planned to write up the necessary paperwork the next day and send in our selection for approval. Now that the interviews were completed I rushed off to a Hot Air Balloon Festival meeting. While at the meeting, another wave of cold sweat and nausea came over me. Again I was in denial when it went away a short time later. I didn't get home until 7:30 pm that evening and didn't feel like much dinner, and decided to go to bed early.

Almost immediately after going to bed I suffered a third episode that was more severe than the first two. Enough was enough. This time I told Margaret but instead of doing what we should have, that is calling 911, I told her to drive me to the nearest hospital in Healdsburg. Even on the trip to the hospital after the feelings of nausea and anxiety passed I tried to convince her all was well and we could return home. As usual, she did not listen to me and continued to the hospital. At the hospital, it was confirmed that I had indeed suffered a heart attack. There was no more denying it now!

The next morning, it was decided that I should be transferred to a hospital in Santa Rosa for further treatment. I was prepared for transport in an ambulance and placed on a gurney. Actually, by now I was feeling fine as the blood thinning drugs I had been given were doing their job. As the ambulance raced down the Redwood Highway I began to roll around in the back of the ambulance. I had visions of the back door opening and me, on the gurney flying out onto the roadway. Since there was no attendant in the back of the ambulance with me I yelled to the driver to stop and secure the gurney. He pulled over to the edge of the roadway and locked down the run-a-way cart. At that time he told me he knew his way around the hospital and he would take me into the hospital via a "short cut".

We arrived at the hospital okay, but instead of driving to the emergency entrance the driver took me to his shortcut which turned out to be a shipping and loading dock at the rear of the hospital. I was carted through a maze of corridors in which the attendant immediately got lost. Finally he had to ask directions to the cardiology area. When we arrived at the right location, there was Margaret waiting for me even though she had left after we did.

It still wasn't clear to me how serious my situation was. I had been told that I would undergo an angioplasty to clear a blocked artery in my heart, but because the operating room was busy it would be an hour or two wait. So there I waited on the gurney in a "holding pen." I decided I might as well make use of the time so I asked Margaret to go down to the car and retrieve the paperwork I needed to complete for Bob LaBelle's appointment to District Superintendent. She did that and so while I waited for my surgery I completed the paperwork (Bob, you owe me Big Time!) and told Margaret to take the documents to the Region Office for processing to

Sacramento Headquarters. Now that is what I call dedication. Others may call it stupidity and it is probably the sort of thing that contributed to the heart attack in the first place.

In the afternoon I was at last wheeled into surgery for the angioplasty. I was somewhat sedated, but awake enough so that I could observe what was happening inside my heart by viewing the nearby television monitor. There was the wire working its way up through the artery to the blockage that was easily visible. The balloon inflated within the artery but the artery would not remain open. Another try and it worked, but the doctor was not optimistic that it would remain clear. As I was wheeled out of the operating room he told me that if I felt anything out of the ordinary to immediately notify the person on duty in the recovery room. For once I listened.

That evening, I didn't feel "right". I couldn't tell you what I felt, but something just didn't seem right. I had no pain, nausea or cold sweating but I could "feel" my heart, and that is something you are almost never aware of when at rest. I was wheeled back down to surgery and again went through the angioplasty procedure. The cardiologist told me this time that if the artery did not remain open and collapsed again he would have to operate. It collapsed. The last thing I remember was the doctor saying to me, "Carl, we're going to have to operate." My last words and response were, "Go for it."

I awoke the next morning with tubes in every orifice of my body and some where there were no orifices (chest). Can't say I felt too good. Family, friends, and coworkers were quick to respond with good cheer and well wishes. Within two days I was up and about shuffling along the hospital hallways. I figured that was good progress after undergoing double by-pass surgery. Five days after the surgery I was sent home. Before returning home I had Margaret drive me to the Region Office where, to the surprise of everyone in the office, I walked in to greet and thank them for their support. Recovery from the surgery was surprisingly fast. The surgery had taken place on June 26th and by July 3rd I had already managed to walk one mile in 20 minutes. The worst part of the whole episode was that we missed the eclipse of July 11th that we had planned to witness in Mexico. In Santa Rosa the solar eclipse was only partial. We would have to try another time.

My forced "vacation" ended on August 19th when I returned to work. My "broken heart" now repaired it was back to the old grind. As I had expected, things had run smoothly without me. I found myself asking over and over again, "Why did this happen to me?" The doctors were not sure. Even without the major markers for heart attack, no excessively high blood pressure or cholesterol levels, healthy lifestyle, and no family history of heart problems there was no denying that the heart attack had occurred. As one doctor explained, I was just one of those statistics out at the end of the normal **Bell** Curve. Let's **ring** it up for science and medicine!

In my own heart, I believe that stress was the problem. Though neither the Department nor State Worker's Compensation agreed with that assessment, I have no doubt that that was the major contributing factor. At the time I felt I had paid the price for leaving the field and moving into a management position. Subsequent events, in later years, would change my mind as other managers in the field also began to have even more disastrous effects from stress on the job than I did. But life goes on, sometimes even with a broken heart.

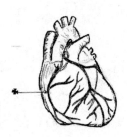

Carl S. Chavez

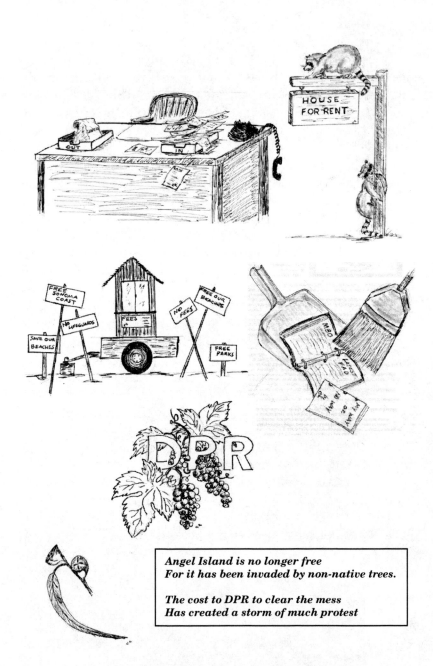

*Angel Island is no longer free
For it has been invaded by non-native trees.*

*The cost to DPR to clear the mess
Has created a storm of much protest*

NORTHERN REGION SKETCHES

THE PATHWAY ENDS

In a career spanning almost 33 years I had the privilege to work with a number of outstanding people. Some of these people became life-long friends, others friendly acquaintances, some remained merely coworkers in my memory, and a few are best forgotten. All of them, even the latter, taught me something that helped me with my career. Those lessons included dedication, grace, honesty, integrity, wisdom, compassion, knowledge, and last but not least-humor. I found that it was so much easier to laugh than cry or get angry about events and circumstances I could not control.

In 1966 when I began my career it was still possible to know almost all permanent field employees in the Department. There were fewer than 1200 employees at that time. Even today, with the many opportunities for training, transfers, and promotions, a ranger at Jedediah

Smith Redwoods has the opportunity to train with his or her counterpart from Boarder Fields State Park at the opposite end of the state. In fact the odds may be good that some day their career paths may cross. I found that to be true as time and again I worked with people I had previously worked with on other assignments. The bonding of a close working relationship never goes away when your "partners" transfer to another unit. That move just becomes another branch in the efficient "grapevine" communications system within the Department.

As difficult as it is to single out individuals for the impact they have had on my career, I still feel compelled to do so. That is why I have chosen to write of Jerry Henderson, Jim Hart, Ken Leigh, Ted Reinhardt and Carl "Andy" Anderson. Each of these individuals though they entered my park experience at different times of my career did a lot to shape that career. In several instances I worked with them on different assignments, sometimes after lapses of many years. In each case, however, we always took up again where we left off, never missing a beat. As productive a worker as each of them was, it was more the camaraderie that we shared that made working with them so enjoyable. It is also my hope that perhaps I had some little part in furthering the careers of Jerry, Jim, Ken and Ted. With Andy it was a different story because he was ahead of me and it took all his wit, skill and patience to help further my career.

Perhaps it is fairer to say that the five people I have chosen to write about are, in reality, representative of all the good people that became part of my "Park Family". I am forever grateful to them for the experiences we shared and the unconditional gift of friendship that became a part of my life. Because I have told stories of events involving some these people in other chapters I have not focused so much on our work together but rather on the relationship that made that work so productive. So, for what it's worth, meet my Cast of Characters.

CAST OF CHARACTERS

JERRY HENDERSON

Jerry Henderson is the odd man out in the cast of five characters portrayed here. He is not in it so much for how he influenced my career, though he did, but more so for the spirit and carefree sense of adventure he demonstrated. He is the person who showed me that with a little bravado, some self-confidence and a lot of audacity you could get away with a whole lot of things.

Jerry began walking with me up this "Pathway Through Parks" on the first day I arrived at Humboldt State College. When I moved into Room #305 in the Redwood Hall dormitory that day in September, 1963, Jerry was there with my new roommate, Craig Phillips. It turned out that Craig and Jerry were friends from Southern California, having worked together previously at a Boy Scout camp. Both Craig and Jerry were a year ahead of me in college.

I quickly learned that Jerry was transferring to Humboldt State from Long Beach State for a year of "R & R". It was understood that he would take classes, but from the beginning he always had plans to return to Long Beach. When I asked where he was to live while going to school at Humboldt, both he and Craig were at first evasive. It wasn't until a trust had developed a week or so later that I was told a secret that few others over the next year would learn. Jerry was living in a **tent** in the school forest behind the Redwood Bowl football stadium. Most weekends, during the entire school year, he would stay in our room and use the dorm facilities for his personal needs. Always he told others that he lived in "Tex's" Hotel on 2nd Street in Old Town Eureka. No one doubted him and many were fooled.

It was during our first week in school, before classes had really begun, that Jerry had his first impact upon my life. He had an old army surplus jeep that he and Craig had driven up in from Southern California. One day a group of fellows from the dorm decided to drive to the Mad River Beach at the mouth of the river. We had the jeep's canvas top down at the time as we were returning to school on one of the narrow, Arcata Bottom farm roads when it began raining. As we passed a group of young college coeds walking down the road they waved and shouted at us to stop. We waved back but continued on, whizzing right past them until the black cowboy hat that Jerry was wearing flew off his head into the wind. The girls picked up that hat and waved their trophy. Jerry stopped and backed up to retrieve the hat but they refused to return it unless we gave them a lift back to Sunset Hall dormitory. We agreed to give them a ride. It was love at first sight (on my part only). My future wife, Margaret was one of those gals! On the ride back to school we discovered that two of the ladies, including Margaret were Home Economics majors, so we coerced them into agreeing to bake us some pies made from the wild Himalayan berries growing so profusely in the area. We all made a return trip to the beach the following weekend with our pies. In my case it was the start of a budding romance.

Living in the dark, damp and downright rainy redwood forest in an old style umbrella tent was not the most comfortable accommodations for Jerry. True, he had been in similar primitive bivouac situations in his Marine ROTC program every summer while in college, but never for this length of time. He generally ate his meals in the college cafeteria but rarely had to purchase food. He was so friendly and likable that just about everybody knew him. They didn't really know where he lived but that just added to his mystique. People would hold up plates with food they did not like or want to eat and Jerry would "graze" around the cafeteria obtaining his fill. He had very little money to spend and he was able to keep his expenses at a minimum this way.

It was the money situation that almost got him and a few others of us in trouble. It seemed some of the administration at the college began to take notice of Jerry's frequent appearance in our dorm room and around the cafeteria. Still, they couldn't pin anything on him directly. Jerry, bold as ever, ignored the "danger" and applied for a Student Loan to help him weather his financial shortcomings. He still had everybody at the college, including the Housing and Loan Officers, fooled as to where he lived. Several of his friends, including Margaret, actually went in to Eureka looking for the non-existent Tex's Hotel with the fictitious address. I was called into the Dean of Housing's office but confessed that I had no idea about where Jerry lived. Somehow, some way, Jerry got his Student Loan. Knowing Jerry, he paid it back too!

Each spring, an annual dance known as the "Spring Fling" was held on campus. As part of the festivities a "Popera King and Queen" for this event was chosen. Usually the winners came from one of the major clubs, sororities or fraternities on campus. Because Jerry was well known on campus as such an exotic aberration, I got the idea that we should enter him and his friend Leneah as candidates. They agreed to my proposal so I filed the necessary paperwork listing our dorm room, "Room #305", as the sponsor. I had figured out that in reality, not too many people actually would vote for a "King" and Queen." It was a pretty stupid exercise in democracy, but on the other hand there were some good prizes for the winner. As Jerry's "Campaign Manager" I devised a strategy worthy of the mystery of this man. Keeping with the musical theme of the event, I took photographs of Jerry in a manner such that his face could not be seen. Thus his head was stuck down a tuba or hidden behind a drum, etc. On the actual day of the voting we organized a group to canvass the cafeteria for people who hadn't voted that day (about 99.9%) and personally escorted them to the voting booth.

There was a stunned audience the night of the Spring Fling when the "Popera King" was announced. Jerry and Leneah had prevailed and many in the audience wondered who the heck they were. Among the other candidates that Jerry defeated that day were the star quarterback of the football team and a future State Assemblyman who was active in school politics. I can still see Jerry, so casually dressed, strutting up the aisle between a row of other formally attired, would be, "heirs to the throne" to reign over the dance and receive their loot. It was a small group of us indeed who whooped and hollered in giddiness over our upset victory.

Jerry did return to Long Beach State the following school year and received his degree in Criminal Science. Upon graduation he was commissioned as a 2nd Lieutenant in the U.S. Marine Corps. That meant Vietnam. Only occasionally while Jerry was serving his country in Vietnam did we hear from him. When we did, we ceased to worry too much about him. It seemed that Jerry had been assigned a position in the USMC that required him to travel about Southeast Asia and Australia purchasing recreation equipment for Marines on R & R duty. Apparently, Jerry had landed on his feet again and was having a good time buying surfboards for our boys in need. For his work above and beyond the call of duty Jerry emerged from the Vietnam War as a captain.

The next time I heard from Jerry was on April 4, 1967. I received a garbled radio transmission from the sheriff's office in Bridgeport informing me that a Mr. Jerry Henderson was at their office requesting that I pick him up. Margaret and I were delighted with this news so I fired up the SnoCat and went out to retrieve Jerry. This was the first time we had seen him in almost 3 years so we had some catching up to do hearing about his Vietnam exploits. Jerry stayed the night and as he was leaving the next morning he mentioned that he thought I had a "neat" job. He requested that if there ever was another civil service examination for park ranger to let him know about it, as he might be interested in taking it. There was a "hiring freeze" on at the time so I told him that a test was unlikely in the near future.

In 1968 when I was working at Point Mugu, Jerry was living and working in Southern California selling real estate. We had infrequent contact, but one important occasion we got together when I participated as an usher in his wedding to his lovely wife Pat. As Margaret and I drove up to the church for the ceremony we were "met" by Jerry as he stumbled out of a side entrance door. He was definitely feeling the effects of an all night "Stag" party and was in the process of regurgitating his sins. Fortunately the timing of our arrival was impeccable, as we were able to use one of Abby's clean, fresh diapers to clean Jerry up and make him presentable before he re-entered the church to "kiss the bride".

A year later an announcement for a State Park Ranger examination came out and I remembered that Jerry had expressed an interest in taking the test. I still had a current address for him so I mailed him an application but did not hear from him again for over year. I had no inkling if he had even filed the application I had sent him, let alone taken the test. You can imagine my surprise when one evening in 1970, the telephone rang and Jerry, on the other end, said, "Carl, guess what? I'm, a Park Ranger at Big Basin State Park!" Indeed he was, having been selected as one of the first "Ranger Trainees" chosen for the new program.

In 1971, Jerry completed the Trainee program and was assigned as a State Park Ranger I at Huntington State Beach. He remained there only 6 months before transferring to Mt. San Jacinto State Park and Wilderness Area. He later promoted to State Park Ranger II while he was assigned to Mt. San Jacinto. In 1978, Jerry resigned from the Department of Parks and Recreation to seek other opportunities in various fields of endeavor over the course of the next 25 years. I completely lost track of Jerry until doing research for this story. Thanks to the computer and the Internet that has developed in the ensuing 25 years since I last talked to Jerry, I was able to track him down and renew our friendship. It was great to find him. He is still that goofy and audacious person I knew in my youth who gave me a gift of laughter. It is good that some things never change.

JAMES (JW) HART

You were first introduced to JW in my writings of Pismo State Beach. That was when I first met him. It was to be the first of three (and one half) times in my career that I worked with Jim and tried, unsuccessfully, to straighten him out.

Jim was a young Ranger Trainee at Pismo who talked a good line, mostly about himself. Unfortunately, he could back up most of his talk with action and knew it. Born and raised in eastern New Mexico, Jim had cowboy daring in his blood. The stories and exploits of JW in the Department would be a book in itself. I related a couple of them but there are many more. For instance, one time I was with him on patrol at Pismo when he decided to allow an unlicensed vehicle operator to drive back to his beach campsite to retrieve his driver's license. We followed and sure enough the individual produced his license along with several of his irate buddies. Jim managed to obtain the license but it was grabbed back out of his hands, which raised the stakes of the game considerably. As I eased back to our vehicle to radio for backup in this ever-escalating confrontation, Jim somehow managed to bluff his way out of the situation without getting us killed.

JW liked to tell jokes and stories but he was also a good sport when he was the butt of a joke or prank. One time he came over to my house in Grover City with a handcuff dangling from his wrist and in obvious distress. It seemed that some of the Pismo park crew had managed to handcuff him to the maintenance yard chain link fence and left him there after work. I'm not sure how long he had been attached to the fence but it was evening before he managed to escape. His wife took pity on him (I'll never know why) and gave him some bolt cutters from the shop so he could free himself. He did manage to cut himself free from the fence but he did not have a handcuff key to free himself of the cuff. Jim decided to drive to my house hoping that I would free him and unlock the handcuffs with my key. Of course, I lied a little bit and told Jim that I couldn't free him because I had left my keys at work. I thought it would be much more fun to watch Jim squirm so I suggested that he go down to the local police department and embarrass himself by asking them to unlock the cuffs. It was one of the few times that I saw JW swallow his pride to get out of a situation.

Later, in 1974, I worked with Jim again when he was the Unit Ranger at Palomar Mountain State Park and I was the Chief Ranger for the Montane Area with Jim under my supervision. Always the cowboy, Jim was in his element and took great delight on one occasion when cattle were running loose in the park from an adjacent ranch. The delight wasn't in the fact that the cattle were running loose, but rather that his Chief Ranger (me) had come over that day to check out the operation and could be included in the "roundup." Before I knew it, with a "Yipee Ti Yi Ay", Jim had me astride a horse that he had managed to commandeer and off we went chasing after cattle through ferns, brush, forest and creeks. He was in his element, I wasn't! I think I managed to corral one of the "Little Doggies"; JW got the rest of them. Being the free spirit that Jim is, I believe he actually thought he was living in the 1880's on the Chisom Trail.

The next time I worked close to Jim was in the redwoods. JW was actually assigned to the Piercy Area as its Chief Ranger when I first became Manager of the

Dyerville Area prior to the two Areas combining. He was still close enough to do damage though! He had managed to start up a horseback riding concession of sorts at Benbow SRA that was having limited success. Against my better judgment, he conned me into moving the operation up to Humboldt Redwoods where it still was only marginally successful. I found out, as I'm sure JW knew, that it was easier dealing with the horses than the concessionaire wrangler! If you can imagine it, I actually had to settle a ruckus between the crusty old cowboy concessionaire and one of his **paying** customers. The concessionaire had punched the customer and knocked him down some stairs after a drinking episode. I still can't believe that we weren't sued over that incident.

If Jim was anything, he was a storyteller and spinner of yarns (or lies) and for the most part the public loved his outlandish tales. I think while Jim was in the Piercy Area he liked nothing better than to regale visitors with his story of a Paul Bunyan-like Banana Slug that could "slime" a person to death. If I heard that story once I heard it a thousand times. JW never got tired of it. What he didn't know was that the rest of us did!

Finally, when I went into the Region office in Santa Rosa, who should amble in but the very same JW. Somehow, despite himself, Jim had managed to scramble up the career ladder to become Technical Services Manager. Under the tutelage of Ted Crane he survived that experience too. His office in the Region complex was unique. In the corner were his saddle, spurs, cowboy hat and lasso. The very same saddle and lasso he once used to rope an employee he had made sit on the saddle as he gave a Corrective Interview. How JW didn't get his own Corrective Interview for that ploy remains a mystery.

Jim had many other (mis) adventures. Everything from getting serious food poisoning from the frozen burritos with broken wrappings that he bragged about purchasing so cheaply, to being stranded in the patrol dune buggy his first time out at Pismo Beach. While a ranger out at the very remote Mitchell Caverns State Reserve he was bitten on the hand by a rattlesnake and almost died. While riding the rails as a young man (he was/is forever young) he once witnessed a stabbing in the boxcar and had to deftly extricate himself from that situation. At Palomar Mountain SP, I watched him stitch up a severe wound on his finger with a regular needle and thread because he didn't want to go to the doctor! Jim really is a cowboy who rode rodeo. Evidence of that was visible as he limped back to work after his days off with a loss of feeling in his legs and arms and a hitch in his "giddyup." He was a refreshing nut to have around and a definite plus on the morale of any operation he was associated with. At Region Headquarters he would frequently get on the intercom speaker and recite cowboy poetry or make other equally inappropriate remarks that were good for a laugh.

When Jim retired at a young age, he moved to Oregon and bought a cattle ranch. He did return for a while as a seasonal ranger in the redwoods before devoting full time to his very prosperous Sage Hollow Ranch. Somehow he succeeded in spite of himself. If nothing else, Jim brought a lively sense of much needed humor to the job. It is a gift that all of us should have.

KENNETH LEIGH

I met Ken Leigh on his first day on the job when he reported to work as a Ranger Trainee at Morro Bay SP. Ken, who grew up on a farm in Nebraska, brought with him a strong work ethic, a college degree in geography, a willingness to continue to learn, a love of boating and canoeing, and a great sense of humor.

It did not take a genius to quickly realize that Ranger Trainee Ken would be one of the few "stars" that would graduate to the ranger ranks from the fourteen Trainees that passed through the San Luis Obispo Coast Intake Area. In fact, of the fourteen, only four of them made a career of State Parks and only three of them, Steve

Hill, Steve Michels and Ken Leigh went on to become District Superintendents. They were the best.

I suppose because Ken was such a likable and social character, it was natural that our families did things together. We had a few camping and claming adventures, but it was the sailing in Morro Bay that I remember most. Ken had rigged up his canoe with an elaborate, homemade sail and stabilizing sideboard paddle system that worked fine. I think he was most proud of it and the pushcart trailer he made for transporting the whole rig to the water. I wasn't too sure how much of a sailing expert this Nebraska native was but if he was as competent at this sport as he was on the job I felt I could trust my life and that of my children to his skills. It was a thrill racing through the shark infested waters of Morro Bay (okay, so they were only 2' - 3' Nurse Sharks) with Ken at the helm.

After I moved on from Morro Bay to Cuyamaca and later to Plumas-Eureka I would only occasionally see Ken at various training classes at the Mott Training Center. When he had completed his Ranger Trainee program, Ken had been selected to stay on at Morro Bay as a permanent Ranger I.

In 1977, when I was Manger at Plumas-Eureka SP, the State Park Ranger I position became vacant due to a transfer. This would be my opportunity to fill the position. At the time I was also serving as an instructor at the Mott Training Center as the trainee classes rotated through for various aspects of training. I was scheduled to drive to Pacific Grove on the Monterey Peninsula to teach a class when I decide to make a wide detour in getting there in order to recruit Ken for the Plumas-Eureka position. This added an extra 8 hours to a drive that was already 8 hours but I figured it would be worth it if I were successful in convincing Ken to apply for the job. I knew it was not a sure thing since Ken really did like life in Morro Bay. Additionally, I was aware that he was reachable on the Ranger II list, and that a person of his ability in all probably would be snatched up for promotion soon after I selected him.

In any event, I did make the long trip from Plumas-Eureka to Morro Bay and made my sales pitch. Ken agreed to apply and low and behold he got the job - surprise, surprise! It was my philosophy that it was always better to have an excellent employee for a short time than an average employee for a long time. That is why I took the chance in recruiting and selecting Ken. He was only at Plumas-Eureka SP for a little over a year before he promoted to Supervising Ranger at Old Town, San Diego. But what a year we had!

Ken should get much of the credit for making what I consider the single most productive year of accomplishments in my career with State Parks. Despite Plumas-Eureka being such a small unit we made the most of our limited resources. Ken had a hand in many of the accomplishments I listed in Chapter 7. Most notable was his work in helping to establish the Interpretive Association, develop a Teachers Aide Kit, improve the trail system and generally upgrade the interpretive programming of the park. He was an excellent "supervisor" in dealing with a large seasonal staff and had willingness and even enjoyed doing maintenance projects. That was the key to our success, as we never made a distinction between visitor service and maintenance service duties. We just did what was necessary regardless of labor relation rules in place at that time. Today conflicting labor rules prevent this level of cooperative work and for this the parks and the public suffer the consequences.

Ken, as my next door neighbor in Johnsville, made winter life a little more bearable. We often cross county skied or trekked in snowshoes up to Grass Lake or to the gorge in Upper Jamison Creek just to check out how things looked in winter. I guess we marked this kind of "work" down on our time sheets as "patrol" though I can never recall seeing a single person on our patrols in winter, at least during the week days.

Ken and his career eventually moved on to San Diego, then to La Purisima Mission near Lompoc, on to the Mendocino District, and finally to the Santa Monica Mountains District and Point Mugu SP (it had been reclassified from a recreation area to a state park after I left). When the Department again reorganized in 1993, he became the District Superintendent of the Marin District. With that move, Ken, once again fell under my supervision after a 15-year hiatus.

It may seem strange to some, but it is normal within the California State Park System that working relationships begin, end, and are re-established, rearranged and yet appear seamless as if there has been no gap in service or relationship. It was as if Ken and I were back together after a short vacation and we easily made the adjustment into our respective roles. It is not, however, our working relationship that turned out to be the most significant impact upon my life that Ken had.

Ken, had known my daughter Abby since she was 5 years old when we lived in Morro Bay. He had watched her grow up at Plumas- Eureka and seen her from time to time after his various moves. When Abby, by now a State Park Ranger at Mount Diablo State Park, became ill with lymphoma cancer, Ken and his wife Kim became a source of comfort and support for the ordeal that our family was experiencing. It was Ken's wife Kim who organized an Education Fund drive within the Department's "Park Family" for Abby's children after she passed away. For that we will always be grateful.

It was a further tribute to Abby when Ken, starting a second family with his wife Kim, named their first child Abigail.

TED REINHARDT

Theodore Reinhardt II was my Chief Ranger at Humboldt Redwoods from 1980-1983. We had first met in 1973 while attending "Cop Shop" (Peace Officer Training) at Modesto Criminal Justice Center. At that time Ted was a Supervising Ranger at Folsom SRA. Quite honestly I don't remember much about him other than the fact he seemed very competitive in the sports activities. I also learned at that time that Ted was a former airline pilot for a small commuter airline. Because of my interest in aircraft, I liked hearing of his flying adventures. I don't think I ever saw Ted again until he came over to Plumas-Eureka from the adjacent Sierra District on his day off for a visit with his wife Jeanne sometime around 1976.

Ted was my surprise choice for Chief Ranger when I selected him in 1980. I did some background checking on him prior to the interview and got reports back that confirmed his abilities. Ted was one of the few who drove to Humboldt Redwoods for an in-person interview, something I hadn't done when I interviewed for my job. It is a long drive from Lake Tahoe to the redwoods no matter what route you take and in winter it can be an especially treacherous drive. I was immediately impressed that he would take the time and drive for 8-9 hours for a half-hour interview for the job. You don't usually do that unless you really want the job. Most of the other candidates opted for a telephone interview. As I recall, Ted sweated through the interview but he answered all of my prepared questions correctly. Later he told me that it was the toughest interview he had ever taken. I didn't think so, but I did wish that he had wiped the chair dry after he left!

When Ted finally did arrive in advance of his family, his first job as you read earlier was to assist in the "murder" of my chickens. I figured that if he could do **that,** he could do anything. Ted was as efficient at killing chickens as he was at every task he took on. I quickly became aware of many of Ted's quirks, habits and idiosyncrasies and he mine, so that we established a great working and personal relationship.

Ted was born in Texas and grew up in San Luis Obispo. He was pretty much a hometown kid attending schools there all the way up to his degree in Biology from

Cal Poly San Luis Obispo. After graduation from college, he obtained a commercial pilot license and worked for several years flying for a small commuter airline. He would later tell me some hair raising tales of his experiences with the airline, such as losing an engine on take-off, getting struck by lightening, or even making a barrel roll with the airliner for the fun of it (thankfully no passengers aboard). Maybe it was the latter incident that resulted in his leaving that line of work.

In any event, in 1972 Ted was hired as a Ranger Trainee at the Folsom Lake State Recreation Area near Sacramento. Upon completing his training he stayed on as a full time ranger but shortly afterwards left to return to flying. This time the California State Police hired him. He was assigned to fly out of the Lancaster Airport in the Mojave Desert and patrol a major water pipeline along the Owens Valley. To say that Ted became bored with the job would be an understatement. Spending many hours in a hot airplane hanger in the desert and flying the same routine flights in a small single engine airplane just did not fill the bill. So it was that Ted returned to State Parks and pursued a career that led him to Hearst Castle, Mount Diablo and Lake Tahoe, Humboldt Redwoods, Sacramento Headquarters and back to Lake Tahoe. Like all of us, Ted's family, his wife Jeanne, and sons Teddy and Eric took a liking to, or at least came to expect, the somewhat nomadic lifestyle of a California State Park Ranger.

Perhaps because of his flight training and the precise nature of that activity, Ted has always been a case study in time management for me. If he says he will meet you at 5:15 pm he does not mean 5:14 pm or 5:16 pm. If you are late or he is early you are sure to find Ted pacing up and down, arms crossed upon his chest, checking his watch every 10 seconds. He will never, never, never miss a deadline whether for work or play.

Ted is also an electronics junkie and must have the latest of entertainment or weather recording gadgets, be it the first 12 foot diameter satellite dish in Humboldt

Redwoods or probably the finest home theater in Graeagle. His theater is a thing of beauty with plush seats, purple and gold velvet drapes, colorful neon lighting on the ceiling and track lights on the floor to direct you to your seats. While his theater is an accurate replica of the real thing, I still can't figure out how he can keep track of the 8 (count them) remote control devices used to operate his electronic menagerie.

When Ted is not watching TV or one of his hundreds of movies you will find him attacking the golf course. I was never successful in converting him to fly fishing though he did go so far as purchasing a fly fishing outfit, but to my knowledge only used it twice (Hey, nobody's perfect). Despite this one flaw in fishing expertise, Ted is passionate about most everything else he does. He has collected and kept years of statistics from following his beloved Los Angles Dodgers and when we were doubles tennis partners he attacked that game as he does most sports activities with absolutely no intention of losing. That paid off as we won several Southern Humboldt County tournaments. About the only thing Ted attacks with more vigor than sports is food. You can almost be assured that while you are still eating your salad, Ted will be finishing up his dessert.

In my entire park career I was fortunate to work with two Ted's who had no equal when it came to Completed Staff Work. In our Santa Rosa Region office, Ted Crane filled that bill but in the field Ted Reinhardt stood shoulders above all others I worked with. He was the best implementer of ideas I ever worked with and excelled at turning many of my ideas into reality.

Because Ted and I knew each other so well we had an easy give and take relationship that was often misread by others who actually believe we didn't get along. At meetings we would sometimes make disparaging remarks in a joking fashion in our attempt to out-do each other. We both took great delight in this but it was not uncommon for people afterwards to ask me if I had a personnel problem with my Chief Ranger! Nothing could have been further from the truth. Ted was a willing participant in this game and could dish out the rhetoric as well as take it. Beyond our playful banter and what we may have accomplished on the job, what we did after working hours remained just as beneficial to our work and the community. Together Ted and I managed both youth baseball and basketball teams in Southern Humboldt County. This provided an opportunity for non-park community members to see park employees in a different light as family folks just like them. Our involvement with the community in sports, I am convinced, went a long way in obtaining support for our Visitor Center and Interpretive Association success with the local residents. There was definitely a lessening of the "We verses Them" syndrome. We even managed to piggyback that success into the schools even more when Ranger Tim Young set up a school "Ranger Ride-Along" program with the local Weott elementary school.

After Ted left Humboldt Redwoods in 1983 for a new assignment in Sacramento Headquarters he again put his analytical skills to great use in assisting the Deputy Director on innumerable special assignments beyond his normal duties as Superintendent for Law Enforcement. We, of course, remained in close contact, and entered a period of our relationship that continues in retirement.

Ted and his wife Jeanne really had not done too much traveling outside of California up to this point in their lives. Once they and Ted's parents had flown a small private plane cross-country to St. Louis, but for the most part they were content to stay put. Margaret and I introduced them to the adventure of travel. Many of our trips hadn't started as adventures but by the time Ted and I nearly ruined them they were. One time we went to Crater Lake in a motor home with a worried Ted fretting about of running out of gas the moment we started the trip. Another time we took a 3,185-mile road trip to Dinosaur National Monument, the Custer Battlefield and Yellowstone National Park in a whirlwind, one-week non-stop driving marathon. The highlight of the trip was the miserable night that we spent with all of us packed like sardines in the back of Ted's Suburban station wagon trying to sleep during a thunderstorm at an appropriately named "Tough" campground somewhere in Wyoming. We also took two trips to Hawaii together and a 19-day cruise of the Mediterranean, which were great but not without our (mis) adventures.

What I learned and love most about Ted is that you can count on him to do what he says. He has no hidden agenda and is a very "easy to read" person. In times of need he was always there, whether for when my career was on the line with allegations of impropriety or when my son Chris was badly injured in a skiing accident and we needed Ted and his folks' assistance to help us through that traumatic event.

Ted followed me into retirement and settled for a while in the Graeagle area in a home around the corner and a few houses up from us. Now that his current passion for golf has got the better of him he has moved on to the warmer climes of Arizona which will be much easier on his ravaged knees (fourteen operations at last count!) and golf game. Our partnership will survive this move too, as we prepare for our next adventure, a rafting trip down the Colorado River in the Grand Canyon.

Ted is more than the best Chief Ranger I ever had - he is a friend for life!

CARL A. ANDERSON

A thump on the bottom of my boots. That's how I first met him. My feet were sticking out from under an old International Travelall truck as I worked on clearing a clogged fuel line. Carl A. Anderson, the Big Swede, better known as "Andy", had come up from the District Office in Stockton to meet the "new kid on the block". He was the first "Big Boss" I was to meet and I was pleasantly surprised to find him a very "unboss like" kind of guy. He was actually very personable, funny, and practical. On top of that he was really nice. We hit it off immediately and thus began a working relationship that was to last almost 25 years as our paths crossed and intertwined through our respective assignments as we moved up and down the State of California. Andy proved to be my mentor, and more importantly my friend, confidant, and advisor throughout my entire park career.

I think what initially endeared Margaret and me to Andy was his real concern for our health and safety in the remote Bodie assignment in the winter of 1966-67, especially once he learned of Margaret's pregnancy. He would constantly check up on us to see how we were doing, something others didn't often do when we were snowbound with limited communications to the outside world.

It was Andy who gave us the news that we would have to move out of Bodie after our daughter, Abigail, was born. He told me to write a letter requesting a transfer. I was to list three parks that I would like to move to in order of preference. Naively, I did so, never suspecting that none of my requests would be honored. It was Andy who told me that we were to be transferred to Folsom Lake State Recreation Area near Sacramento. So it was in October 1967 that I telephoned him from Bridgeport to inform him that we were enroute to Sacramento to look for a place to live. "Whoa, hold your horses", he said. There had been a change of plans it seemed. The Folsom position had been filled and now we had the choice of three Southern California beach parks. I choose the one that was brand new and hadn't even been open to the public yet. That was Point Mugu State Recreation Area of which I have previously written. This was the first amicable parting of our ways, but it was not to last to long.

Carl Anderson, up to this point, and even later, had a wonderful park career. He and his wife Luella had lived and worked in a number of parks, some of which I, too, would later be assigned to. Among these were Cuyamaca Rancho State Park and Humboldt Redwoods State Park at opposite ends of the state. Prior to starting his park career, Andy had trained as a Navy pilot in World War II. Ironically, his early first duty station was out of Portola, California at what is now one of the Plumas County airports in Beckwourth, just 15 miles from where we now live in Graeagle.

Upon discharge from the Navy, Andy tried his hand at carpentry work but he proved all thumbs at this to the extent that he sawed off one thumb and left it on the job. Lu laid down the law and said, "enough is enough, find another line of work before you kill yourself". That new line of work proved to be with State Parks when he accepted his first position as a ranger at Cuyamaca Rancho State Park. That was followed with assignments at Doheny State Beach, Richardson Grove State Park, Patrick's Point State Park and Humboldt Redwoods before moving on to the Stockton District Office where I first met him.

In any event, shortly after we left Bodie for our new assignment at Point Mugu, Andy received a promotion to the Central Coast District Office in Monterey as the Acting District Superintendent. As things turned out, Andy never did get a permanent appointment to the Monterey position. Despite this, he was nevertheless in the right place at the right time when Director William Penn Mott selected Andy as the first Deputy Director appointed to the new Southern California office that opened on Olvera Street in downtown Los Angeles. Andy was the perfect fit for this highly visible public relations and liaison position which needed someone to deal with the myriad politically sensitive issues facing the Department in that part of the State.

As much as Andy enjoyed the "hobnobbing" and intrigue of wheeling/dealing in the politics of Southern California, his first love of parks was working "in the field" of Northern California. The opportunity to do that came with the Department's reorganization in 1970 when he was appointed the Area Manager of the Sierra District. Five years later I followed him north when I was appointed

Area Manager of the Plumas-Eureka SP. Later, when word came that Andy was being promoted and transferred from the Sierra Area to District 1 Headquarters in Eureka I was thrilled that Andy and Lu would be returning to the redwood country they loved so much.

It was only a year or two later that I was again to follow Andy. I loved my assignment and family lifestyle at Plumas-Eureka but I did not find it a particularly challenging job after four years. I felt that I had accomplished most of what I could and wanted to do there, so despite saying "I would never leave this park" I found myself staring at a promotional job announcement advertising the Area Manager position at Humboldt Redwoods State Park. It would be a major change and increase in scope and responsibility going from one of the smallest parks in the State Park System to what was then the second largest in the state after Anza-Borrego Desert State Park. Should I try for it? After discussing it with my wife Margaret, I decided to "sort of try for it". That is, I wouldn't bother to drive up to Eureka for the interview since I already knew the area from my time in attending college at Humboldt State in nearby Arcata.

It was my belief that I would have an interview with District Superintendent Allan "Tiny" Philbrook whom I had only met once before at our Clam Feed in Morro Bay several years earlier. Much to my surprise, and delight, when I called in April 1979 to set up the interview I found that Andy would be the one conducting the interviews! As I recall we talked on the phone for about 45 minutes as he questioned me and told me of the problems with the local community, and asked me what I could do and bring to the assignment. Although I felt good about the interview I was still concerned that since I hadn't made the effort to drive up to Eureka that that might prove to have a negative effect on the outcome of the selection.

One week, then two weeks, came and went with no word of the outcome. I assumed that I hadn't been selected for the position because it usually did not take so long to receive notification of the results one way or another. At last I could stand it no longer so I called Andy and asked what the heck was going on? I did not expect the answer I got. I remember exactly what Andy said to me. It was this: "Well, Carl, you are the only person I interviewed who bothered to call back so I guess you get the job". I was stunned. So it was in May, 1979 that I headed back to redwood country where I would once again be working with the Big Swede.

When Andy retired in 1983 after more than 36 years of dedicated service he remained active with parks and was always available for advice and the perspective of "one who has been there" when times were a little tough. Occasionally, after Andy retired he would come down to Humboldt Redwoods and he and I would drift fish the South Fork of the Eel River and he would revel me with stories of the Great Flood of 1955 and we discussed parks, family, and life in general. He and Lu remained and settled in Eureka after retirement and I would often stop by to see them even after I had moved on to Santa Rosa and Sacramento. I think one of the finest compliments Andy ever paid me was not in words, but in action when he became a member of the Board of Directors for the Humboldt Redwoods Interpretive Association which I had founded in 1979. Andy also served as the representative for the Save the Redwoods League in the North Coast region until his death on January 4, 2000.

The California Department of Parks and Recreation, the Save the Redwoods League, his family and friends have recently paid the highest compliment and recognition to the Big Swede by setting aside the 3,500 acre **CARL A ANDERSON NATURAL PRESERVE** in the Rockefeller Forest area of his beloved Humboldt Redwoods State Park. I cannot think of a more fitting tribute to the man who did so much to preserve the redwood giants of this and many other parks and still had the time and patience to keep me straight on my "Pathway Through Parks".

Now that Andy is gone one must remember that he was not only a man of action but also of words. All who knew him can attest to his humor and his way with words. Andy was a poet and in fact, his wife Luella, published a collection of Andy's poems entitled "Poems & Reflections of a State Park Ranger". The cover of Andy's book of poems is graced with artwork sketches of the ducks that he was forever doodling. With Lu's permission what follows is my favorite poem from that collection harking back to 1964 when the great battles to save old growth forests of the north coast redwoods from destruction was surrounded by controversy with proposed creation of Redwoods National Park and the Prairie Creek freeway bypass.

CUT'EM DOWN
The Redwood Parks Controversy Song
1984

Cut'em down, Cut'em down, they're only
Worth cash on the ground
Our econ-o-mee depends on that tree,
So crank up the saw- -Bring 'em down.

Cut'em down, bring 'em down. the parks
take up too much ground.
And they don't pay taxes, so sharpen those
axes
And crank up the saw- -Cut'em down.

Hack 'em down, whack'em down, through
intelligent research we've found
One old redwood tree is plenty to see,
So crank up the saw- -Cut'em down.

Cut'em down, cut'em down, they grow
where our freeway is bound.
We will brook no refinement of our chosen
alignment,
So crank up the saw- -Cut'em down.

Chop'em down, saw'em down, they're over
mature and unsound.
Seedlings can't grow in their shadows you
know,
So crank up the saw- -Bring'em down.

Cut'em down, bring'em down, let our
tractors crawl over the ground.
'Though the hills start to slide, by the
"rules" we abide,
And it's "not guilty" we will be found.

Chop 'em down, saw'em down, let the rain
fall on bare ground.
"Though we fill up our rivers with silt,
stumps and slivers,
The "Corps" will not let us drown

Cut'em down, cut'em down, 'though our
salmon no longer are found.
We'll plant plenty of catfish 'cause we found
out that that fish
Can almost live on dry ground

Cut'em down, chop'em down, 'though the
pulp mills may smell up our town.
They use up the small trees, so now we take
all trees.
Crank up the saw- -Cut 'em down.

Cut'em down, bring'em down, our
reforestation is sound.
Please shed no tears, for in two thousand
years,
They'll be just as they were when first
found.

ANDY'S DUCKS

Andy has returned to the forest-a giant among giants.

LEGISLATIVE LAMENTS

Twenty-five to thirty years ago field personnel were not encouraged to deal directly with members of the California State Senate or Assembly. In fact in many instances there were direct orders not to do so. "Sacramento", meaning DPR Headquarters, in most instances would take care of "the problem(s)". How times have changed. Now, not only must the Park Superintendent take on that sometimes sensitive chore, they are expect to or at the very least maintain a working relationship with local legislative aides. Sometimes I wish it weren't so. A righteous legislator on the loose with a special interest in a park can be a terrible waste of time and money. The true purpose of a park and its resources can be pushed aside in the name of expediency in an effort to satisfy an individual constituent or larger constituency. I saw this happen more often then I like to remember. The truth of the matter it seemed to me was that when it came to dealing with the Legislature the DPR often was in the embrace of that all to familiar "Love/Hate" relationship.

State Parks were often a jewel within a particular legislator's district. They provide a positive affirmation for what is good about government. They also cost money to operate, with much of the cost unseen by both the general public and the legislature. Additionally, it seems that many of the legislators believe that it is okay to collect fees, raise fees, or institute new fees as long as none of the aforementioned occurs within parks inside boundaries of their voting districts.

As a Ranger I, Supervising Ranger II, and even as a Chief Ranger III I can not recall ever having dealt directly with a Senator, Member of the Assembly, or their aides. That includes never talking face to face, on the telephone, or through correspondence. It just wasn't prevalent to do so (at least in my case) in the period from 1966-1975.

That changed quickly when I moved to Plumas-Eureka SP in 1975. In the space of a two or three months I was suddenly dealing with a Senator in person, on the phone, and via the mail, who had a vested interest in "our" little park. It did not matter that the park was not located within his home district because it turned out that he in fact had a private home in Johnsville which for all intent and purposes was right in the middle of the park!

One time I remember receiving a telephone call after hours at home from the Senator complaining of noise in town (not park property) while I was in the middle of dinner with my family. As disconcerting as that can be it is even more upsetting to then receive, a short time later, a second telephone call from the Director of State Parks after **he** has received a complaint from this same Sacramento Solon. Then too, there can be the touchy matter of dealing with a Senator's friends and family who may think that policies, rules and regulations, and laws do not apply to them. One must carefully walk a fine line in tactfully balancing the protection if park resources and maintaining professional, if not cordial relations with this special park visitor. One way I tried to do this was to provide appropriate help to the Senator whenever possible. This usually involved some aspect of assistance for a youth camp that was sponsored by the Senator. The camp was located about 10 miles from the park and reached only by a very poor USFS dirt road. For example, one year Ranger Leigh and I drove back into the camp to help install a windmill for the camp water supply. Eventually, I learned the boundaries of our relationship and was witness to the benefits of working with a powerful legislator. A new water system, a fire truck, and group campground are evidence that things worked out okay in the end despite a few bumps in the road.

Perhaps the best working relationships I ever had in my dealing with those in power at the State Capitol was through the legislative aides of a Senator and Assemblyman while I was managing the redwood parks of Southern Humboldt and Northern Mendocino Counties. Both of these individuals were reasonable, practical and persuasive without being pushy. The job was made easier by the fact that both of them truly loved parks and they had the best interests of the park in mind. Often it was they who would make a suggestion for a solution to a problem that a constituent was complaining about that would satisfy that person and their bosses, while not compromising the park. I marveled at the tact and skill they constantly demonstrated. One of them needed all of that skill one day to mollify me after I had hired her daughter to work in one of our parks and she promptly wrecked a park vehicle!

By the time I had gotten to the Region Office in Santa Rosa, I was an "Old Pro" as were most of my peers in dealing with the politics of parks. Outlined earlier were some of the problems we faced with wine, beach fees and eucalyptus trees. There were many others too and almost every one involved as part of the solution a component that would satisfy the demands of a legislator or at least provide a face saving action that could stand the scrutiny of a sometime irate constituency.

Of all the meetings I have had with legislators or their aides there is only one that I can say stands out in my mind to the point of remembering the time and date. It was October 17, 1989. On that day I had picked up the local Senator and Assemblyman's legislative aides to take them on a tour of the Russian River District parks. The units along the Sonoma Coast were not only at the ocean's edge but they were the center of a sea of constant turmoil in a storm of protests. It seemed that the media was searching for a story, any story, as long as it was emotional. With a captive audience in my vehicle this trip gave me the opportunity to explain our programs and policies and show the two aides first hand the results of our actions away from the glare of the spotlight on radio, television and newspapers. I was able to do this. The aides and I spent the entire afternoon together and were returning to the office in Santa Rosa with the car radio on as we listened to the start of the World Series between the

San Francisco Giants and Oakland A's. The radio went dead at 5:05 pm. **EARTHQUAKE!** We didn't feel a thing. I guess we weren't the "movers and shakers" we thought we were.

The closer that I got to the State Capitol, the more evident it became how petty some legislators could be. The Resource Building is only two blocks from this institute of democracy. This close physical proximity resulted in "opportunities" to meet any particular legislator in person should a problem arise, and we did, usually at their beck and call.

I quickly developed empathy for the park management staff of the State Capitol Museum crew that had to work under the microscope of the legislature on a daily basis. What a pain in the --- that could be. Perhaps the worst abuse of power and pettiness I observed and was involved in, concerned the alleged lack of performance by one of the park staff at the Capitol Museum. Management had clearly documented some performance deficiencies of an employee and was prepared to take personnel action. It so happened that the employee's spouse was a lobbyist with direct connections to a legislator. Faster than you can dismiss an employee, **we** were called on the carpet and meeting with the legislator defending our action and that of the Capitol Museum Management staff. I guess in the eyes of some it is okay to sleep on the job with a newspaper over your face. I did not doubt the documentation provided by park staff since I had personally observed less than stellar performance in action by the employee. Once, while on lunch break I went over to the Capitol to view an art exhibit. Since I was not in uniform and the employee did not know me I was free to observe this individual in in-action. You would think that at a minimum the employee would greet visitors and be available to answer questions, as well as provide the security needed to protect the artifacts and artwork on exhibit. In this instance, the employee never looked up from the newspaper or the crossword puzzle that was so engrossing and took precedence over the task at hand. Due to the interceding of a legislator I was able to watch the wheels of "due process" grind to a halt.

At least in this next instance of legislative involvement there was a semblance of actually trying to work out a compromise solution to solve a problem. Columbia SHP is in the foothills of Calaveras County. This historical park is a popular destination for tourist and school groups to get a taste and feel for the gold rush environment of a rich boomtown. Not a synthetic Disneyland re-creation of a mining town or a true ghost town like Bodie, Columbia is somewhere in between those extremes. Restored structures have been modified through "adaptive use" and the proprietors wear period costumes and conduct "Living History" that will hopefully provide the visitor with a quality educational and interpretive experience. Commercial businesses operated by concessionaires under contract with the Department sell goods and services.

As you might guess, occasional disputes can occur in interpreting the meaning and intent of a contract of this nature as the Department attempts to maintain the historic integrity of the unit and the concessionaire attempts to keep operating cost as low as possible. The primary concerns in this instance dealt with the renewal of a number of the concession contracts, the length of time it took to get them renewed and unauthorized modifications to historic structures.

Many of Columbia's concession contracts were considered by some to be quite lucrative. Some of the proprietors, especially family run businesses, had been in place for many years under contract and did not feel the State was obligated to put the contracts out for bid when their contracts expired. That, and the fact that because it was a lengthy process to put a contract out to bid, sent many of the incumbents on a rampage directly to their representative in the State Capitol. Couple that with a politically active entrepreneur who feels wronged over contract requirements and you have a recipe for a very long and drawn out dispute that is sure to be carried out in the spotlight of media attention – and was.

In one instance the proprietor of a Blacksmith Shop concession took us to task. Despite the fact that the contract for this concession was clear (at least to us) that authenticity was an important element of the presentation to the public, the blacksmith was unwilling to modify the shop and remove the propane forge he was utilizing. He further felt that he should not have to pay rent to the department and felt that the department should pay him for the privilege of presenting what he thought were his unique blacksmith demonstrations. It doesn't work that way.

The culmination of this lengthy and highly public dispute was several "Town House" meetings at the local Junior College down the road from the park. Well attended by both proponents for and against concession operations, we found ourselves in the all too familiar role as moderator directing the two highly vocal opposing groups and park staff down the path to compromise. Ironically, for whatever reason, the legislator who arranged these meetings only managed to briefly attend one of the meetings and thus missed the full impact, wrath, and abuse that some of us had to endure. I sometimes wished I could arrange my schedule the way that legislator did! Oh, as for the blacksmith shop, new bids were solicited for the concession and a contract for an authentic blacksmith operation was awarded. It is still in operation today.

The most frustrating thing about this whole situation was that the process took from February to September to resolve the problems. In that 8-month period the number of meetings, telephone calls, controlled correspondence was staggering and, it could be argued, of dubious benefit. Oh well, the Public spoke its piece, the Concessionaires had their say, the Park maintained its integrity, and perhaps most importantly of all, the Politician was unscathed by criticism.

MTC

I have always felt that the California Department of Parks and Recreation left the Dark Ages and entered the Age of Enlightenment with the advent of the William Penn Mott Jr. Training Center (MTC).

Prior to about 1969, training for employees was a rather "hit and miss" affair with no coherent, coordinated effort within a District, much less the State. About that time the Department undertook the first of several major re-organizations which modernized the State Park System, and a decision was made in Sacramento Headquarters that placed more emphasis on training. That and the mandated training requirements for Peace Officers were the catalysts that brought training to center stage.

I first learned of the upcoming changes in early 1968-69 when Jim Kruger, who headed up the Training Office in Sacramento, made a visit to Leo Carrillo SB to outline the new program for Area Manager Jim Geary. Though I didn't attend the meeting, I met Mr. Kruger later that evening at a potluck held in the park shop complex. I remember being excited at the prospect of the new program he outlined that was to include a statewide training center, something called "Intake Areas", and a new classification of employees called Ranger Trainees.

The geographic location for the new training center was to be on the Central Coast in Pacific Grove at the Asilomar Conference Center. Asilomar was and still is a unit of the State Park System. The beautiful setting of the Monterey Peninsula would only add to desirability of this location. That and the fact that there were already accommodations that could be used to house and feed employees gave the Department a jump-start on the new training program.

In 1969, the Training Center began operations with the initial classes held in what had been a small two-bedroom house on the property. It was quaintly known as the "Outside Inn". The classroom was what must have been the living room of the house at one time. It was small, not very user friendly but somehow we managed. I can not remember the first class I attended there but I believe it was a two-week management class. After a couple of days in that cramped classroom and the excitement of an extended stay in beautiful surroundings had worn off the days could get a little long.

Despite ourselves I think most of us absorbed much of what was taught. For me, however, the chief benefit was the opportunity to meet and exchange truth and lies with other park professionals from all parts of the State. Perhaps the best learning came after hours over another of "Chef Eddies" evening meals or after a class trip to the Bear Cave in nearby Salinas. The new training center was a centralized place to exchange ideas, meet new people, renew old acquaintances and make lifelong friends.

It was during a later training sessions that I first noticed the construction taking place across the street from the Outside Inn and learned that this was to be our permanent Training Center. A modernistic, 2-classroom building for instruction and three 2-story lodges were to be built.

The William Penn Mott Jr. Training Center was completed in 1974 and immediately put to good use in moving the Ranger Trainee Program into the new facilities. In addition to the modern classroom, the 3 lodges, Treetops, Deer Lodge, and Live Oak each of which housed two Trainees to a room, were a luxury beyond our expectations after our time in the Outside Inn.

Over the years the MTC has had an excellent cadre of staff that have cycled through at the Training Center as Director, support, and specialist staff positions in the various disciplines Visitor Services, Maintenance Services and Administrative Services. Many of these folks such as

Ken Jones, Mary Wright, and Denzil Verardo moved up through the Department to positions of greater responsibility at the Deputy Director level in Headquarters. Certainly the individual with longest tenure at the MTC is undoubtedly the recently retired Director Broc Stenman. Broc was one of the original Ranger Trainees who began his career at Mt. Tamalpais SP and later moved on as a Supervising Ranger in the Channel Coast District before being assigned to the MTC in 1974.

Broc was in place at the MTC in 1975-76 when I was first recruited into the Training Program as an instructor. This was when I was working at Plumas-Eureka SP. My first teaching assignment was as an instructor for Administration and Business Management. Later I was also to be an instructor in a Continuing Interpretation course. The most enjoyable instruction I led, however, was in the Law Enforcement segment of the Ranger Trainee/Cadet classes. This entailed Discretionary Decision-Making and Law Enforcement Ethics. Interspersed with these programs I occasionally participated as course leader for Secretary Seminars. In total I was an instructor several times a year for almost 25 years until my retirement. It was always a special joy for me to meet the bright new trainees and cadets who were just beginning their career with the same high hopes, aspirations and ideals that I hoped I still shared with them. In any event, Broc kept asking me back so I guess I didn't put all of the students to sleep.

"BANG! BANG! YOU'ER DEAD

I have spent many, many hours, days, weeks and months as both an instructor and student at the Mott Training Center at Asilomar over the course of 33 years. The facilities and the training that is provided are excellent. There was one incident in particular that stands out as most memorable for the shocking impact it had on the participants of one management class in which I took part. For the protection of the innocent and all parties involved I have omitted names in this account.

I'm sure many of you have attended training sessions or regular high school or college classes where there is one individual in class who is always disruptive with loud, boisterous and inappropriate remarks. These individuals interrupt not only the instructor but also other students who might have something meaningful to contribute to a discussion. It has been my experience both as an instructor and participant that usually a low-key reprimand is sufficient to take care of the problem or sufficient peer pressure from other students will curtail the offender's comments. That did not happen in this instance.

Our instructor, a highly respected member of the Training Center staff, was doing a fine job of covering the material for the class. Granted, sitting in a training session all day can become boring no matter how interesting the subject, but usually with friends and colleagues you know well, there is sufficient interaction to make for lively and appropriate conversation and banter. Once in a while, however, someone just gets on your nerves to the point you want to strangle them. I noticed as our "friend" got bolder and bolder with his inane remarks that there was much more fidgeting, glancing in his direction, and finally downright ugly stares trying to will (or maybe weld) his mouth shut. The instructor was having more and more difficulty controlling the class and it seemed as if the disruptive person was enjoying every minute of it. At one of the breaks several of us told the individual to "cool it" but when class resumed so did the disruptive comments. Several of us made some more pointed suggestions to the effect that we had heard enough from this interrupter. He seemed to cherish the spotlight and took our comments for what they were worth to him - nothing. There seemed like no solution to the problem, but we had underestimated our instructor.

After the next break the same scenario started up

once again. Enough was enough. Suddenly, the instructor reached under the podium and pulled out a .38 cal revolver. He shouted, "I've had enough of your damn interruptions ___" and pointed the gun at the disruptive student and fired two "shots"! People were stunned when the Instructor pulled out the gun and some folks actually "hit the deck" when the shots were fired. Our offensive friend was more than stunned, he was petrified. You can imagine the sound of two **blank** gunshots fired in an enclosed classroom. Our ears were ringing from the reverberation of gunshots echoing off the walls. This action was so unlike the Instructor's normal demeanor that we at first didn't know what to think of it. As we recovered our composure we noticed how quiet it had become at last. Our disruptive student was still and looked to be in a catatonic state. Hands straight out on the desk in front of him, eyes staring straight ahead and most importantly, MOUTH SHUT! The Instructor certainly had regained control of the classroom, albeit by unorthodox methods, but there would be no further classroom interruptions from this class member for the remainder of the week. We had heard the last of his stupid stories and were better for it.

I'm sure under normal circumstances this would have been a "firing offense". Under these circumstances the instructor should have been awarded a marksmanship badge. He was right on target!

"NO, NOT THAT DOOR!"

I have been a participant in many interviews, both as interviewee and as an interviewer. As the person being interviewed most of my interviews were a little strange. Some were almost "non-interviews" such as I had when I was selected for Bodie, transferred to Point Mugu or promoted to Supervising Ranger at Morro Bay. In fact, with the exception of my Regional Director interview, they were all pretty short and straightforward affairs. The promotional examinations on the other hand, which often consisted only of an oral interview, could cause anyone to sweat a little. I must admit it was much easier to be a member of the interview panel asking the questions than it was to be the one on the "Hot Seat" trying to answer them.

Once I had reached the supervisory and management level in the department, I was often asked to participate as member of examination boards. It was a task that I really did enjoy, and it was a great opportunity to assess candidates who I might want on my own staff some day (or who I wouldn't touch with the proverbial ten foot pole!). I might even discover which "rising star" out of the candidate pool might be my boss in the future. As grueling as some of these examinations might be for the candidates, they could be even more so for the panel members. Even with notes, we often struggled to remember what a particular candidate had to say as the interviews tended to blend together. I must say though that I always felt that the panels seemed to be able to maintain a fair objectivity in the process. Sometimes it took a lot of humor to maintain our sanity. We would talk to as many as 80 candidates in the period of a week, allotting half an hour for each candidate, so that after the second or third day of day-long interviews things tended to get a little fuzzy.

Perhaps the most difficult part of the examination process was evaluating the pre-examination reports that each candidate's supervisor had prepared. I can remember one panel I was on when about 38 of 40 candidates were rated "Outstanding" by the candidate's supervisor. Personally, as a panel member, I knew the abilities of some of those candidates and I knew some of them certainly were not "Outstanding". It was a case of supervisors "passing the buck" and failing to objectively rate employees. Ironically, in those instances it was often the case that the panel members spent as much time discussing and evaluating the candidate's supervisor as the candidate himself. Goofy things did happen at times even during these promotional examinations. I recall one occasion where we began an interview with a mid level manager who produced a little stuffed bear that he placed on the table in front of us for some unknown reason. I think it was his attempt to bring a little levity into the situation. Unfortunately for him, we were not in a laughing mood at the time.

Perhaps one of the strangest interview sessions I encountered involved the hiring interviews for a Ranger Cadet class that was conducted at the Mott Training Center. There were four teams of two people each, who made up the four interview panels. At the end of each day we would discuss and merge our lists in priority order to obtain the final rankings.

In my case, I was teamed up with Supervising Ranger Jill Dampier, whom I must say was a delightful, dedicated individual who accepted the task of selecting the next generation of state park rangers as seriously as it deserved.

We had conducted several interviews when the first of two memorable interviews began. We had a series of prepared questions that each candidate was to be asked, as well as a box full of miscellaneous hand-held objects that would be used for an impromptu interpretive presentation. We could also intersperse our own questions as the course of the interview developed.

There was an expectation that the interviewees would exhibit some degree of nervousness. That was normal. On this occasion, however, the individual was really "up tight". He came in carrying a handful of 4"x 6" cards, at least 25 of them. On each card he had written prepared answers and/or statements for potential questions we might ask. As we proceeded with the questions he would "shuffle his deck" until he found what he thought was an appropriate answer. At no time during the interview was he spontaneous and forthcoming with any answer. I had never seen this level of "preparation" before during an interview. We could not break his pattern in using those cards. At one point he dropped them on the floor which flustered him even more and even solicited some sympathy on the part of Jill and me for this pathetic performance.

For the grand finale we asked him if he had anything to add at the end of the interview. Now he was in his element as he produced his summary card and read it to us. With the interview concluded we thanked him and he left the room. Immediately as the door closed Jill and I put our heads down on the table trying not to laugh so loud that we might be heard in the lobby. We had no sooner done this when our card carrying candidate burst open the doors to the interview room waving another card and saying he had one more thing to add. In as straight a face as I could muster under the circumstances, I politely told him the interview was over.

Jill and I did not think we would ever have an interview like that again. We were right about that but wrong about the degree of nervousness a candidate could bring to the interview. During another interview we did have empathy for a poor, shaking fellow. He tried his best and did a fairly good job answering the questions and making his interpretive presentation. When it came time for him to leave, what little poise he retained failed him as he became disorientated in the room. Jill and I watched in amazement as he walked over to a closet door and walked in! We had heard stories about such things happening but here was living proof. The embarrassed candidate came out and I said, "No not that door, the other one" as we pointed him in the right direction. We attempted to make light of the situation so he wouldn't go completely off of the deep end.

For candidates who were successful in the interviews and went on to become park rangers, I hope that the doors of opportunity have opened for them as they did for me.

THE FINEST RANGER

I met the finest ranger I ever knew on June 23, 1967 in Bridgeport, California when I was a ranger at Bodie State Historic Park. This person wasn't a park ranger when I first met her and I didn't know that she would grow up to become a park ranger. I certainly did not know that her career would be all too brief or that it would have such a profound impact on my life as a park professional and more importantly as a father. This person is my daughter, the very same "Bodie Baby" you were introduced to in the beginning of this book.

Abigail Rose Chavez Cushenberry was a "Park Brat" if I ever saw one. Her first home was in the State Park at Bodie and her last home, 29 years later, was also in a state park, at Mt. Diablo. The intervening years were special. You have read some accounts of her adventures. Abby was headstrong, stubborn and ever so independent. She loved animals and raised everything she could get her hands on that her parents would allow in or around the house. Horses were her specialty. Introduced to riding at Cuyamaca and Plumas-Eureka State Parks she always figured a way to be around those critters. At Humboldt Redwoods when I started a horse stable concession she was soon found to be leading rides.

Abby had an early start with state parks. Her first working experience was as a volunteer for the Humboldt Redwoods Interpretive Association in 1980. At age 13 she was staffing the sales counter and providing information to park visitors. In 1981 at the age of 14 she already had her first job as a seasonal maintenance aide at Richardson Grove State Park in the adjacent Piercy Area. This required her to live on her own in a small cabin for the summer. She worked two summers at Richardson Grove until the Piercy Area merged with the Dyerville Area to become the Eel River District. Since I was Area Manager of the Eel River District I would not allow her to work in the same District. Either I would have to move or she would. She did.

Abby's next summer work was at Prairie Creek Redwoods State Park, north of Eureka in the Klamath District. Her duties were that of a park aide in Visitor Services staffing the contact station. Her second season at Prairie Creek found her working at the more isolated Gold Bluff Beach sub-unit of Prairie Creek. I know she much preferred the freedom and independence that came with that assignment.

All of Abby's seasonal work was summer employment only. The rest of the time she was attending college and driving her father crazy! I think it was her plan to attend every California State College that began with the letter "S." First she went to San Diego State. Next she went to Sacramento State, and finally she went to Sonoma State. Somewhere along the line she also managed to attend Santa Rosa JC to acquire both her Emergency Technician (EMT) and her National Park Service (NPS) Law Enforcement Certification. By this time in 1988 she had two park jobs. One as a park aide at Gold Bluff Beach for State Parks, and the other, a Seasonal Ranger for the National Park Service at Redwood National Parks where she worked during her park aid days off. Incidentally, in the NPS law enforcement training class she finished #2 in the class of about 25-30 cadets.

1989 brought profound change in my daughter's life. That summer she accepted a seasonal park aide job at Grover Hot Springs State Park near the town of Markleeville in the Sierra District. It was there that she met a lifeguard named Craig Cushenberry. I won't go into to details of what happened but I bet you can guess. Abby had taken the State Park Ranger Trainee examination early that summer and passed the rigorous screening and background tests. It was decision time for her as she was offered the opportunity to be one of 22 cadets in Basic Visitor Services Training Class #9 at the William Penn Mott, Jr. Training Academy at Asilomar in Pacific Grove.

She decided to accept the position and forego her last year of college. It was not a decision she regretted. On September 17, 1989 she started a career as a California State Park Ranger that was to be all to short.

Abby was the youngest of the 22 Cadets in the class, but certainly not the least experienced. It was fun for me to have the opportunity to be an instructor in her class. Few of the other cadets knew of our relationship. She did well as a cadet and finished #2 in the class (or so she told me). In any event, on February 2, 1990, after six months of training, it was a proud father and Regional Director that pinned Badge #721 on Abigail Rose Chavez.

State Park Ranger Abigail Chavez was first assigned to Pescadero State Beach along the San Mateo Coast, which was a unit of the Bay Area District. She seemed to like all aspects of the job. She made good use of her EMT and Law Enforcement training on this dangerous stretch of coast highway and beach south of San Francisco. She also had the opportunity for many interpretive activities in leading school groups around Pescadero Marsh or driving the Park's interpretive trailer to local schools and special events. She became friends with a ranger at an adjacent park who had horses so that she could indulge herself in her favorite horseback riding activities on her days off. There was, however, one thing missing from her life. That was a guy named Craig, still living and working at Grover Hot Spring SP. It was a 200-mile commute and long distance relationship that didn't last very long.

Craig and Abigail were married on September 19, 1990. It took another few months for Craig to finagle a transfer and change of classification to a maintenance position at Pescadero SB, but it was done. After that things happened fast. Work continued, of course, but there must have been some play too, because on December 12, 1992 they became parents of Cody Craig Cushenberry. Most of 1993 Abby was off on maternity leave, basking in the glory of motherhood.

In mid to late summer of 1993, Reorganization again raised its ugly head and park people's lives were disrupted for the sake of "operational efficiencies." The direct result of this was that Abby and her family were transferred to Mount Diablo State Park. Actually, in her case, she couldn't have asked for a better transfer. She was to become the horse patrol ranger at Mitchell Canyon near the community of Clayton. She would have not one, but two horses and could basically ride to her heart's content. The family lived in the park and quickly adapted to the life style they had hoped for. Abigail excelled at her job, ever so much a better ranger than I ever was at that stage of my career. Abby was first and foremost my daughter so we rarely, if ever, discussed park business. After all, I was "Management" and she was "Rank and File". It was fun to constantly tease each other about this.

This was a job Abigail loved almost more than anything else in her life except for her family, and the family was growing. On December 21, 1994, Hailey Claire Cushenberry was born. Craig was no longer working for Parks, having taken on a supervisory EMT position with a Bay Area ambulance company. Abigail was once again off on maternity leave. The next few months were everything that Abby and her family could hope for. Family, fun, health and prosperity. How fleeting those can be.

In September 1995 Abigail was diagnosed with Non-Hodgkin's Lymphoma. Our world shattered. A daughter, wife, mother only 26 years old with a bright future ahead of her was in a battle she could not win. To say it was a struggle would be an understatement. I will just say that Abby battled with all her heart and soul to remain with her family. I saw not only the best in her, but also in the Department of Parks and Recreation during her year of illness. With her sick leave exhausted, the "PARK FAMILY" throughout the state came to her rescue and donated over 2900 hours of sick leave to her so she could remain at home in the park receiving treatment and be with her family. The park staff at Mt. Diablo, under the leadership of Manager Larry Ferri made every accommodation possible on Abby's behalf.

Abigail did rally and actually managed to return to work briefly in October 1996. She even went on horse patrol again. But alas, in November the signs of cancer returned. The last days of Abigail's life were remarkable. Two days before she passed away she went on one last wild horse ride with her friend Sue. The wind blowing through her beautiful black hair that had finally grown back after radiation and chemotherapy treatment, she whooped and hollered her good-byes to the park she loved so dearly.

The night before she died she baked her children their favorite pie, pumpkin. I have now learned to do that for them. Lastly, the most beautiful thing she did was write a letter to Cody, who was then age four and his sister Hailey who was two years old. The letter, of course, is too private and special to share in its entirety, but there was something she said in the letter that can be shared. She told the kids that when they heard the coyotes howling, that was her saying "hello", and when they looked up in the sky and heard a red-tail hawk screeching as it soared overhead, that was her watching over them. Abigail Rose Chavez Cushenberry passed away quietly in her sleep on November 19, 1996.

But the story does not end here. A "Celebration of Life" was held for Abby at the Mitchell Canyon picnic area in Mt. Diablo SP on November 30th. As preparations for the gathering were being made in the morning, two red-tailed hawks soared above the picnic area. As I began speaking to a gathering of some 200 friends and relatives, movements in the audience caused an interruption. Everyone turned to look and see a coyote loping up the hill behind them. Surely Abigail's spirit was with us that day. A week later I returned to work in my office on the 14th floor of the Resource Building in downtown Sacramento. I looked out my office window and was stunned to see two red-tail hawks flying outside the window and soaring higher and higher. I couldn't believe it. I called to my

Secretary, Linda to come and look at this. Linda knew of Abby's letter to the children. All we could do was hug each other as tears streamed down our cheeks. **It was time to say good-bye to the finest ranger I ever knew.**

THE WIZARD OF "ODDS"

When the Department under took yet another "down sizing" reorganization in 1993 it was to prove to be a very stressful situation for many employees throughout the State Park System. A group of employees that came to be known as the "Phoenix Committee" was charged with the task of recommending and implementing the changes to be made. For the most part this group was successful in mitigating the loss of jobs but still found it necessary to institute a number of employee transfers and downgrades which in itself could be upsetting.

I was one of those individuals who was impacted by the reorganization. My position as Regional Director in the Santa Rosa Northern Region Office and my home in nearby Windsor where we had resided comfortably for the previous 7 years were about to be turned topsy turvy. As a result of the reorganization our office in Santa Rosa was to be closed and the majority of positions in it were to be eliminated or transferred either to other Districts "in the field", newly created Service Centers, or to Sacramento Headquarters.

In one stroke all 5 Regional Offices were eliminated along with the 5 Regional Director positions in charge of them. I had the good fortune to be one of the Regional Directors to survive the cuts. That was the good news. The bad news was that I would have to move to Sacramento to fill the newly created position of Northern Division Chief. The Phoenix Committee had chosen to combine and enlarge the District and thus reduce the number of superintendents reporting to any one supervisor. The state was essentially divided in two, with half of the superintendents reporting to me in the

Northern Division and the other half reporting to my counterpart, Southern Division Chief Dick Troy. Dick and I shared a secretary whose office separated our respective offices on the 14th floor of the Resources building. Dick and I hit it off very well and worked together pretty much as a team. Dick did not have the field experience I had but, on the other hand, he was much more suave and adept in public relations, and the inner workings of the department's interaction with individuals and organizations that thrive in Sacramento's political climate. This served Dick well as he was later promoted to Deputy Director, a position he held until his retirement in 2002.

The changes that were made did not actually increase my workload as much as I had expected. I still had approximately the same number of Superintendents reporting to me. It was the understaffed, enlarged districts and their superintendents who actually absorbed most of the burden of increased workload which was passed on to them (work, like water runs downhill in DPR!). That is not to say there was not stress with the job. Perhaps most difficult for me was the issue of fees and revenue again. Placed under the gun again by the legislature we were poked and prodded to the brink of a financial cliff to the new marching orders of "revenue generation". The budget of a district was held hostage by its ability to generate revenue. Suddenly it seemed that revenue generation, not; resource protection, interpretation, facility maintenance or even public safety was the unspoken core mission of DPR. This "new" direction left a very unsettling feeling in ones stomach or conscience, or in my case, in my **heart.**

Though no one could prove that job related stress was the cause my second heart attack, of that I have no doubt. I know I wasn't alone in this feeling. In the space of a year we lost several outstanding individuals and superintendents to heart attacks or other potentially stress related illnesses. Foremost among these were Dave Bartlett, Carl Maier and Hal Bradshaw. The common denominator, or coincidence, that each of these people shared was that they were all superintendents of the Lake Oroville District within a time period I was their supervisor.

Margaret and I, having gone through the most traumatic and stressful situation any parents could go through with the loss of our daughter Abby less than a year and half previously, now looked forward to a vacation to experience one of our life goals. That was to see a total eclipse of the sun. You may remember that I had had my first heart attack and subsequent surgery only two weeks before we were scheduled to depart for the total eclipse in Mexico in 1991.

This time we were successful in meeting our goal on a wonderful Caribbean cruise. The total eclipse of February 26, 1998, was awesome and everything we hoped for as we viewed it from the luxury liner Galaxy offshore from the erupting volcano of Montserrat. Just as in ancient times, however, when people feared and foresaw a total eclipse as a harbinger of ominous events to come, that is how it seemed to affect us.

We returned to Sacramento on March 1st only to learn that my friend Dave Bartlett, the only superintendent that ever called me "Chief", had passed away suddenly the previous Saturday from a heart attack. I was stunned. Here was a wonderful, fun loving park professional, a husband and father taken too young at the prime of his life. It affected me greatly, perhaps more than I would admit to others or myself. Because I had been away when Dave died, I was one week behind the rest of the department in the grieving process and in my efforts to console Dave's family.

Less than ten days, later on March 9th, I suffered my second heart attack. That morning at work I had been discussing arrangements for Dave's memorial service with Superintendent Bob La Belle (I guess eclipses, Bob La Belle, and heart attacks go together!) I felt fine, but sad, so after lunch I took a walk downtown. As I was returning to my office in the Resource Building I felt some chest discomfort and began to suspect something was wrong. Stupid as I am, I said nothing about it and finished out the day and again said nothing to Margaret when I got home lest I worry her. Double stupid.

I came to my senses the next morning and realized that something serious was occurring. Not all, but some of the classical heart attack symptoms were in progress. Again, instead of calling 911 for an ambulance I had Margaret take me all the way to the hospital in Davis, about a half hour drive away- Triple Stupid. While in the emergency room I had a definite heart attack but the doctors quickly stabilized me. To make a long story short, I missed Dave Bartlett's memorial service because I had to undergo angioplasty surgery to have a coronary stent implant on March 12th. Again there was good news and there was bad news.

The good news was that the procedure was successful even though complications arose. The bad news was that I was told that I would still need heart by-pass surgery relatively soon. I knew in my heart (as bad as it was) that for all intents and purposes my park career had ended on March 9th. I had made the decision that as wonderful as parks are, there are more important things such as my wife, my son, and my daughter's children. It was not a hard decision to make. I was ready to start a new life in Graeagle.

My recovery from the angioplasty procedure took much longer than I had anticipated and was actually more uncomfortable than my open-heart surgery in 1991. In any event, during my convalescence in March plans were in the works for my Grand Finale Retirement Party and a date for the party was set for April 18th. The doctors at the hospital had wanted to do the second by-pass operation the first or second week of April. I told them that that was impossible because I had to attend a party! We finally compromised when they agreed to postpone the surgery if I would come in the day after the party for the operation.

Now I must tell you about State Park Retirement Parties, Inc. Within the Department of Parks and Recreations there is a cadre of individuals (read "Ring Leaders") who are so creative and have such an outrageous sense of humor it is frightening. The so-called "honorees" of this attention have been known to wince at the prospect of being the focus and "object of the affection" of this talent.

Russian River Superintendent Bob La Belle and Dave Bartlett were the heart and soul of this "underground" production company. At their beck and call were the talents of many others. To name a few there was Bill Berry, Joe Mette, Ron Brean, Rick Rayburn and Dick Troy and in my case almost every superintendent from the Northern Division.

A retirement party put on by this group was not for the faint of heart, yet here I was. Stodgy decorum was the exception, not the rule. Each party generally had a theme that was well thought and played out. There have been O.J Simpson Trial and Elvis Parties. Mine was to have a Wizard of Oz theme with the "Oz" turned into "Odds"

I, like many of my predecessors, winced too. Why had they chosen this theme? At first I wondered and was uneasy about it. On reflection, however, I began to think about it and actually liked the idea as I thought about my career especially the last few years as it began to wind down with my Headquarters assignment as Northern Division Chief.

To me, it seemed like I never did fit into the general mold of the management team in Sacramento. For one thing almost all of my contemporaries wore a suit and tie. I detested that "uniform" and only rarely could be found wearing that outfit. On the other hand, as a consequence of not wearing a tie I was probably the most comfortable person attending meeting after meeting. Also, when it came to lunch, I rarely went "out with boys" to the local restaurants. I was the only one who consistently took a lunch to work. I would usually walk over to Capitol Park and eat my tuna sandwich while watching the people and squirrels go about their daily lives. I always enjoyed it, however, when my friend, Resource Management Chief Rick Rayburn (also a tuna fish fan), would join me. Then again, Rick was one of the few people who understood my weird sense of humor and suffered through the "**pun**ishment" of it. I think the bottom line was that I was a product "of the Field" and in my heart and mind really wished I were still working in it. I liked the feeling of actually seeing the direct results of action rather then viewing it from afar.

In any event, on the evening of April 18th, five days , after my 54th birthday, Margaret and I drove to the Dante Club in Sacramento to attend the "Wizard of Odds" festivities of my retirement party. Our emotions ran high and we were stunned by the turnout of friends, coworkers, and family who were in attendance. Over 200 had come. I was so pleased that my parents and four of my five sisters were able to make the trip to Sacramento for this event.

Once the speeches, lies, and presentations were made the full impact of the amount of work the Bob La Belle and all of the other participants of the production that was to follow hit us. As the curtain on the stage parted there was a complete set for the Wizard of Odds constructed and painted by persons unknown to me. Next, superintendent after superintendent paraded on stage with their part in a lavish parody of the original production. Great artistic license was taken to include the "Odd" character here and there such as Ron Brean in a complete "Chicken" costume. There was John Kolb dressed as Dorothy, Bill Berry as the Lion, Ron Schafer as the Straw Man and John Knott as the Tin Man. Supporting cast included The Munchkins (Ken Leigh and Bud Getty), Auntie Em (Peggy Dalton) Uncle Henry (Bob La Belle), The Wicked Witch (Dick Troy) and last but not least, Rick Rayburn (complete with tutu) as the Fairy Queen. Without a doubt this skit proved that as the Wizard of the Northern Division I truly did direct a crew of very uninhibited "Odd" characters!

As the play neared it's final act I was dragged not quite kicking and screaming, back stage where I donned my Wizard of Odds costume. Placed at center stage in a throne of "honor" of sorts I proceeded to embark upon my short acting career. Fortunately for all those in attendance it was brief and sweet. Mercifully my grandkids, Hailey and Cody, who joined me on the stage, proceeded to upstage me. It was a fitting and emotional tribute to my daughter that all who were there could remember her through her children.

The Grand Finale came when Margaret, my partner down this winding pathway I had taken, joined me on stage. We climbed aboard the basket of the balloon that was to launch us into retirement. As midnight approached we bid our family and friends farewell as we embarked upon the next phase of the journey we call "LIFE" – but first...

Early the next morning I drove myself to the hospital for the pre-op test needed for my open-heart surgery. Afterwards I returned home to spend the day with Margaret before facing the uncertainty of the operations. I checked into the hospital in Sacramento that evening with the surgery scheduled for the following morning. The next day all went well as I underwent a triple by-pass operation. During my 5-day stay at the hospital I was again blessed with knowledge that I had many caring friends. Many of them visited me and I know that played a significant role in my quick recovery. Four days after the operation I was walking ½ mile circuits around the nurses station and by the time I got home the next day I was walking ½ mile 3 times a day. One of the nicest things that happened during my recovery occurred when we got a knock at our condo door in Sacramento and who should appear but Dick Troy and Rick Rayburn. They had come with all the fixing for a complete and elegant pasta dinner, which they prepared for us! What a wonderful surprise that was from the finest drop-in chefs I have ever known.

It was a month before the doctors officially released me so that we could move full time to Graeagle but when that day came on May 15th I could hardly wait. I knew my recovery was complete when on May 19th I joined Ross Henry and others on a hike to the summit of 7197-ft Mt. Penman. Though retirement would not officially begin until July 1, 1998 I knew that my Pathway Through Parks had ended and a new path was about to begin

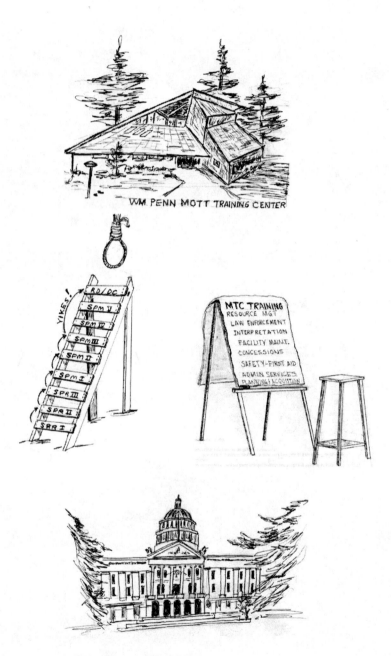

WM. PENN MOTT TRAINING CENTER

YIKES!

RD/DC
SPM V
SPM IV
SPM III
SPM II
SPM I
SPR III
SPR II
SRR I

MTC TRAINING
RESOURCE MGT
LAW ENFORCEMENT
INTERPRETATION
FACILITY MAINT.
CONCESSIONS
SAFETY-FIRST AID
ADMIN SERVICES
PLANNING/ACQUISITION

NORTHERN DIVISION SKETCHES

ISBN 141202273-8